Transfigurations of the Maghreb

Transfigurations of the Maghreb

Feminism, Decolonization, and Literatures

Winifred Woodhull

University of Minnesota Press
Minneapolis
London

Photographs on pages 38 and 39 are reproduced from Malek Alloula, *The Colonial Harem*, © University of Minnesota Press, 1986, all rights reserved. Photographs on page 44 are reproduced from Marc Garanger, *Femmes algériennes 1960*, by permission.

Portions of chapter 1 were originally published in *Genders* 10, University of Texas Press, Spring 1991, and in *SubStance* 69, University of Wisconsin Press, 1992. Reprinted in revised form, by permission. Portions of chapter 3 were originally published in *Yale French Studies* 82, 1993, and in *SubStance* 62-63, University of Wisconsin Press, 1990. Reprinted in revised form, by permission.

Published by the University of Minnesota Press
2037 University Avenue Southeast, Minneapolis, MN 55455-3092
Printed in the United States of America on acid-free paper

Library of Congress Cataloging-in-Publication Data

Woodhull, Winifred, 1950-
    Transfigurations of the Maghreb : feminism, decolonization, and literatures / Winifred Woodhull.
      p. cm.
    Includes bibliographical references and index.
    ISBN 0-8166-2054-7 (hc : acid-free). — ISBN 0-8166-2055-5 (acid-free)
    1. North African literature (French)—Women authors—History and criticism.   2. Feminism and literature—Africa, North.   3. Women and literature—Africa, North.   4. Decolonization in literature.
5. Africa, North, in literature.   6. Colonies in literature.
I. Title.
PQ3988.N6W66   1993
840.9′9287′0961—dc20
                                               92-46725
                                                CIP

Contents

Acknowledgments

I wish to thank Dean Stanley Chodorow of the University of California, San Diego, for his generous support of this research. UCSD also supported my work with a Chancellor's Summer Fellowship (1990) and an Affirmative Action Pre-Tenure Award (Fall 1990). During the 1991-92 year, I had the pleasure of completing this book at the Cornell University Society for the Humanities, where the staff was of invaluable assistance, as were the staff of Cornell's Olin Library and the UCSD libraries, and Mr. Nour-Eddíne Mekki of the Centre Culturel Algérien in Paris.

Thanks are also due to the following friends and colleagues who read parts of this work or discussed various aspects of it with me: Nancy Armstrong, Réda Bensmaïa, Mária Brewer, Page duBois, Susan Kirkpatrick, Donna Landry, Françoise Lionnet, George Lipsitz, Lisa Lowe, Susan McClary, and Ronnie Scharfmann.

Introduction

je suis ce nom perdu
qui chante toute rive

[I am this lost name
that celebrates every shore]

—Amina Saïd, *Sables funambules*

Tunisian poet Amina Saïd's evocation of a "lost name that celebrates every shore" is inscribed in a practice of unnaming close to
that of Moroccan writer and theorist Abdelkebir Khatibi, who promotes the production of a "plural" Maghreb freed from unitary,
theological notions of national and cultural identity.[1] For Khatibi,
the effort to pluralize the Maghreb is synonymous with decolonization, a process requiring a double critique of Arab-Islamic institutions and culture on the one hand, and of the universalizing, colonizing dynamics of Western metaphysics on the other. In his
account, decolonization of the Maghreb through a process of unnaming is inseparable from a necessarily global challenge to transnational capitalism and the deadening, or even deadly, uses to
which it puts science, technology, and the mass media.

In Khatibi, the process of decolonization is associated with the
bi-langue, a space in which body and language, voice and writing,
feminine and masculine sexualities, native and foreign languages,
hegemonic and marginalized cultures mingle without merging to
form a new unity.[2] Because of his emphasis on the *bi-langue*, Khatibi's writing suggests fruitful ways to read various bodies of work
that are at issue in this study: "nomadic" poststructuralist theories

of language, subjectivity, and social relations; Maghrebian literatures in French; French literature about the Maghreb; and literature dealing with Maghrebian immigrants in France, whether by French, Maghrebian, or "Beur" writers (the Beurs being young people of Maghrebian descent who were born in France or have lived most of their lives there. Originally a pejorative slang term for "Arabs," "Beurs" was appropriated by Maghrebian-French youths critically negotiating their cultural identity). In my introduction, then, I want to look briefly at Khatibi's writings in terms of their contribution to rethinking Maghrebian cultural politics and understanding decolonization as a process in which peoples of both the "East" and the "West" must participate critically. At the same time, though, I want to indicate some of the limitations of Khatibi's approach, particularly its emphasis on the transformative power of a subversive poetics removed from what is conventionally referred to as the political sphere. By discussing Khatibi's work in connection with that of Jean-François Lyotard, I hope to show that, historically, in France, a subversive poetics has gradually *replaced* work for change in the political field: for Lyotard, and for Khatibi as well, poetic language has come to be associated with an "other" politics radically divorced from social institutions and from material relations of domination. I also hope to suggest that Khatibi's notion of a subversive poetics is problematic in light of recent feminist work on literature, culture, and decolonization in both the "first" and "third" worlds.[3] For the poetics promoted and practiced by Khatibi often reinforces a patriarchal law that is assumed to be immutable, rather than effectively challenging that law.

Samir Amin reminds us at the beginning of *The Maghreb in the Modern World* that "Maghreb, in Arabic, signifies the West," indicating that this region occupies an ambiguous geopolitical position that is at once "Western," from the standpoint of Arabs in the Mashreq (the Middle East), and "oriental," from the standpoint of Europe.[4] According to Khatibi, this ambiguity makes of the Maghreb an especially potent site for dismantling the opposition between occident and orient. He writes in *Figures de l'étranger dans la littérature française* that the Maghreb, like other parts of Africa, is a "mosaic of *interlangues* between the oral and the written, between the national and the extranational or the transnational," and between sacred, profane, and popular religious and cultural traditions.[5] Moreover, in his view, Morocco, Algeria, and Tunisia embody and are capable of fostering a "concrete internationalism" (210) by virtue of being plurilingual societies in which Berber dialects, Arabic dialects, and literary Arabic cohabit with French as well as Spanish (in Morocco) and Italian (in Tunisia). The "African map of writing" (204) is said to provide the basis for a theory of what Khatibi calls "the laws of hospitality in language" (203), which acknowledge, welcome, and enable the articulation of the strangeness, or foreignness, inhabiting every language, every subjectivity, every nation and culture:

> Diglossia, bilingualism, or plurilingualism do not merely involve external relations of one language to another—of a source to its target, as the linguists say. Rather, they are *structural elements of every act of writing*, every exploration of the unknown translated by words. In each word, each name, each given name and proper name there is the sketch of other words, its hospitable calligraphy. In each word: other words; in each language: the sojourn of other languages. The completely-other always watches over poetic force. (205; Khatibi's emphasis)

For Khatibi, "poetic force," or "the power of the word," can challenge "the word of power" (*Maghreb pluriel*, 61). It is an alternative not only to the silence imposed on Maghrebians and other third-world peoples by Western powers but also to its audible twin, the threat of "war, destruction, and vile guilt" coming from various parts of the third world with the aim of "turning the West against its own self-sufficiency and ethnocentrism, now elevated to a planetary scale" (*Maghreb pluriel*, 50). The third world, says Khatibi, can take a third route: "neither reason nor unreason as the West has thought them in its totality, but a subversion that is, in a sense, double, and that, giving itself the power of word *and action*, sets to work in an intractable difference. To decolonize ourselves and each other would be another name for this other-thought" (*Maghreb pluriel*, 50-51; my emphasis).

While implicitly or explicitly acknowledging his debt to the work of Jacques Derrida in nearly everything he writes, Khatibi maintains that the "African map of writing" itself invites an analysis of decolonization that takes account of the "laws of hospitality in language." My reading of Khatibi is that he has appropriated deconstruction for third-world peoples and for reflection on third-world cultural politics, much as Hélène Cixous has appropriated it for women and for reflection on sexual difference, if not for feminism. (In fact, Khatibi's work on the body, sexual difference, and "feminine" or radically bisexual modes of writing are very close to Cixous's. I will return to this point later.) The problem is that his use of deconstruction and other modes of philosophical inquiry, as well as Freudian psychoanalysis, often uncritically mimics the increasingly conservative uses to which they have been put in France in recent years.

Particularly troubling is the degree to which Khatibi's writing tacitly endorses a view advanced by many French philosophers, such as Jean-François Lyotard, Philippe Lacoue-Labarthe, Jean-Luc Nancy, and Maurice Blanchot: the view that, today, we must proclaim the end of politics because Marxism's grand narrative of worldwide proletarian revolution is historically obsolete. Instead of revolutionary politics, according to this view, we should promote a philosophy or a poetics—"other-thought" in *Maghreb pluriel*, "other-literature" in *Love in Two Languages.* For philosophy and poetics alone are considered capable, in our time, of bearing witness to the irreducible otherness inhabiting and unsettling every system, including capitalism.[6] I think we should be suspicious of the fact that so many theory writers declare philosophical-poetic work—that is, their own work—to be the only activity capable of resisting capitalism and other oppressive systems while remaining faithful to an otherness variously referred to as the feminine (or the maternal), intractable difference, singularity, the uncanny, and the unpresentable. In this connection, it is worth noting the resonances between Lyotard's concern with "faithfulness" to "intractable difference" (*l'intraitable*)[7] and Khatibi's "passion for language," an "intractable love" to which he remains "unreservedly faithful" (*Love in Two Languages,* 57, 115). For we find inscribed in Lyotard's work a history of the depoliticization of irreducible otherness, a history that suggests a need to rethink the relation between cultural discourses and a supposedly prediscursive intractable difference.

Lyotard situates intractable difference in a space apart from "the politics of 'intellectuals' and politicians."[8] At the same time, he links it with the need not just to challenge but to destroy capitalism. This linkage is especially apparent in his 1982 essay "A Memorial for Marxism," where he writes of intractable difference in terms of his "differend" with Pierre Souyri, a friend with whom he collaborated from 1954 to 1964 in the Socialisme ou Barbarie collective. The collective's journal, *Socialisme ou Barbarie*, was dedicated to the critique of new forms of class oppression developing under bureaucratic socialism:

> I have testified here to what I can evoke without betrayal, this differend itself [with Pierre Souyri], which betrayed each one of us to the other, and in which I experienced, to my surprise, what in Marxism cannot be objected to and what makes of any reconciliation, even in theory, a deception: that there are several incommensurable genres of discourse in play in society, none of which can transcribe all the others; and nonetheless one of them at least—capital, bureaucracy—imposes its rules on the others. This oppression is the only radical one, the one that forbids its victims to bear witness against it. It is not enough to understand it and be its philosopher; one must also destroy it.[9]

In addition to addressing the basic problem of capital, Lyotard speaks of the differend in terms of specific cases of "wrongs" and "damages" suffered, for example, by holocaust victims who cannot phrase their experience in the idiom of those who claim that no victim can prove the existence of gas chambers at Auschwitz since to have seen one is to have died there (*Differend*, 3-6). And, like Khatibi, Lyotard is concerned with differends arising in the postcolonial situation, for example, the inability of Martinicans to bear witness to the wrong they suffer by virtue of being French citizens, when the only idiom in which testimony is possible is that of French law:

> It might be [a matter for litigation] under private or public international law, but for that to be the case it would be necessary that the Martinican were no longer a French citizen. But he or she is. Consequently, the assertion according to which he or she suffers a wrong on account of his or her citizenship is not verifiable by explicit and effective procedures. These are examples of situations presented in the phrase universes of Ideas (in the Kantian sense): the Idea of nation, the Idea of the creation of value. These situations are not the referents of knowledge phrases. There exist no procedures instituted to establish or refute their reality in a cognitive sense. That is why they give rise to differends. (*Differend*, 27)

Both Lyotard and Khatibi attempt to phrase differends that would otherwise "be smothered right away in a litigation" (*Differ-*

end, 13); both attend to silences that indicate phrases in abeyance, *en souffrance de leur événement* (*Differend,* 57). Khatibi's "L'oriental-isme désorienté" shows, for example, how the Christian values informing the work of Henry Corbin and Louis Massignon silence aspects of Islamic experience such as the suffering associated with the "specifically Islamic ordeal" (*Maghreb pluriel,* 121). Similarly, his "Sexualité selon le Koran" is concerned to "translate [sexuality] from one language to another, from one civilization to another. The essential thing in such an undertaking is to specify, first, the use of notions and concepts put into question, and then to indicate the effects of their transformation so that 'sexuality'—both sign and thing—be rendered to the word that can say it and to the body grafted to it" (*Maghreb pluriel,* 150). The task of translation is equally important in conveying subjective experience; only the *bi-langue* or *pluri-langue*—"a question of translation"—can express "the asymmetry of body and language, of speech and writing—at the threshold of the untranslatable" (*Love in Two Languages,* 101, 5).

It is interesting to note that on two occasions in the late 1980s Lyotard links the question of phrasing differends, or bearing witness to intractable difference, to the memory of the Algerian War. His essay "A l'insu," which argues that all politics is a politics of forgetting intractable difference, appears in a 1988 issue of *Le Genre humain* on the politics of forgetfulness, dedicated to the memory of "those days of October 1961 when Algerian men, women, and children were massacred, thrown into the Seine."[10] One year later, Mohammed Ramdani publishes *La Guerre des Algériens,* a collection of Lyotard's articles on Algeria written for *Socialisme ou Barbarie* from 1956 to 1963, accompanied by an author's note titled "Le Nom d'Algérie."[11] In the latter piece, Lyotard credits the Algerian city of Constantine with "awakening" him politically when he was sent there to teach in 1950 (39). When he begins to write about the Algerian War for *Socialisme ou Barbarie* in 1955, he criticizes France's political responses to the conflict as well as the hierarchies and vanguardism developing within the National Liberation Front (an organization he nonetheless supports in various practical ways). He does so, he says, as a combatant who is "neither French nor Algerian, but internationalist" (36).

Lyotard claims that his task in Algeria, and generally speaking the task of the Socialisme ou Barbarie collective, resembles an endless analytic cure, "a free-floating mode of listening to the live con-

temporary struggles where intractable difference continues to signal its presence" (35). Other names given to intractable difference
in "Le Nom d'Algérie" are "the secret from which all resistance
draws its energy" (35) and the "inventiveness of the immediate
practice of these [workers' and third-world] struggles [that] is so
natural that its value goes unnoticed. Its value is that this inventiveness is *already* emancipation" (34; Lyotard's emphasis). The role
of the revolutionary organization, he says, is "not to lead the struggles, but to give them the means to deploy the creativity that was
being exercised in them, and to become conscious of them so that
they may lead themselves" (34).

   In the aftermath of the Algerian War it became clear, however,
that an oppressive bureaucratic socialism was a structural problem
of global proportions that would have the effect, in the newly independent nation, of defeating the Algerians who had revolted
against colonialism. At this point, Lyotard claims, "Marxism is fin-
ished as a revolutionary perspective"; "the intractable voice or the
voice of intractable difference no longer makes itself heard, in
Western societies, in social or political channels" (37). This "depoliticization" does not result in a complete absorption of intractable
difference by the system (May '68 is one of its postrevolutionary
manifestations), although the system "assimilated everything that
could be assimilated from the legacy of the social and political
struggles of the oppressed for more than a century" (37), effectively thwarting political forms of resistance. For Lyotard,

> it is inaccurate, and intellectually dishonest, to place in activities
> of free spontaneity—those of youths, immigrants, women,
> homosexuals, prisoners, or peoples of the third world, which
> destabilize the system here and there—the hope that we, as
> Marxists, could only place in the revolutionary activity of the
> industrial proletariat. This is not to say that these initiatives are
> negligible. But thought must bend to the evidence that the master
> narratives of emancipation, starting (or ending) with "our own,"
> that of radical Marxism, have lost their intelligibility and their
> substance. (37-38)

Lyotard closes by offering his essays as testimony to "this intractable thing that, for a time, bore the name of Algeria, and that per-
sists" (39).

   I have cited Lyotard at length in order to show that he locates the moment of depoliticization in the aftermath of the Algerian War (or even during the Algerian War),[12] effectively neutralizing all extrapoetic Algerian struggles after independence *and* using "the name of Algeria" to designate intractable "inventiveness" and "creativity," which, from now on, will necessarily manifest themselves elsewhere, "in a literature, in a philosophy, in a politics perhaps" (*Differend*, 13) (although by "politics" he seems to mean a politics of "other-thought" or "other-literature," to borrow Khatibi's terms). In "A l'insu," Lyotard suggests that the function of literature and philosophy is both to disclose the activity of the intractable thing and to signal the oppressive and potentially genocidal consequences of thinking that it has a face—"Medusa's face?"—or that it can be captured in a name—" 'the jews,' for example" (44), particularly when these thoughts are instituted politically, as in Nazism.[13] Echoing Maurice Blanchot's *The Unavowable Community* and Jean-Luc Nancy's *The Inoperative Community*, he declares that intractable difference "has no place, not having taken place and being 'present' only outside representation: in death, in birth, one's absolute and singular dependency, which prohibits any instantiated disposition of oneself from being unitary and total. I could just as well say 'sexual difference,' in the most radical sense of a heteronomy that does not belong to the space-time of representation" (44).[14]

Given the way Lyotard has framed the questions, it is impossible to contest his restrictive definition of an effective politics without assuming the aspect of a totalitarian oppressor. (Or is it Medusa in the guise of such an oppressor?) Moreover, because he links "the name of Algeria" to phrases implying that certain experiences of intractable difference—birth, death, sexual difference—are *always* outside representation, his formulations naturalize existing cultural configurations, discouraging the imagination of *other* systems in which "Algeria" and "sexual difference" might be positioned differently. In a different material/symbolic regime, Algeria would not necessarily occupy the place of the "beloved woman" to whom a smitten Lyotard addresses his articles in *La Guerre des Algériens*, "love letters" sent by a man who "laments the knowledge that she will not have the fate she merits by virtue of her valiance and beauty" ("Le Nom d'Algérie," 39). Why should we assume that no politics is possible, other than a quiescent poetic one, because the world is writing memorials to Marxism? Even if we accept the dubious proposition that "the voice of intractable difference no longer makes itself heard, *in Western societies,* in social or political channels," why should we suppose that manifestations of it in those and other channels elsewhere in the world cannot effectively combat capitalism and bureaucracy (not to mention patriarchy) without a unitary revolutionary politics ("A l'insu," 37; my emphasis)? Why not try to imagine new ways of linking the inventiveness of various groups of third-world peoples to that of women, immigrants, homosexuals, prisoners, and other groups in the first world—without assimilating others' struggles to one's own?

What is compelling about Khatibi's work is that, in its best moments, it *does* link manifestations of intractable difference in the third world to the prospect of significant social change worldwide, change to which he gives the name "decolonization." The "third route" he proposes in *Maghreb pluriel,* which involves seizing the "power of word and action" (50), seeks to enable intellectuals and activists around the world to carry out, by postrevolutionary means, the very task Lyotard had set for revolutionary organizations at the time of the Algerian War: "not to lead the struggles, but to give them the means to deploy the creativity that was being exercised in them, and to become conscious of them so that they may lead themselves" ("Le Nom d'Algérie," 36). In *Maghreb pluriel* Khatibi says, "A thought that is not inspired by its poverty[15] is aways elaborated in order to dominate and humiliate; a thought that is not a minority thought—marginal, fragmentary, and incomplete— is always a thought of ethnocide" (18). Pointing to Maghrebian leftists' uncritical adoption of a dogmatic Marxism on the model of the French Communist party (due to the fact that in the 1960s "no other revolutionary theory seemed to us to be operative on a national and global scale"), he calls for a double critique of "a simplified Marxian thought and, in parallel, the theological ideology of Arab nationalism" (16). The failures of the past contain their own regenerative force, he says, and what is required now is "a strategy without a closed system, but rather the construction of a play of thought and the political. . . . To decolonize ourselves and each other is this *chance* of thought" (16).

Now, granted, in many ways Khatibi's presentation of the political task at hand echoes that of Lyotard (and of Blanchot, Nancy, and Lacoue-Labarthe), for instance in avoiding the term *la politique* (politics), which refers to existing networks and practices generally termed "political." Instead, Khatibi uses the term *le politique* (the political) to suggest an "other" politics.[16] In the same way, Khatibi shares with his French counterparts a suspicion of homogenizing, unitary appeals to solidarity; for him "the 'we' that I name is this unthought, unprecedented unsettling, in the face of all forms of tyranny" (*Maghreb pluriel*, 18). Still, when Khatibi invokes notions of poverty and marginality to characterize a mode of thought and political action, he links them to the material impoverishment and sociopolitical marginalization of a less ambiguous "we" in the Maghreb and other parts of the third world (17), underscoring the urgency of addressing their situation concretely, since what is at stake is nothing less than survival.

Unfortunately, however, few of Khatibi's texts are as historically and geographically grounded as "Pensée-autre" and "Double critique" in *Maghreb pluriel*. Much of the time, he ignores or downplays the different historical, social, and geopolitical contexts in which inventiveness and resistance are at work, for instance in his reading of Tunisian writer Abdelwahab Meddeb's *Talismano* in "Bilinguisme et littérature" in the same volume.[17] In that analysis, Meddeb's critique of Islamic fundamentalism and Arab nationalism as they manifest themselves in language, culture, and politics are extracted from the context in which the novel situates them — namely, postindependence struggles against the power of the Tunisian state — and are dealt with only in relation to a poetic practice deemed capable of unsettling them regardless of how they may function in particular historical situations. For example, Khatibi sees in *Talismano* a transhistorical encounter between the fragmented body and the symbolic, figured in a child's recitation of the Koran. Khatibi says that while the recitation ushered the boy into a mode of thought governed by theological unity ("There is no God but Allah" [202]), it simultaneously ushered him into the field of writing, in the Derridean sense: "Through the reproduction and endless repetition of the sacred text, theology opens onto writing in the powerful sense of the term; it opens onto the time of the trace, of vocalization, of the breath and the syntax of the body, toward the call of the Other, the Absent, the Invisible" (203).[18] Extracted from the historical context in which Meddeb situates it, the tension between the body, the symbolic, and writing is assigned a single, endlessly repeatable meaning and social function. And whereas Meddeb's novel links an exploration of relations between the syntax of the body, the mother tongue, and "maternal" modes of writing with the question of women's speech (notably in the figure of the witch Saïda, who presides over the assembly of an idol from scattered parts of various bodies, a process bound up with a challenge to state power), Khatibi is interested only in the general question of "the scansion of the spoken body, rhythmed by all the idioms of memory and amnesia" (200). It is as if the stakes of the particular struggles at issue here were of minor importance by comparison, and as if the process of writing the body had the same consequences for women as for men, whatever their class, race, nationality, or historical circumstances may be.

Now, it is true that in *Love in Two Languages* Khatibi stages two very different, gender-related experiences of radical alterity. On the one hand, there is the pleasure/pain of the "he" figure who actively assumes his divided subjectivity and plays with it in language. And on the other, there is the melancholy of the "she" figure whose exile from self, native language, and home takes her to the limit of madness and death before she finds the strength to "face the mother tongue" and "present the chasm of her memory to this future which is continually translating itself" (113).[19] Moreover, Khatibi goes so far as to suggest that radical social transformations may be wrought as women, like the "she" figure in his text, "capture these singular and inalienable rights of speech and observation," that is, as they move beyond "suffering" and "renunciation" to "affirmation" of the future open to "orphans" lacking any full instantiation in language, family, or culture (106-7).[20] However, when faced with a concrete instance of women's challenge to existing symbolic structures, as in Fatima Mernissi's published interviews with Moroccan women,[21] he has the defensive response that has become the hallmark of the theorists associated with the International College of Philosophy, namely that while women's social equality with men must be affirmed in principle, feminism must be seen as an instance of phallogocentrism that is unfaithful to a supposedly prediscursive intractable difference. In Khatibi's foreword to Mernissi's *Doing Daily Battle: Interviews with Moroccan Women*, this intractable difference is figured as sexual dissymmetry:[22]

Law is divided/shared [*la loi se partage*]; its principle of rigor obeys rules. For example, we have said that inegalitarian dissymmetry fixes this principle in terms of two territories: the sexual (on the feminine side), the economic and the political (on the masculine side). This patriarchal and phallocentric regulation is denounced today. Fine. But the utopia of an absolute and paradisaical equality is excluded for us. Of course, we *must* have economic, legal, and political equality, but how can one think the sexual outside of all dissymmetry? How can it be rendered equal to itself? How can it be divided/shared equitably? This seems to me absurd. I mean that dissymmetry is insoluable in itself, and must be regulated by a thought that thinks that which is impossible to divide/share. (8-9; Khatibi's emphasis)

To my mind, nothing in the interviews or in Mernissi's presentation of them suggests that feminist demands in Morocco presuppose thinking the sexual, or any other aspect of social relations, "outside of all dissymmetry." In fact, it is not feminism's ostensible phallogocentrism that poses a problem so much as the attachment of Khatibi and other theorists to a particular patriarchal version of sexual dissymmetry, according to which the polymorphously perverse body exists prior to marking by sex, is repressed by the paternal law, and subsequently finds expression in a poetic language coded as feminine, "the mother tongue . . . [that] initiates one into the speaking of the not-said of the confusion with the mother's body" ("Bilinguisme et littérature," 191). When Khatibi says in *La Mémoire tatouée*, "Sign of signs, sex is the end [*la fin*] of disordered memory" (55), we should understand that sex, as a symbolic structure that fixes gender identities in a relation of hierarchized opposition, is the reified *outcome* of a psychosexual development that represses the polymorphous perversity and the disordered memory of the androgyne. But we should also understand that sex, in its inegalitarian dissymmetry, is the disavowed *aim* of that supposedly resistant form of memory.[23] As Judith Butler has shown in *Gender Trouble,* this version of sexual dissymmetry is evident in prevailing psychoanalytic discourses on bisexuality and homosexuality:

Within psychoanalysis, bisexuality and homosexuality are taken to be primary libidinal dispositions, and heterosexuality is the laborious construction based upon their gradual repression. While this doctrine seems to have a subversive possibility to it, the discursive construction of both bisexuality and homosexuality within the psychoanalytic literature effectively refutes the claim to its precultural status. The discussion of the language of bisexual dispositions is a case in point.[24]

Citing Foucault's warning, in the *History of Sexuality*, against using the category of sex as a "fictitious unity . . . [and] causal principle" and relying on a repressive, rather than a productive, notion of power,[25] Butler argues compellingly that "any theory that asserts that signification is predicated upon the denial or repression of a female principle [such as the mother's body] ought to consider whether that femaleness is really external to the cultural norms by which it is repressed" (93). Significantly, Butler does not jettison psychoanalysis. Instead, she argues that

in order to avoid the emancipation of the oppressor in the name
of the oppressed, it is necessary to take into account the full
complexity and subtlety of the law and to cure ourselves of the
illusion of a true body beyond the law. If subversion is possible, it
will be a subversion from within the terms of the law, through the
possibilites that emerge when the law turns against itself and
spawns unexpected permutations of itself. The culturally
constructed body will then be liberated, neither to its "natural
past," nor to its original pleasures, but to an open future of
cultural possibilities. (93)

Tellingly, in his foreword to Mernissi's book, Khatibi implies that in Morocco patriarchal law should be adjusted so as to insure women's economic, legal, and political equality, yet he assumes that the law must remain patriarchal and repressive, allowing, at most, for the possibility that "a song arise from these mute [women's] lips" (10), *le chant d'avant la loi*, in Hélène Cixous's terms.[26] Khatibi's foreword is out of tune with Mernissi's book, whose aim is to produce a discursive space in which the paternal character of the law may be challenged at its very basis, so that the critical speech of Moroccan women can be heard and be widely disseminated. Throughout the Arab world one finds feminist work similar to Mernissi's, for instance, that of Egyptian feminist Nawal al-Saadawi, in whose novel *Woman at Point Zero* "a fresh discursive field is imperceptibly traced for other Arab women," according to Algerian writer Assia Djebar.[27] For Djebar, such writing creates "a point for take-off. A combat zone. A restoration of body. Bodies of new women in spite of new barriers." Unlike Khatibi, Djebar, al-

Saadawi, and Mernissi are able to affirm women's historical agency without making it contingent upon an immutable paternal law.[28] Far from naively attempting to abolish inevitable dissymmetries, these Arab feminist writers proceed as if dissymmetries were capable of producing what Butler calls "an open future of cultural possibilities" in which no repressive paternal law need prevail.

Regarding the interpretation of Maghrebian literary texts written in French, Khatibi's notion of the *bi-langue* is indispensable, for many of these texts produce what Khatibi calls *identités folles*, mad identities that resist the constraints of a dualistic sex/gender system, as well as those of other bounded systems such as language, nation, and culture (*La Mémoire tatouée*, 180). The *bi-langue* challenges the very concept of Francophone literature, which implies the hegemony of French literature in relation to the literatures of the former colonies—a hegemony supported by the structure of French departments in the United States, where the one "Francophone" specialist (if there is one at all) is presumed capable of covering the vast and heterogeneous field of literatures in French. At the same time, the *bi-langue* counters the complementary concept of an authentic, autonomous Maghrebian literature in Arabic. And finally, by attending to the strangeness, or foreignness, inhabiting every language, it discloses the inadequacy of structuralist approaches to Maghrebian literature that dominated the critical field in the 1970s, approaches that presuppose that both language and text constitute closed systems. Khatibi writes: "As long as the theory of translation, of the *bi-langue* and the *pluri-langue*, has not advanced, certain Maghrebian texts will remain impregnable by means of a formal and functional approach."[29]

Khatibi's writing conveys the urgency of generating discourses of "love" that open subjects to the other rather than participating, directly or indirectly, in what Cixous calls "the murder of the other." And like Cixous, he is committed to exploring the uncharted territories traversed by peoples and subjectivities whose identities are shifting, multiple, and conflictual. A Jew of Moroccan, Spanish, German, Austrian, Hungarian, and Czech descent born in colonial Algeria, Cixous writes of the nonplace she occupies in terms that are close to Khatibi's, that is, in terms of "a meeting of two trajectories of the diaspora":

At the end of these routes of expulsion and dispersion that mark

the functioning of western History through the displacements of
Jews, I fall. —I am born, right in the middle of a scene that is the
perfect example, the naked model, the raw idea of this very
process: I learned to read, to write, to scream, and to vomit in
Algeria. . . . I am (not) Arab. Who am I? . . . Who is this "I"?
Where is my place? . . . Which language is mine? French?
German? Arabic? (70-71)

Like Khatibi, Cixous wants to give voice to an otherness—"an
economy of femininity"—that has historically been associated not
only with women but with Jews, Maghrebian Arabs, African-
Americans, and other marginalized groups. "There is a link," she
says, "between the economy of femininity—the open, extravagant
subjectivity, that relationship to the other in which the gift doesn't
calculate its influence—and the possibility of love; and a link today
between the 'libido of the other' and writing" (91-92). It is this understanding of writing that enables Cixous to defy Freud's association of femininity with the "dark continent," saying, "the 'Dark
Continent' is neither dark nor unexplorable. . . . We [women] are
'black' *and* we are beautiful" (68-69; Cixous's emphasis).

The problem is that, in Cixous's writing as in Khatibi's, the "link
between the 'libido of the other' and writing" is made in such a
way as to obscure or even obliterate the difference between various
manifestations of intractable difference, with the result that various
figures of otherness—femininity, Arabness, Jewishness, black-
ness—circulate indifferently in a space of "immemorial bewitch-
ment" divorced from the particular intersecting histories of these
groups (*Love in Two Languages*, 80). Because dehistoricized poststructuralist readings of Maghrebian texts have dominated the critical scene for some years now—in response, it is true, to pressures
to read them only in terms of the quest for national identity—I
worry that, in the name of affirming the resistant poetic force of
Maghrebian writing in French, critics have developed a habit of
reading this body of work in strict conformity with current French
philosophical and literary norms as a way of "elevating" it. As Edward Said has noted, "The notion of black skin in a white mask is
no more serviceable and dignified in literary study than it is in politics."[30] Rather than arguing against theory, I am making a case
for a consideration of the historical contexts from which a cosmopolitan Maghrebian writing emerges, and of the national and

global conflicts that encumber its efforts to displace restrictive identities.

To avoid isolating Maghrebian literature on a disciplinary continent of its own, I have undertaken the feminist analysis of a number of the most frequently discussed texts in Algerian literature in French (chapters 1 and 2) alongside readings of "nomadic" thought in French poststructuralist theories and in Leïla Sebbar's writing on Maghrebian immigrants in France (chapter 3), as well as analyses of contemporary French fiction on the Maghreb (chapter 4). I have tried to respect the particular historical and cultural determinations of each set of writings, pointing, for example, to the differences between women's struggles in Algeria today and the struggles of "Beur" women in France as they are figured in literary texts. Writing as I do in the wake of the Rushdie affair and the Gulf War, I see this work as part of a collective effort to resist an impulse that is disturbingly evident in the United States—the impulse to demonize and do violence to Muslim peoples while exploiting the powerful resources of global media networks to foster ignorance of their diverse histories and the myriad historical forms and functions of Islam.

Chapter 1

Recasting the Colonial Gaze

Gender and sexuality as key forces in the ongoing negotiation of national and cultural identities are a central concern in cultural studies in the United States and are beginning to attract attention in French studies as well, particularly in work focusing on the situation of racial and ethnic minorities in France and on relations between France and its former colonies. It is obvious that in the texts of widely read Maghrebian writers such as Abdelkebir Khatibi, Tahar Ben Jelloun, Nabile Farès, Mohammed Dib, and Assia Djebar, women's negotiation of these identities in both the Maghrebian and French contexts is a crucial issue, yet critics, when they have not ignored the matter altogether, have often taken a postfeminist approach to it, analyzing "woman" as a textual marker of intractable difference without considering its relation to women's historical and material reality. Alternatively, critics have taken a feminist approach devoted mainly to studying images of women (as mothers, militants, and so on), leaving aside the problem of the texts' staging of the social processes by which human subjects are constituted as women in particular cultural and historical circumstances.[1]

Critical neglect of women's constitution as historical subjects in literature is perhaps nowhere more apparent than in readings of Kateb Yacine's *Nedjma* (1954), for although readers readily recognize in Nedjma (the character) an emblem of the contradictory forces at work in Algeria's search for national identity on the eve of the revolution, they rarely consider *Nedjma*'s significance for Algerian women's liberation and never see in it what is nonetheless easily discernible from today's standpoint, namely a figuration of the revolution's potential failure to ensure social equality for women.

1

In this essay, I want to offer a reading of *Nedjma*—the most highly acclaimed and frequently studied novel of the Algerian Revolution—that takes account of Algerian women's present situation as historical subjects who are not so much excluded from national life (as Germaine Tillion, David Gordon, and others have argued) as they are called upon to *embody* contemporary Algeria's irreducibly contradictory identity and contain the nation's dangerous conflicts, at great cost to women. At the same time, though, I want to situate *Nedjma* with respect to other cultural texts addressing the relation between Algerian women and Algerian national identity in an effort to reconnect literary analysis to a broader cultural-political critique of nationalisms, both French and Algerian.

The cultural texts considered here include colonial texts such as the reflections of French intellectuals and government officials on Algerian resistance to assimilation, and mass cultural events such as the centenary celebration of the French conquest of Algeria in 1830, which go hand in hand with and help to shape the policies of the French army and administration. Since the feminization of colonial Algeria in the French cultural imagination is often alluded to but rarely demonstrated except in analyses of orientalist painting and photography, I hope to show how Algeria is feminized in the writing and social activity of some influential Frenchmen, particularly the Algerian governor general Maurice Viollette, in the years preceding the independence struggle. Alongside the colonial material, I will examine anticolonial texts like Marc Garanger's photographs of Algerian female detainees during the revolution, Frantz Fanon's 1959 essay "Algeria Unveiled," and Malek Alloula's 1981 critique of the colonial gaze cast on Algerian women by postcard photographers in the early twentieth century. I want to argue that despite their focus on Algerian women both as objects of colonial domination and as subjects of resistance, the Fanon and Alloula essays hinder women's liberation in the present political context insofar as they ignore feminism's conflicts with nationalism in Algeria—conflicts that Kateb's *Nedjma* confronts head-on.

Before discussing these questions in detail, however, I think it would be well briefly to map the field of scholarly and political work in which my own study is situated, that is, feminist work on third-world women attempting, on the one hand, to analyze the complex and conflictual relations between feminism, nationalism, and anti-imperialism and, on the other, to take account of the ways race, class, ethnicity, nationality, religion, and other factors inform those relations for particular groups of women. The need for such work in the study of Algeria can be indicated by reference to the fact that in two key texts to be dealt with in this essay, Kateb's *Nedjma* and Fanon's "Algeria Unveiled," the Algerian nation and, by implication, all Algerian women are embodied in a single female figure—as if women in Algeria comprised a homogeneous, monolithic group. If Kateb's novel successfully stages some of the processes by which women are constituted as actors in history—and are limited in their ability to act in nationalism's confrontation with colonialism—it nonetheless makes one woman, Nedjma (however fluid a figure she may be), stand in for women generally. Similarly, Fanon's "Algeria Unveiled" analyzes the processes by which the meaning and function of veiling change as women increasingly participate in the struggle against colonialism, but assumes nonetheless that women compose an undifferentiated social entity. For both writers, the possibility of imagining a cohesive (though not unitary) national body relies on the rhetorical strategy of reducing the multiple, heterogeneous identities of Algerian women to a single figure, woman—a strategy that is particularly evident in the titles of their texts: *Nedjma* and "L'Algérie se dévoile," where Algeria is personified as one woman.

Yet Kateb and Fanon are not isolated cases, for a similar reduction is at work in much Western scholarship—including feminist scholarship—on the women of Algeria and other countries in the Maghreb and the Middle East. This is perhaps most obvious in work less subtle than Fanon's dealing with the practice of veiling. It is well known that, historically, the veil has been seen in the West as the sign of women's oppression in Muslim societies, as if all women were equally and identically oppressed in those societies, as if their oppression stemmed uniquely from the power of Islam (rather than the power of Western imperialism), and as if Islam and "Muslim society" themselves were monolithic entities impervious to historical change and, above all, to Western enlightenment.

Reductive representations are typical not just of scholarship on veiling and Muslim women, however. More generally, as Chandra Talpade Mohanty has shown, they characterize Western feminist discourses that take third-world women as their object. Mohanty argues eloquently and persuasively that, however diverse the intentions, political allegiances, and goals of Western feminist discourses, they rely on analytic strategies or implicit principles that have the effect of "discursively colonizing the material and historical heterogeneities of the lives of women in the third world, thereby producing/re-presenting a composite, singular 'Third World woman.'"[2] Thus, despite the relative marginality of feminist discourses in the West, they contribute to the production and perpetuation of Western power and privilege, for in those discourses, Western subjects—specifically, Western women—are identified with modernity, rationality, individual autonomy, and freedom, all of which depend symbolically and materially on the backwardness, mystification, subordination, and unfreedom of their third-world other-opposites.

In recent years, many feminists have been productively criticizing this scholarship and generating alternative studies that take account of various social practices—conjugal and family relations, child-rearing arrangements, work inside and outside the home, religion, education, and so on—that constitute women in particular ways that change dramatically over time and across class, ethnic, cultural, and national frontiers. In addition to Marnia Lazreg's general critique of Western social scientific feminist discourse from the standpoint of Algerian women's experience, a good example of the work being done by feminists from Muslim countries is Homa Hoodfar's "Return to the Veil: Personal Strategy and Public Participation in Egypt," which examines the shifting significance of veiling in Egypt since the 1920s, particularly in the lives of educated lower-middle-class women in Cairo since the 1970s.[3] Hoodfar shows, for instance, that reveiling among married women in this group, employed as white-collar workers in the public and government sector, is linked to the effects of rising prices and housing costs in the seventies and early eighties: the wages they were earning became insufficient to justify keeping a job, given the high costs (in child care, transportation, suitable clothing for work) associated with married women's employment. Under these circumstances, for both economic and ideological reasons, men began using "their Islamic right to limit their wife's mobility, which, in modern Cairo, is popularly interpreted as their right to prevent their wife from 'working'" (111).

As a way of acknowledging their domestic responsibility and thus justifying their claim to their husband's financial support, while simultaneously securing for themselves an independent income and control over their own resources (which is of vital importance in cases of divorce or widowhood), many of these women reveiled. Hoodfar shows that reveiling at once permits women's continued activity in the public sector, enables them to circulate in public without being molested, affirms their adherence to Islamic values that recognize the importance of work and child-rearing responsibilities in the home, reduces their husbands' insecurities and thus dispels a certain amount of domestic tension, considerably reduces expenditures for clothing, and allows women of this class to publicly differentiate themselves both from upper-class women who generally wear a modest version of Western-style clothing as well as from *balady* (urban lower classes whose neighborhoods they now inhabit on the outskirts of Cairo) and *felaheen* (peasants), who wear different types of veils.

Hoodfar's method of examining reveiling in relation to the social practices and ideological concerns of a specific group of women allows her to theorize the meaning of reveiling *for those women in their context.* In doing so, she not only avoids clumsy, dangerous generalizations about "Muslim women" and "the veil," but above all grants the women she has interviewed the status of historical subjects who, far from being impotent victims of a monolithic patriarchy or religion, are actively and skillfully negotiating ways to affirm their own religious or cultural values while simultaneously protecting their economic and social gains in public employment. Yet, even as she affirms the resourcefulness and critical consciousness of the women she studies, Hoodfar never loses sight of the need for political networks capable of bringing about broad economic and ideological change. Speaking of a young single woman who reveiled in order to escape harassment while working and traveling by bus at night—a tactic that allowed her to "invest her energy in her top priority: going to school"—Hoodfar observes: "Considering her lack of power to change prevailing attitudes, *a change which would require collective efforts and social and political support,* she used the social institution at her disposal in order to protect herself" (118; my emphasis).

Hoodfar's strategy of maintaining tension between widespread but unorganized resistance by women on the one hand and collective political activity on the other is an important one, for it is only by attending to the contradictions and resistances in the lives of particular groups of women that effective political action can be organized. In this connection it might be useful to contrast Hoodfar's method with Mai Ghoussoub's in "Feminism—or the Eternal Masculine—in the Arab World," which focuses on the near impossibility of oppositional feminist politics in Muslim countries, thanks to the ways in which Islam and nationalism collude in women's oppression. Ghoussoub writes:

> The bitter reality is that Arab feminism, in the modern sense of the term, exists as a force only in the student milieux of Europe and America to which a privileged few can escape, and in a growing but still very modest academic literature. The double knot tied by the fatal connexions in Arab culture and politics between definitions of femininity and religion, and religion and nationality, have all but throttled any major women's revolt so far. Every assertion of the second sex can be charged—in a virtually simultaneous register—with impiety to Islam and treason to the nation.[4]

Because she doesn't acknowledge the forms of latent or protofeminism in the Muslim cultures she discusses, Ghoussoub is open to charges of "bourgeois feminism" leveled by her critics, Reza Hammami and Martina Rieker, who claim that in counting as feminist only the types of organizations and activities found in the West, she symbolically disempowers Muslim women in the third world, especially poor and uneducated women.[5]

Yet it seems to me that Ghoussoub's effort to underline the importance of organized feminist movements is a worthy one that Hammami and Riecker are wrong to dismiss. As Hoodfar's essay implies, affirmation of resistance in the lives of individuals and isolated groups is no substitute (although it may be the precondition) for political action. In my view, Ghoussoub's essay has the merit of forging strategic links among heterogeneous groups of women within and across Muslim cultures with the aim of denouncing (presumably as a step toward dismantling) the various configurations of Woman/Islam/Nation that do in fact oppress women in Muslim countries, even if they also act in women's interest by resisting imperialism.

The logic of Ghoussoub's essay is similar to that organizing collections of essays that have appeared in recent years linking various analyses of women, or the literary production of women, in widely differing Muslim cultures.[6] The networks formed in these academic projects are structurally similar to those generated by feminist activists in organizations such as Women Against Fundamentalism (in Britain) and Women Living Under Muslim Laws (in France), which intervene in practical ways to combat the laws and cultural practices that oppress Muslim women both in Muslim societies and in the West.[7] Projects like these are vitally important because they constitute international networks that can begin to change existing power relations between the West and "the rest," and at the same time challenge the hierarchies of culture and "development" that inform them. It is thus counterproductive to suggest, as Hammami and Riecker seem to do, that essentialism and orientalism necessarily underlie the identification of common problems and goals among Muslim women across class and national frontiers. On the other hand it is crucial to acknowledge the strategic and provisional nature of those ties rather than presenting them as "fatal connections," as Ghoussoub does at certain moments.

The problem of the composite Third-World woman that obliterates the material and subjective reality of women in the third world is of course relevant as well to the situation of third-world women living in the West. Readers of this volume are undoubtedly familiar with feminist work by women of color in the United States addressing this issue. Where Maghrebian women living in France are concerned, it seems to me that much impressive work is being done to break up the composite other/woman both by writers (Leïla Sebbar, Assia Djebar, Tahar Ben Jelloun) and by social scientists who, in Rabia Abdelkrim-Chikh's words, "cast doubt on the clear-cut opposition between, on the one hand, a culture founded on the sacred, which muzzles and even asphyxiates women, and on the other, a culture founded on secularism and the rights of man, which liberate women."[8] Abdelkrim-Chikh's analyses of interviews with "exogamous women" from the Maghreb who have married French citizens (whether "naturalized" Maghrebians or native Frenchmen) convincingly demonstrate that these women are "double agents . . . who dare to play against each other two systems that unceasingly clash and emphasize their differences" (245). In this negotiation, "woman is not given but always a construction in a relation of force" (246). Through their way of naming their children, their verbal exchanges with their daughters, and their insistence on circumcising their sons, they mark their differences from a French culture to which they refuse to assimilate. At the same time, they loosen the constraints of traditional Maghrebian culture while maintaining their affective bond with it.

In the pages that follow, I hope to problematize further the stark oppositions between French and Algerian politics and culture without losing sight of France's power and privilege in the colonial and postcolonial contexts. Focusing mainly on French and Algerian nationalisms as they have affected women in Algeria, I will try to indicate the importance of debates generated by feminists from Muslim societies for an analysis of Algerian feminism's relation to nationalist and anti-imperialist struggles.

The National Guise

In 1964, Germaine Tillion, a French ethnographer known for her extensive work on male-female relations in Algeria, writes that "on the Muslim side of the Mediterranean, the veil . . . constitutes not just a picturesque detail of costume, but a veritable border. On one side of this border, female societies stagnate; on the other side there lives and progresses a national society which, by virtue of this fact, is but half a society."[9] To her credit, Tillion painstakingly emphasizes, in the essay in which this sentence appears, the lines of continuity between social practices in the northern and southern parts of the Mediterranean (including women's obligation to cover their heads) in order to counter the view, widespread among her compatriots, that women's oppression in Muslim societies stems uniquely from the supposed barbarity of Islam. As a survivor of the concentration camps, Tillion is keenly aware of Europe's capacity for savagery toward its own people, and as a critical observer of her country's relation to Algeria, she repeatedly calls her readers' attention to the abuses of colonialism, particularly as they have affected women.[10] Yet in the sentence quoted above, Tillion poses the question of women and nationalism in contemporary Muslim societies in terms that, today, obstruct, as much as they enable, feminist analysis of the problem.

In setting the tradition-bound female sphere in opposition to the modern nation and in underscoring women's exclusion from national life in Muslim societies, Tillion's formulation is typical of much Western scholarship on women in Algeria since the nation achieved independence in 1962. For example, David Gordon stated in 1968 that

> with the dawn of independence, confused and economically ominous as the atmosphere was, the expectations of and for women were high. But the force of the legacy of centuries was soon to make itself felt. The gap between promise and reality, law and fact, was to widen. . . . While one does, of course, see women unveiled in the streets, working in ministries, serving as deputies, working by the side of men in welfare centers and such, the role of even these "evolved" women is peripheral.[11]

Nearly twenty years later, Catherine Delcroix poses the problem in similarly dichotomous terms, saying that "in view of the Algerian woman's higher level of education today, her underrepresentation [in political institutions] can only foster frustration and obstruct the evolution of her personal status, and thus, of her emancipation."[12] Delcroix contends that responsibility for women's exclusion lies with the traditionalist mentality of the electorate, both female and male, and with "the ideological system itself, which doesn't sufficiently mobilize the female population for fear of seeing woman transgress her role as guardian of traditional values" (138-39). Like the veil, then, which Tillion had identified as "a veritable border" internally dividing the national territory, "the ideological system" is said to bar women from meaningful participation in public life.

The opposition that structures the arguments of Tillion, Gordon, and Delcroix bears testimony to conditions that prevailed during the Algerian Revolution and at the time of independence, when the emerging nation still held the promise of social equality for women, whose role in the war had been recognized by the National Liberation Front (FLN). Despite women's subordinate role as militants in the liberation struggle, documented in an exhaustive study by Djamila Amrane, the FLN's formal commitment to women's equality was actualized in certain situations—for example, in the wartime tribunals before which couples were married based on the partners' mutual consent—and was continually reiterated in statements printed in its newspaper throughout the revolutionary period. Here are the remarks of an FLN combatant in a published interview:

> Since 1954 there have been many changes. In most households, men are absent—they are in prison, in combat, or dead. Women

have learned to get along on their own; they work, they manage their own money, they take care of their children. It is an established fact of the Revolution; there is no turning back. Habits have changed, too. . . . I think men understand that it is in their interest to give their wives some responsibilities, and that they will let them take some initiative, even when peace has been restored.[13]

Unfortunately, however, the promise of social equality for women faded after 1962, and this failure on the part of the nation that had played an exemplary role in anticolonial struggles provoked bitter disappointment, as Fadela M'rabet's work, for example, makes clear.[14] The realignment of women with tradition and their consequent exclusion from public life were considered by feminists to be a betrayal both of the women who had fought for the nation's freedom and of the revolution itself. The oppositional relation between women and men, and between tradition and the modern nation, thus accounted for an important dynamic of the 1960s, one that is undoubtedly still operative in Algeria today and that has a place in feminist analyses, which must, of course, affirm the possibility of a modern nation in which women are on an equal footing with men.

Since independence, however, a quite different relation has emerged between Algerian women and the nation, one that must be taken into account, I believe, if women's situation in Algeria is to be changed. An articulation of this other relation is already discernible in Gordon's 1968 study, which maintains that "as far as many women are concerned, Algeria lives *between* two worlds, the modern and the traditional" (83; my emphasis). Remarking on the tension between the contradictory aims of the Algerian Revolution—the establishment of a modern socialist nation on the one hand and, on the other, the restoration of a culture that French colonialism had all but destroyed—Gordon goes on to suggest that "women are the victims of this tension, and their present condition might be seen as its symbol." Here, women are identified less with tradition as such than with Algeria's "betweenness," its traversal by irreconcilable modern and traditional currents. Tillion situates women in a similar fashion when she says that they are "the principal victims of the irresistible slippage that draws nomadic populations toward the towns and cities [insofar as the migration to urban centers results in stricter practices of seclusion and veiling]. This slippage lies at the source of a conflict, persisting into the present, between two types of structures: the society of citizens and tribal society. There is conflict between individuals and within each one of them. . . . In this conflict, the 'noble personality' opposes the promiscuities that the human density of the cities or towns apparently makes inevitable, for the daily contact with non-relatives will wound and irremediably compromise this 'personality.' "(30)

As the embodiment of conflicting forces that simultaneously compose and disrupt the nation, women are the guarantors of national identity, no longer simply as guardians of traditional values but as *symbols that successfully contain the conflicts of the new historical situation.* At the same time, women are the supreme threat to national identity insofar as *its* endemic instability can be assigned to *them.* Gordon's and Tillion's analyses imply, further, that women symbolize and are called upon to stabilize Algeria's irreducibly contradictory identity in and through their "present condition" of subordination. They are subject to discrimination, to be sure, but not, as it still appeared in 1968, simply by virtue of their exclusion from a national life that could have included them as equals; rather, women's exclusion increasingly *constitutes* the Algerian nation after independence, just as their veiling—now a powerful national symbol—plays an important role in producing and maintaining both Algeria's difference from its colonial oppressor and the uneasy coalition of heterogeneous and conflicting interests under a single national banner.

Writing in 1987 in the wake of Algerian feminism's twenty-five year struggle against the forms of exclusion and appropriation that have prevailed under the socialist state, Peter R. Knauss recasts the problem Gordon had broached regarding women's symbolic function in the revolution and its aftermath, observing that "Algerian women became both the revered objects of the collective act of national redemption and the role model for the new nationalist patriarchal family."[15] Granted, Knauss's rhetoric often echoes Gordon's in its use of antithetical formulations that oppose traditional Algerian culture to modern nationalism as if each were a self-contained entity, albeit one capable of dressing up in the other's clothes. (Knauss speaks, for instance, of "the ideology of cultural restoration wrapped in the mantle of radical nationalism" [xiii].) Nonetheless, Knauss's analyses of present-day male-female relations show that the government's legitimation of traditions that disempower women works to "contain the social consequences of significant changes that have taken place in education and employment" and does so (this is how his position differs from Delcroix's) in the name of "patriarchy which has become part of the warp and woof of Algerian political culture" (137, 141).

The patriarchal texture of Algeria's political culture is evident in the persistence of traditional social practices dictated by Islamic law, practices that the state formally sanctioned in the family law of 1984, adopted from the Shari'a, the historical principles of Islamic law and ethics. Under this law, women remain legal minors, for example, until they marry, whereas men attain adult status at age eighteen whether they are married or not; a woman's, but not a man's, decision to marry must be authorized by a guardian; the dowry system is maintained; married women must obey their husbands; and it is difficult and costly for women to initiate divorce, whereas men retain the rights of polygyny and repudiation of their wives.[16]

If the integration of women into public life is significantly hindered by the family law, it is impeded by other factors as well. Despite gains in recent years, large numbers of women continue to be excluded from education or from jobs for which their education qualifies them, and birth control is still widely discouraged by both Muslim conservatives and Algerian nationalists who regard it as "unnatural" interference in the production of children, an important source of national wealth and family honor.[17] Moreover, because Islamic fundamentalism has gathered new force in Algeria since the Iranian Revolution, there is at present little possibility of change that would ensure women's equality with men. In fact, in the municipal elections of June 1990, "the Islamic Salvation Front (FIS) swept every major city in the country, capturing all 33 municipal councils in the capital city of Algiers, even those councils in well-to-do neighborhoods populated by wealthy businessmen and Cabinet ministers."[18] The stunning electoral victory of the fundamentalists bears grim testimony to the growing strength of the claim made nearly a decade ago by President Chadli Bendjedid in response to feminist protests of a 1981 draft of the family law: "No place whatever exists for anarchy [that is, feminist opposition to government policy] in a society that is building itself and constructing the foundations for its future."[19]

Ever since independence, feminists have deplored the cynicism of political regimes that have promoted regressive interpretations of Islamic law and dismissed the relevance of basic civil rights to "the Arab and Muslim Algerian woman."[20] The state's sanction of oppressive traditions directly contradicts the 1964 Charter of Algiers, which proclaims women's political equality with men in the new socialist state, calling for their integration into every level of the work force as well as national political organizations. If Algerian feminists such as Ratiba Hadj-Moussa, Rabia Abdelkrim-Chikh, and Marie-Aimée Hélie-Lucas are right to argue that the current political function of misogynistic customs is to forge solidarity among men who are otherwise deeply divided, while maintaining what is perceived as a crucial distinction between Muslim and Western societies, then it is reasonable to say that the oppression of women has become indispensable to Algerian nationalism in its present form.[21]

There has been a vast unemployed or underemployed male population in Algeria for twenty-five years now, as well as ongoing strife between the petty bourgeoisie and the wealthy elite. The events of October 1988 in particular—mass riots of the underclass to which the government responded with shootings and torture—mark the degree to which economic divisions are threatening to rend the social fabric in Algeria. The outcome of these violent conflicts was sadly predictable where women's rights are concerned: when the government moved to institute economic reforms, eliminate widespread corruption, and give political parties some freedom to assemble and air their demands, political groups—including the Parti de l'Avant-Garde Socialiste (the reincarnation of Algeria's Communist party)—refused to call for a single change in the family law despite pressure from feminists groups like the Association for Equality before the Law, headed by Khalida Messaoudi.[22] In its effort, then, to mute economic conflict between men and forestall violent struggle between fundamentalist groups such as the Muslim Brothers and "progressive" nationalist factions, the state has fixed upon "the Arab and Muslim Algerian woman" as the indispensable unifying force, a symbol whose power is turned against Algerian women, whether rich or poor, Arab or Berber, Muslim or nonreligious, in the name of national cohesion and stability.

This is not to say that state policy affects all Algerian women in the same way, or that all women respond to it in the same way; clearly, their responses vary according to class, region, generation, education, and their conception of what constitutes political action in today's Algeria, as is apparent from the interviews published in the Delcroix study cited earlier (166-82). Yet despite the multiple, contradictory, and overlapping positions of Algerian women and the resistance of many to state policy, the government has nonetheless had alarming success in exploiting the symbol "woman" in order to erase differences among women, neutralize women's differences with men, and overcome men's differences with each other. The underside of this strategy is the fundamentalists' designation of woman as the *cause* of the differences from which conflicts are arising in Algeria today. In their version, woman embodies *fitna*,[23] the dangerous force that disrupts the community of believers: "To all the social ills from which Algeria is suffering," writes a group of Maghrebian intellectuals in January 1990, "the fundamentalists ascribe a single origin: woman. They intend to find a way out of the real crisis the country is experiencing by depriving Algerian women, as a group, of their civil and moral rights."[24]

Clearly, something more than women's exclusion from the nation's political life is at stake in Algeria in the 1990s. For although women are indeed underrepresented in political institutions, silenced in public debates, and denounced as anarchists whenever they make themselves heard, they nonetheless embody Algerian national life, whether in its "progressive" or regressive guise. More than any other social group in Algeria, women are made to bear responsibility for the nation's conflicts and assume the risks of its uncertain identity. In this context, an important social function of the veil is to cover up the social and psychic divisions in the Algerian "personality." Yet when the cover-up inevitably fails because of the intensity of social conflicts in Algeria today, women — whether veiled or unveiled — become objects of fear, hatred, and vitriolic attacks, both verbal and physical. Because the women of Algeria have been fashioned as living symbols of the independent nation, feminist analysis must come to terms with and begin to dismantle this aspect of national identity. It is no longer enough to call for women's integration into an order whose very constitution depends on their exclusion as producers of social meanings that contest tradition or, more dangerously still, attest to and presume to negotiate the "betweenness" of Algeria that has been projected onto them.

This is not to discount the view, recently put forth by Fatima Mernissi, that "the conservative wave against women in the Muslim world, far from being a regressive trend, is on the contrary a defense mechanism against profound changes in both sex roles and the touchy subject of sexual identity."[25] Mernissi's strategy of underscoring the reality of progressive change in Muslim women's lives constitutes an important challenge to the self-representation of conservatives who claim that Muslim societies are inherently traditional and that "their women miraculously escape social change and the erosion of time" (8). Still, it seems to me that her flat denial of fundamentalism's regressive character obscures another, equally important reality, namely, fundamentalism's regressive effects in the social field where it *is* working to reverse feminist gains by restricting women's mobility and visibility. More and more women of all social classes are veiling again, whether as an expression of religious faith; a sign of class, national, or pan-Arab solidarity; or a means of escaping harassment. In the case of Algeria in particular, even as we follow Rabia Abdelkrim-Chikh in affirming women's acts of resistance in donning a colorful, "attractive" *hijeb* ("Enjeux politiques," 276), it is essential to acknowledge the mobilization of the veiled woman as a national symbol. Until the fundamentalist victories in the 1991 elections at least, this symbol not only defended against the progressive changes Mernissi points to but also helped to produce a new social configuration in which "betweenness," rather than a simple archaism, worked to constrain women. Because it is the political effectiveness of a representation that is at issue here, the border dividing culture from politics in feminist analysis must be opened. In Abdelkrim-Chikh's words:

> It is not so much a matter of consuming secularism as of producing women's identity articulated to a culture and a history, while simultaneously contributing to the deconstruction of all models and monopolies. This elaboration of women's identity, which must pass by way of equality without being fixed there, will make possible the birth of . . . a world that will no longer destroy alterity by virtue of its inscription solely within the abstract rights of "man," but will instead produce concrete

plurality in which difference will not be discriminated against.
("Enjeux politiques," 277)

The Feminization of Algeria in Culture and Politics

The cultural record makes clear that women embody Algeria not only for Algerians in the days since independence, but also for the French colonizers who conquer them militarily, control them administratively, study them as sociologists, ethnographers, and historians, and represent them in both high and popular forms of art and literature. In the colonialist fantasy, to possess Algeria's women is to possess Algeria. Mostefa Lacheraf has disclosed the "colonial perversion" infusing the official and unofficial writings of the military officers who "pacify" the country between 1830 and 1870. Montagnac, for example, "one of the most excited young officers of the Conquest," according to Lacheraf, writes in a letter to a friend: "You ask me . . . what we do with the women we capture. We keep a few as hostages, exchange others for horses, and auction off the rest like beasts of burden [to the troops]. . . . This, my friend, is how one must go about fighting Arabs: kill all the men over fourteen years of age, capture all the women and children, fill the warships with them, send them off to the Marquesas Islands or elsewhere—in a word, annihilate everything that doesn't grovel at our feet like dogs."[26]

No less than its military officers, France's colonial administrators view the control of Algerian women as indispensable to their "civilizing mission." For example, the liberal politician Maurice Viollette, who twice served as governor general of Algeria, states that "one cannot envisage the question of relations between Europeans and natives without devoting a special chapter to the native woman."[27] Viollette aligns himself with "enlightened" (that is, wealthy, French-educated) native men who, writing in the assimilationist publication *La Voix des Humbles*, propose to "help the French of good faith who want to extend a helping hand to us, but who dare not act because of this sort of superstitious fear inspired in them by the veil that we throw in the face of our women like a shroud before death" (421; Viollette is citing one of their articles). Viollette likewise enjoins the French women of his class to be kind and encouraging rather than critical in their treatment of upper-class native women in their social contacts at tea parties, and notes with approval the "serious movement [toward Europeanization] in feminine circles" (415, 417-18).

Alhough he obviously applauds natives' efforts to assimilate, Viollette joins Léon Blum in an unsuccessful attempt, in 1936, to persuade his compatriots to grant citizenship and political rights to Algerians without requiring that they relinquish their personal status, which was governed by the Shari'a.[28] In the debate on personal status, the fate of Algerian women is centrally important, for French opponents of the Blum-Viollette bill express moral outrage at the institutions of polygyny (which had all but disappeared by this time), repudiation, and child marriage, claiming that no Muslim who adhered to his code could respect the French laws that citizens are bound to obey. Feminists all around the Mediterranean are criticizing these institutions in the early twentieth century; yet it is clear that their denunciation by Viollette's opponents is, more than anything else, a political ploy.[29] As Jean-Robert Henry and François Balique observe, "the assertion of this juridical unshakeability" is intended first and foremost to point up the Muslim's "natural inequality" and thereby obstruct his passage from subject to citizen.[30]

As governor general, Viollette works to apply French social legislation to the native population, and here, too, women are a central concern. At the heart of Viollette's policy is "assistance to mothers and nurslings, which afforded me the additional opportunity of making great moral and material progress not only in assistance properly speaking, but in Hygiene, since assistance to mothers and nurslings entails, alongside the problem of subsidies, that of medical care for the native family" (153-54). This is accomplished by establishing a "corps of female nurses, preferably midwives," since Algerian women refused the care of male physicians. Although Viollette notes that this effort is considered "superfluous" by French conservatives—in light of the natives' rapidly increasing demographic superiority, disease and infant mortality are, in their view, a boon—it provides an invaluable technique for regulating the native population through infiltration of the family (388). In Viollette's scheme, the nurse's labor is complemented by the charity of the colon's wife, who "often undertakes good works for her natives and sometimes makes truly heroic efforts" in this regard (392). However "heroic" they may be, though, these efforts are insufficient to enable the French to overcome their racism, for "as a group, the French *grand colons* of Algeria, barring exceptions, have been able to establish cordial relations with [native] individuals, but there is on their part no moral disarmament with respect to the Muslim and the Arab" (392).

According to Viollette, philanthropy and government-funded welfare, together with higher salaries, will not remove the native's incentive to work, as many *colons* contend, but rather will "improve" conditions throughout Algeria, that is, make them favorable for optimal colonial exploitation: "Who does not see that the day our six million natives acquire needs and become consumers, Algeria will experience an unprecedented commercial and industrial prosperity from which the metropolitan center will benefit?" (150). Clearly, the regulation of the female sphere—in part, through mobilization of French women in the colony—is integral to the governor's plan to empower France by "uplifting" the native population of Algeria.[31]

A less sanguine observer than Viollette, the Islamicist Octave Depont, writes in the same period that assimilation of the Algerian natives is impossible without drastic changes in the lives of their women: "As long as . . . the miserable condition of the native woman is not improved, as long as endogamy causes Muslim society to close in on itself, the door to this society will open to outside influences only with difficulty. We can attempt rapprochement and fusion, but these efforts are liable to weaken, if not shatter, at the feet of this woman, unyielding and faithful guardian of the home, its traditions and, in a word, the preservation and conservation of the race."[32] Depont deplores the Maghreb's "incomplete opening" to France, which, in comparison with the Eastern Mediterranean countries, makes her less prepared "to receive the emancipatory seed." Nonetheless he musters enthusiasm for an education campaign that can foster at least partial assimilation of the Algerian natives, most of whom will of course receive only vocational instruction. For women, this means instruction in running a household and in manual tasks such as needlework: "Let us thus hasten to open . . . schools everywhere, above all girls' schools" (49), for "the native woman," says Depont, citing approvingly the Kabyle financial delegate Hacène, "must not undo at home what the teacher has done at school" (49 n. 12). Like Viollette, Depont applauds French women's efforts to assist native women in matters of hygiene, saying that the latter will be freed from their slavery "by the implementation of the 'household pol-icy' advocated by Mr. Pierre Bordes [Viollette's successor as gover-nor general], the bases of which were explained by Georges Grand-jean in the June 24, 1928, issue of the women's illustrated magazine *Eve*" (50 n. 12).[33]

For Depont, women embody not just native society in Algeria, but the ancient soul of the orient that supposedly survives in the Maghreb under the guise of Islam. Quoting the orientalist scholar Maspero, he maintains that in Babylonia "the women seldom went out to pray in the temples or visit friends in the neighboring har-ems, veiled and surrounded by their entourage . . . most of the time [they were] secluded at home, idle. . . . Woman's influence works silently through intrigue, or through crimes of the palace that dishonored the Persian Empire." Depont then asks his reader in a confidential tone, "*All things considered*, isn't this more or less the image of our Islamic and Islamicized [Maghrebian] families?" (50-51; my emphasis).

As Depont's hallucinatory reflections indicate, French intellectu-als, like their military and administrative compatriots, make of Al-gerian women key symbols of the colony's cultural identity. Women—or rather a single, undifferentiated Algerian woman modeled now on the wealthy woman of the harem, now on the poor city or country dweller whose need for "assistance" will be guaranteed by the managers of colonial domination—are at once the emblem of the colony's refusal to receive France's "emancipa-tory seed" and the gateway to penetration. This is as true of anx-ious and hostile conservatives like Depont as of liberals like Viol-lette or his contemporary, René Maunier, professor of sociology at the University of Paris and member of the Académie des Sciences Coloniales. Maunier envisages with pleasure not just the penetra-tion and domination of the native race by its French conquerers, but "a fusion between the peoples" in which influences will be re-ciprocal. "A very ancient author noted," writes Maunier, "that the principal agent of linkage and fusion of races is woman; and he said that durable and permanent contact is made only through women. It is, indeed—let us say it with him—the sexual union of peoples, or rather, exogamy in the very broad sense of the word, which is the superior form and the major form of contact between races."[34] In Maunier's account, however, the sexual hierarchy maintained between the European (cast as a male) and the Algerian native (cast as a female) ensures that the supposed "fusion" of races will leave European power and authority intact.

Thus, whether the imagined contact between races or peoples involves a perilous siege or easy pleasure, a key point of contact, where Algeria is concerned, is the veiled or secluded woman. Not surprisingly, in the face of French aggression, including its medical, hygienic, philanthropic, pedagogic, and social forms (such as the tea party), Algerians respond with various "attitudes of refusal" that, according to Abdallah Laroui, mark the emergence of nationalism and the delegitimation of French rule in the 1930s. These attitudes of refusal, which include "withdrawal into private life, noncooperation, personal and familial independence, disobedience, slovenliness, and finally, destructive individual revolt,"[35] are retroactively symbolized in terms of the veil by Frantz Fanon when, in 1959, the fifth year of the Algerian Revolution, radical changes in women's situation make it possible to ascribe to the veil a "historic dynamism" dating back to the rise of nationalism in the 1930s. Challenging the idea that Algeria is mere "prey disputed with equal ferocity by Islam and the Western power, France," and that cultural regression—including anachronistic forms of women's oppression—is Algeria's only alternative to assimilation, Fanon rearticulates the symbolic link between the veil and Muslim traditions in his essay "Algeria Unveiled."[36]

In the early phases of the independence struggle, he says, wearing the veil signaled women's allegiance to cultural traditions and forms of existence, such as the extended family, that enabled the emerging nation to forge an identity. This identity, then, grew out of resistance to France's strategy of combating nationalism by "unveiling" Algeria, that is, regulating private life through assistance campaigns aimed at women and children and promoting the so-called liberation of Algerian women through education—"encouraging" them, as Maurice Viollette put it, in their movement toward Europeanization. Subsequently, according to Fanon, the veil became an instrument in armed resistance to the French forces, once women actively engaged in guerrilla activity and began hiding explosives under their veils. Later, Algerian women carried out their militant actions in Western dress, concealing bombs in their purses rather than in the folds of their veils. When these tactics were discovered by the French, however, militants again wore the veil in order to escape detection by the occupiers. The readoption of the veil came in response, too, to a demonstration that followed the army officers' revolt of May 13, 1958, when officers' wives presided over the public unveiling of Algerian women who had been persuaded, paid, or forced to adopt the slogan "Let's be like the French woman."[37] In this context, says Fanon, donning the *haïk* shows that "it isn't true that woman liberates herself at the invitation of France and General de Gaulle" (46).

Fanon's outline of this development is fleshed out by his attention to the historic dynamism of Algerian women's bodies in relation to the veil. It is by means of the veil, he writes, that the nubile body is "revealed" to the Algerian woman; that is, the veil "covers the body and disciplines it, tempers it at the very moment when it knows its greatest effervescence," but also "protects, reassures, insulates." According to Fanon, who was a psychiatrist at the hospital in Blida-Joinville, dream material showed that the woman accustomed to wearing the veil was disoriented when she began to move about in public space unveiled; for instance, she had trouble judging distances in the street and even found it difficult to mark out the contours of her own body: "The unveiled body seems to get away from itself, to go to pieces. There is an impression of being improperly dressed, even nude." Accordingly, Fanon argues that during the revolution, the Algerian female combatant in Western dress entered the European district of the city "completely nude," and so had to "relearn her body, reinstall it in a totally revolutionary way" (42).

Undeniably in 1959 when Fanon's "Algeria Unveiled" was first published, it was strategically important to affirm a "historic dynamism of the veil" unfolding within a cultural territory free from French influence. This is true, first, because as we have seen, the colonizers had positioned Algerian women as living symbols of both the colony's resistance and its vulnerability to penetration. It was therefore essential that the national liberation movement wrest women's liberation from French control. Beyond, this, however, it is important to note the hypocrisy and brutality of France's official stance toward Algerian women at the time of Fanon's writing. Shortly after the wives of the rebellious army officers induced a number of Algerian women to "liberate" themselves by making a public spectacle of their unveiling, the army opened women's prisons for the female combatants they were capturing and subjecting to torture.[38] And clearly, the extension of voting rights to Algerian women in 1958 was intended primarily to weaken the nationalist movement by promoting women's support for a French, rather than an independent, Algeria. (By contrast, when the Paris government proposed the same move in 1947, the French in Algeria opposed it, since they were in a much stronger position at the time and thus saw no need to make this concession. They responded to the bill with irony—because Algerian women were considered too ignorant and backward to vote—and even made outlandish statements in defense of "the veil that was being trampled": "Tomorrow the young girl, the wife, the mother will be summoned to the disputes of the forum," they lamented, calling on their [male] "Muslim friends to stop the evildoers who are weakening the age-old foundation on which our households rest."[39] Here, as in so many other instances, the veil signified, for the French, both Muslim tradition *and* the means to effective colonial domination.)

Fanon's insistence on the "historic dynamism of the veil" does not necessarily indicate that he has succumbed to the inevitable limitations of a French-educated secular intellectual in underestimating the force of Islam and its effects on women, as critics of the time claim.[40] Nor does he necessarily allow his *engagé* zeal to blind him to the importance of the colonial relation itself—the implantation of an industrial economy and Western ideologies—in preparing the ground for the radical transformation of women's lives during the revolution, as André Adam contends.[41] The writing of "Algeria Unveiled" cannot be accounted for by invoking the opposition between scholarship (with its supposed disinterestedness and historical accuracy) and polemic and situating it, however sympathetically, on the side of the latter, as Adam and others have done. Rather, Fanon's essay must be understood as a cultural-political intervention in a historical process whose outcome, in 1959, remained uncertain; "Algeria Unveiled" tries to *enable* the liberation of Algerian women in a form that complements nationalism and simultaneously challenges Western ideologies, including feminist ideologies, that ignore the specificity of the Algerian situation.

In light of developments since independence, however, it is important, from a feminist standpoint, to note that Fanon's strategy of articulating Algerian feminism as a purely indigenous force wholly compatible with the progessive changes wrought by the nationalist movement works, in today's context, to obscure tensions that have always existed between nationalism and feminism in Algeria—tensions that, in the new forms they have taken in the past decade, underlie current attempts by the two most powerful nationalist groups, the government and the fundamentalists, to crush feminism. Quite rightly, Fanon denounces the French myth that Algerian women liberate themselves "at the invitation of France and General de Gaulle," and condemns the colonial regime's hypocrisy in instituting legal reforms whose chief aim is to weaken the independence struggle. Yet Fanon's emphasis on Algerian feminism's harmonious integration into the nationalist movement—which implies feminism's unqualified rejection of French reforms—discourages investigation of problems that are important for women, such as the ways Algerian women actually used the colonial apparatus to take advantage of certain reforms, for example the 1959 laws forbidding child marriage and requiring that divorce proceedings be brought before a judge. Studies contemporary with Fanon's essay suggest that many Algerian women were not in a position simply to refuse recourse to the French legal system; rather, they successfully manipulated ambiguities in both the Muslim and French legal codes, exploiting the conflicts and gaps between them in order to improve their economic and social condition.[42] Further investigation of such questions might enable more nuanced analyses of feminism's relation to nationalism in Algeria and throw light on the situation of women whose lives are governed by conflicting legal codes in our time, for example, Muslim women who are living in, but are not citizens of, France and other first-world countries. Which laws, we might ask, are to be enforced regarding marriage, divorce, adultery, child custody, employment, and the right to political asylum in the lives of Algerian women in France or Pakistani women in Britain? How do Algerian, French, Pakistani, and British nationalisms affect decisions to invoke one legal code or another? How do they affect the ways the codes are used to advance or undermine women's interests? Historical perspectives of Algerian women's engagement with the legal apparatus in the colonial period may suggest ways to rethink and reshape current struggles.

Fanon's strategy of casting Algerian feminism not only as a movement wholly compatible with a progressive nationalism but as a purely indigenous movement poses other problems as well, for it invites readers to consider Algerian feminism in isolation from or in opposition to Western feminism, as if the latter were by definition at odds with, or irrelevant to, third-world nationalisms and anti-imperialist struggles. Granted, Fanon mentions the European women of Algeria who are arrested for supporting the liberation struggle in the mid-1950s (44), but he never speaks of *feminist* support for the revolution, support that is manifest most clearly two years after "Algeria Unveiled" in 1961, when Simone de Beauvoir and other French women working in concert with the Tunisian lawyer Gisèle Halimi protest the arrest and sexual torture of militant Djamila Boupacha by the French forces.[43] Moreover, in writing that the Algerian female combatant in Western dress enters the European district of the city "completely nude" ("nude" being a common way of translating the Arabic term for "unveiled"), Fanon strips her of the attire that could be interpreted as symbolically linking her to currents in Western feminism engaged in anticolonial struggles. The unveiling performed by Fanon's text, while clearly intended to enable the Algerian woman to "relearn her body, reinstall it in a totally revolutionary way," nonetheless establishes between Western and third-world feminisms a border that today's most productive feminist activity is reopening, both at the level of political action and in scholarship.[44]

Refashioning National Identities

As I have tried to show in my discussion of Fanon's "Algeria Unveiled," it is important to acknowledge that even the most progressive cultural texts may be used to underwrite the exploitation of women by various nationalisms—fundamentalist and conservative, secular and "progressive."[45] Where Algeria is concerned, a reading of Kateb Yacine's *Nedjma* can be exemplary in this regard, for the novel directly addresses women's status in the anticolonial and nationalist struggle, yet is almost never read with this problem in mind. Leila Ahmed presents the question of women and Algerian nationalism in these terms:

> Algeria, exceptional among Arab countries in the protracted duration of its colonization (integration into France in 1848), in the numerical size of the colonial presence (nearly one million French), and generally in the harshness and brutality of the colonization, was to be where the confrontation between the Arabicate world (or one distinctive sub-culture within it) and the

West was to emerge at its fiercest and most explicit: and women
and the status of women were to become openly and blatantly
mere counters (it is difficult to credit that for *either* side they were
anything more than counters) in the cultural, moral and military
battle between the French and the men of Algeria.[46]

I do not wish to suggest that *Nedjma* entirely supports Ahmed's
claim that women became mere counters in Algerian nationalism,
much less that the novel authorizes the use of women as counters.
Rather, I want to argue that *Nedjma* exposes the risks of using
women in this way, underlining the costs *to women*, albeit women
conceived as a fairly homogeneous class.

Written during the Algerian War when Kateb was in exile in
France, *Nedjma* deals with four young men caught in a cycle of violence in the period between the Setif rebellion of 1945 and the eve
of the revolution (1952). What unites them—but also divides and
sparks violence between them—is their common obsession with
Nedjma, a beautiful married woman born of a French Jewish
mother and an Algerian father of uncertain identity. Like her
mother, who is ravished three times, Nedjma is carried off to a
cave in the mountains of the Nadhor by an old man, Si Mokhtar
(possibly Nedjma's father), and one of the young protagonists,
Rachid. Her ravishment is inscribed as the repetition of an event
that figures in a founding myth of their tribe: a virgin's sacrifice to
the ancestor Keblout in the name of tribal unity.

Through Si Mokhtar, we are given to understand, however, that
the journey to the Nadhor has been undertaken in a historically
progressive rather than a nostalgic spirit. In terms later echoed by
Fanon's account of emergent Algerian nationalism, Si Mokhtar
says to his companion:

> Tu dois songer à la destinée de ce pays d'où nous venons, qui
> n'est pas une province française, et qui n'a ni bey ni sultan; tu
> penses peut-être à l'Algérie toujours envahie, à son inextricable
> passé, car nous ne sommes pas une nation, pas encore, sache-le:
> nous ne sommes que des tribus décimées. Ce n'est pas revenir en
> arrière que d'honorer notre tribu, le seul lien qui nous reste pour
> nous réunir et nous retrouver, même si nous espérons mieux que
> cela.

> You should remember the destiny of this country we come from;
> it is not a French province, and has neither bey nor sultan;
> perhaps you are thinking of Algeria, still invaded, of its

inextricable past, for we are not a nation, not yet, you know that: we are only decimated tribes. It is not a step backward to honor our tribe, the only link that remains to us by which we can unite and restore our people, even if we hope for more than that.[47]

In this context, the figure of Nedjma, as Abdelkebir Khatibi notes, bodies forth both a woman and the search for the nation.[48] Insofar as she is confined to her grotto, Nedjma, "whose beauty and 'family resemblance' had struck our relatives" (178), is, as Khatibi claims, a "refuge of values" safeguarding Algeria's traditional cultural identity (104).

However, Evelyne Accad observes that even in this guise Nedjma is no mere passive receptacle, for, like Radia in Mohammed Dib's *Cours sur la rive sauvage,* she is a revered primeval force, "the underpinning of all human life and the force of continued social existence."[49] This feature of Nedjma's identity is especially apparent in a passage dealing with her conception as a "star of blood" that ensures the life of the tribe:

> Rachid ne saurait jamais jusqu'à quel point Nedjma, la femme faite adversité, n'était pas tributaire du sang versé dans la grotte: Nedjma dont les hommes devaient se disputer non seulement l'amour, mais la paternité. . . . Et c'est alors que Nedjma fut conçue, étoile de sang jaillie du meurtre pour empêcher la vengeance, Nedjma qu'aucun époux ne pouvait apprivoiser, Nedjma l'ogresse au sang obscur. (179)

> Rachid would never know to what degree Nedjma, the woman made adversity, was not a tributary of the blood shed in the cave: for men were to dispute not only Nedjma's favors but even her paternity. . . . It was then that Nedjma was conceived, a star of blood sprung from the murder [of one abductor by the other] to obstruct vengeance, Nedjma whom no husband could win over, Nedjma the ogress of obscure blood. (239-40; translation modified)

As "ogress," Nedjma also figures an important dimension of the text's signifying activity. In this connection, Accad notes that *Nedjma* is "a symbolic nexus which is almost exclusively female-procreative—it is not the matrix but the paternity of the Algerian people which is called into question by the intrusion of colonialism. Likewise, the stability of the national matrix assures that paternity will ultimately be reestablished" (91). The female figure of Nedjma is thus cast as a productive force in, rather than the static ground for, emergent nationalism's affirmation of the cultural heritage. Although Accad emphasizes the "female-procreative" aspect of Nedjma's potency rather than its semiotic aspect, I believe she implicitly ascribes to Nedjma (as character and text) the same task that Barbara Harlow, writing nearly ten years later, ascribes to the poetry of organized resistance movements: "to preserve and even to redefine for the given historical moment the cultural images which underwrite collective action, military as well as ideological, of a people seeking to liberate themselves."[50]

Nedjma's aspect as an ever-renewable reserve of cultural images (an "amazon of the attic," 104) is linked to another, quite different, aspect, as a warrior who not only defends the culture's integrity but embodies and propels its evolution. The bridge between the two is the figure of Kahina, the legendary Berber heroine of the Aures with whom Nedjma is associated. The name Nedjma, which means "star" in Arabic, evokes the modern "warriors" — Algerian immigrant workers — who in the 1930s formed the secular anticolonial movement called the Etoile Nord-Africaine.[51] Yet as a "star" Nedjma recalls not only the tribal bond whose renewal in the Etoile Nord-Africaine is to propel the forward-looking nationalist struggle, but also the atavistic aspect of that bond: she is both a "star of blood" and "our loss and our ruin, the evil star of our clan" (252). Nedjma thus embodies Algeria's "betweenness" because of her multifaceted, contradictory, and shifting identity encompassing past and future, tribal and national society: she is of culturally mixed and uncertain parentage and has symbolic ties to France ("Nedjma speaks in French" [321]) not only through class privilege and education, but also through her association with revolutionary immigrant workers who are themselves cultural hybrids; she at once recalls Algeria's repeated conquest, resistance, and cultural renewal ("virgin after each rape") and fuels the male protagonists' revolutionary activity. "So elegant, so untamed, with her incredible gazelle's bearing" (141), a woman "capable of electrifying public opinion" (112), Nedjma bodies forth the convergence of contradictory historical forces that are transforming Algeria in the mid-twentieth century. At the same time, she affords a glimpse of the future heterogeneous nation, "the irresistible form of the virgin at bay, my blood and my country" (234). Viewed from this angle, Nedjma (as well as *Nedjma*, itself a hybrid "novel-poem," according to Jacqueline Arnaud [257]) can be seen as a figure for the task

Harlow assigns to narrative in resistance literature: "[It] analyzes the past, including the symbolic heritage, in order to open up the possibilities of the future" (82). The pleasure/pain of historical, psychic, and bodily dynamism is metaphorized in terms of the adolescent Nedjma's "breasts that were as painful as nails, swollen with the bitter precosity of green lemons; her spirit is still unbroken" (104).

As I mentioned earlier, critics of *Nedjma* have readily identified the elusive woman and the text that bears her name as emblems of the unstable convergence of contradictory currents in Algerian nationalism: atavism (Algeria as femme fatale) and historic dynamism (the emerging modern nation that, far from simply adopting Western models, develops by reconfiguring its own history and traditions in relation to Western forms, which, be they imposed or freely adopted, are themselves transformed in the Algerian context).[52] This convergence functions now to mobilize the male protagonists in their collective struggle, now to immobilize them in endless reverie or condemn them to aimless wandering and random violence. The continual vacillation between (and intertwining of) atavism and historic dynamism is habitually read as a mark of the riskiness and uncertainty of the nationalist undertaking. However, no reading makes women—the living symbols of that risk and uncertainty—its central concern.

It is possible, of course, to place the "woman question" at the center of a reading of *Nedjma* and still come up with a fairly sunny account of the way the text's (and Nedjma's) unceasing mobility guards against a totalizing fixation upon a single, "pure" national origin in order to forestall the designation of a scapegoat— woman—as the single origin "of all the social ills from which Algeria is suffering." Nedjma is an unstable and heterogeneous figure, at once animal, mineral, and machine:

> Le climat marin répand sur sa peau un hâle, combiné à un teint sombre, brillant de *reflets d'acier*, éblouissant comme un vêtement mordoré *d'animal;* la gorge a des blancheurs de *fonderie*, où le soleil *martèle* jusqu'au coeur, et le sang, sous les joues duveteuses, parle vite et fort, trahissant les énigmes du regard. (78-79; my emphasis)

> The sea air produced a bloom on her skin combining the dark tint with the brilliance of *metallic* reflections, mottled like some *animal;* her throat has the white gleams of a *foundry*, where the sun

hammers down to her heart, and the blood, under the downy
cheeks, speaks loud and fast, betraying the enigmas of her gaze.
(104-5; my emphasis)

As a long-legged little girl who, "when she ran . . . looked like
high carriages that swerve left and right without leaving their
route" (104), Nedjma seems invulnerable to capture as a living
symbol, for this fleet-footed girl-carriage eludes enclosure within
any identity. Similarly, in her resemblance to the "polyandrous
widows" of conquered cities—"the conserving widows who transform defeat into peace, never having despaired of sowing" (245)—
Nedjma seems to elude entrapment. She holds the promise of cultural renewal and national triumph, "for the lost terrain smiles at
sepulchers . . . for this country has not yet come into the world"
(245). At the same time, she promises new life, new love *for women.*

Yet it seems to me that in light of present circumstances it is no
longer enough to underline the force of Nedjma's "irrepressible
starlight" (182), relegating to the shadows her symbolic work as
emblem of the dark side of "betweenness." It is not just the nation's fate that hangs in the balance in *Nedjma*, as critics invariably
suggest, but women's as well. The abduction scene I referred to
earlier is crucial in this regard. In it, Rachid sacrifices Nedjma to the
mad black guardian of the tribe who will veil her, "protecting" her
from the indiscretions of both the French usurpers *and* hybrid creatures like her abductors, "whose fathers had let themselves be de-
ceived by the French, abandoning the Twin Peaks for the cities of
the conquerors" (178). Nedjma's literal seclusion is preserved in
her relation to the black man, but sublated and recast as a fantasy
("the maddest of monologues") in her relation to Rachid:

Pourquoi ne pas être restée dans l'eau? Les corps des femmes
désirées, comme les dépouilles des vipères et les parfums volatils,
ne sont pas faits pour dépérir, pourrir et s'évaporer dans notre
atmosphère: fioles, bocaux et baignoires: c'est là que doivent durer
les fleurs, scintiller les écailles et les femmes s'épanouir, loin de
l'air et du temps, ainsi qu'un continent englouti ou une épave
qu'on saborde, pour y découvrir plus tard, en cas de survie, un
ultime trésor. Et qui n'a pas enfermé son amante, qui n'a pas rêvé
de la femme capable de l'attendre dans quelque baignoire idéale,
inconsciente et sans atour, afin de la recueillir sans flétrissure
après la tourmente et l'exil? (138-39)

Why not stay in the water? The bodies of desired women, like the cast-off skins of vipers, like volatile perfumes, are not made to waste away, rot and evaporate in our atmosphere: phials, jars, and bath-tubs, that's where flowers should last, scales gleam, and women bloom, far from time and air, like a sunken continent or a scuttled ship, to be discovered later, a survival, an ultimate treasure. And who has not imprisoned his mistress, dreamed of the woman who could wait for him, jailed in some ideal bath, unconscious and naked, in order to receive him unscarred after torment and exile? (182-83)

The sacrifice of Nedjma marks Rachid's historical progression, since it requires that he give up certain practices (here, seclusion and veiling) intended to enact the atavistic fantasy of totally possessing and eternally preserving a beloved woman seen as refuge of values for family and tribe. As a result of the sacrifice, Nedjma, in her dual relation to Rachid and the black man, becomes the symbol of "betweenness" that is supposed to enable the formation of what Tillion calls a national society of citizens.

Now, this solution is unacceptable to Nedjma, who openly protests her sacrifice to the black man and, implicitly, her sublation as well; in other words, she resists not only the brutal measures instituted by the black man to enact the fantasy of possession but also the fantasy itself, which survives in Rachid's monologue and in the minds of the other male protagonists as well. The passages dealing with the scene on the Nadhor show clearly that Nedjma neither embraces the traditional role assigned her by the black man nor accepts her confinement in the remote mountain camp. For although Rachid remarks (before her abduction by the black man) that Nedjma "did not seem dissatisfied with her lot" (178), the narrator observes that as the black man prepares to confine her to the tribal homeland, Nedjma is "sobbing" (195) and is "led by main force to the women's encampment" (199) *after trying to escape.* Yet despite unmistakable textual evidence of Nedjma's resistance to a fate imposed on her by force, critics invariably disavow the coercion to which Nedjma is subject in order to save their faith in the purity of Algerian nationalism. Jacqueline Arnaud claims, for example, that "it would be very inept to discern here [in the account of Nedjma's sacrifice] a reactionary myth" (42). I want to insist, on the contrary, that to deny the reactionary dimension of this myth is to ignore the history of women in Algeria since *Nedjma*'s publication in 1954 and to lend credence to a now dangerous ideology that holds that *this* symbolization of woman still has revolutionary potential in Algeria.[53]

Arnaud's denial of the historical failure of this myth leads her to assert, against all textual evidence, that Nedjma accepts her sacrifice: "The unveiled woman of the novel, the libertine, reveils herself and returns to her traditional role; her molt is subordinated to that of the country" (312). Ironically, Arnaud justifies her interpretation through reference to Fanon's "Algeria Unveiled," ignoring the fact that reveiling, for Fanon, had nothing to do with returning to women's traditional role; in Fanon's account, reveiling was "stripped of its exclusively traditional dimension" and imbued with "historic dynamism" (47). While it is true, as Fanon claims, that reveiling acquired a positive social meaning during the revolution and was practiced strategically both to affirm Algerian culture and to enable women to carry out dangerous military missions, Nedjma's forced reveiling at the time of her imprisonment on the Nadhor is of a different order altogether: it signals a loss of freedom imposed on her against her will, not her deliberate rejection of a "false freedom," as Arnaud claims (312 n. 66).

Nedjma's resistance stands in dialogic relation to the endorsement of the sacrifice by the black man, Si Mokhtar, and Rachid; it is neither discredited by the male characters' views nor suppressed in later parts of the novel. In fact, the effects of her sacrifice to the black man and her sublation by Rachid resurface repeatedly in forboding forms that stand in contrapuntal relation to the liberatory figurations of Nedjma. For instance, the swift girl-carriage of Part 2 becomes, in Part 4, a woman *enclosed* "in a train or carriage" (244). Of the impassioned, elusive Nedjma it is said that "it is as though she no longer existed" (244). Although in the latter sequence she is no longer "kept . . . by force on the Nadhor," her return to the city brings not freedom but continued tutelage: "She travels under guard, veiled in black now, from Bône to Constantine, from Constantine to Bône" (245).

It is important to note the ambiguity of the veiled Nedjma's mobility in the passage just quoted. On the one hand, by virtue of its location on the road between Bône and Constantine and its ongoing character, it links her to the male protagonists, Lakhdar and Rachid, the "two shadows [who] fade on the road" in the last line of the novel—insubstantial beings who may or may not fulfill the historic mission figured in the text by what Kristine Aurbakken calls "the rectilinear order of the 'road' of the national chronicle."[54] Insofar as she is still part of an emerging nationalist collectivity, then—one whose emancipatory potential for women is affirmed— Nedjma continues to embody the hope, however shadowy and uncertain it may be, of women's liberation in her country. On the other hand, though, Nedjma's mobility is divorced from the progressive features of the nationalist collectivity since it is always "under guard": in this guise, the woman-symbol is "no longer anything but a final gleam of autumn, a beseiged city fending off disaster" (244), the counterpart of the "polyandrous widow" who brings new life to "conquered cities" (245).

Now, it is true that in the last pages the text circles back to and even repeats verbatim earlier scenes (in terms of the fiction's chronology) in which Nedjma's sensual and symbolic potency work in her favor, for instance, when she walks proudly into the "café of the future": "without a veil, she looks like a gypsy" (320). By virtue of her inassimilable quality in relation both to France and to traditional tribal society, she is aligned with Mustapha, Mourad, and Rachid, the young men from the city who have defied French colonial authority by maintaining their solidarity with Lakhdar when he is arrested for physically attacking their villainous foreman, Monsieur Ernest, at the construction site. To a certain extent, then, the structure of the narrative affirms Nedjma's liberation by subverting the fiction's chronology and negating the social meanings it imposes. Yet, as a "gypsy"—a cultural outlaw—Nedjma also resembles the young men in their guise as "outsiders" who "get blamed for everything," (40) not only by the French authorities, but also by their rural compatriots: "The people, including the workers who have more than once been victimized by the foreman, are annoyed to see a stranger from the city settle straight off an old dissension" (338). Just as the young men are continually threatened with imprisonment either in jail (in the case of Mourad and Lakhdar) or in a hashish-induced stupor in the *fondouk* (in the case of Rachid), Nedjma is repeatedly subject to confinement. Unlike the men's imprisonment, however, the woman's confinement has a dual aspect: it signifies both the historical failure of Algerian nationalism *and* (as we saw in the analysis of Rachid's reverie on the Nadhor) its potential triumph.

The ambiguity of Nedjma's position in the final sequences of the novel thus underscores the uncertain meaning and outcome of Algeria's social transformation. A related function of this ambiguity is to point up the stakes and perils of the subjective transformation that accompanies and enables social change. For instance, Nedjma's adulterous encounter with a lover generates, in Lakhdar's mind, a fantasy that dislocates the traditional order, opening a path for the articulation of a new order whose "cardinal points" (344) would be the four male protagonists:

> Le vent avait rasé le salon, proscrit toute vision, et le tourbillonnement du sang ne permettait à aucune idée de se fixer, comme si la ville, à la faveur de l'orage, était délivrée des feuilles mortes, comme si Nedjma elle-même tournoyait quelque part, brusquement balayée. (246)

> The wind had razed the living room, proscribed all vision, and the whirling blood permitted no idea to settle, as if the city, on account of the storm, were suddenly freed of its leaves, as if Nedjma herself whirled somewhere, suddenly swept away. (329-30)

Together with that of the "city," Lakhdar's identity is set in motion by the "whirling blood," as is that of the lover, Mustapha, whom Lakhdar has mistaken for Mourad.

In many respects, Lakhdar's fantasies in the final sequences replay Rachid's fantasy on the Nadhor by reenacting the "sacrifice" of Nedjma—that is, the male dream of possession/dispossession of the mother-lover-cousin—as a way of producing and perpetuating the community of nationalists. Just as Rachid turns Nedjma over to the black man, Lakhdar leaves her to Mustapha (Mourad), in a gesture of painful self-sacrifice that disrupts both the infant's tie to the mother and the organization of the social world along familial and tribal lines: when Mourad takes Lakhdar's place in Nedjma's room, the infantilized Mourad falls "headlong into the woman's games, her laughter nailing Lakhdar to the living room floor and leaving a mournful legend in his mind . . . 'I can't be everyone's brother and cousin' " (325). Further, when Lakhdar discovers he has mistaken Mustapha for Mourad—discovers, that is, the futility of his attempt to simultaneously "risk sounding [his] passion" *and* control his own dispossession by locking Mourad in the room with Nedjma—"images pierced him like nails" (330). Another version of this scene of dispossession (the positions of the protagonists are redistributed) is presented a few pages earlier when Rachid and Mustapha catch the eye of Nedjma in her garden. The young men are fascinated by Nedjma's power as she "turns a little further, intrigued, as though to kill a fly on her glowing shoulder"; but upon seeing Lakhdar with Nedjma, Rachid and Mustapha "run down the hill with the humility of two foxes leaving a third at the hencoop door to deal with a rare bird that would have driven them to fatal conflict had they not withdrawn" (324).

Already evident in these scenes, however, is an element that threatens to contain Nedjma's whirling revolutionary force, namely her terrifying power over the young men, particularly Lakhdar, who is alternately paralyzed by Nedjma and moved to paralyze *her* as a way of neutralizing the power he attributes to her. In the scene examined above, Lakhdar is "nailed to the floor" by Nedjma's laughter not only because he has *abandoned* the infantile position that Mourad now occupies in a playful mode (falling "headlong into the woman's games") but also because he has *taken up* Mourad's position in fantasy—with the difference that he fears engulfment by the woman rather than enjoying the headlong fall into her games as Mourad does. Lakhdar's relation to Nedjma's games is close to the one inscribed in Mustapha's notebook, where it is claimed that "Nedjma's fatality derived from the atmosphere she was surrounded by as a little girl, when the already devastating games of the sacrificed Vestal glowed in her rarest adornments" (247). Lakhdar's paralyzing fear is thus inextricably bound up with his desire to be enclosed in (or with) Nedjma in some ideal space, such as "the nuptial chamber" of her house—a space that doubles "the nuptial cave where the Frenchwoman [Nedjma's mother] entangled her lovers" (240):

> Nedjma retenait Lakhdar dans la chambre nuptiale. Elle lui avait apporté des cigarettes; Lakhdar se retrouva sans parole sur le lit où il ne pardonnait pas à Mourad de s'asseoir; il ne fit plus de mouvement pour sortir. (244)

> Nedjma kept Lakhdar in her room. She had brought cigarettes; Lakhdar found himself speechless on the bed where he could not forgive Mourad for sitting; he no longer tried to escape. (327)

The deadly consequence of Lakhdar's terror is manifest—again, at the level of fantasy—in his reaction to the insouciance of Nedj-ma's husband, Kamel:

L'argent et la beauté. Un bijou pareil, je l'attacherais à mon lit.
(239)

Money and beauty. If I had a jewel like that, I'd chain her to the bed. (321)

This fantasy obviously recalls Rachid's dream of "the woman who could wait for him, jailed in some ideal bath, unconscious and na-ked," (183) and thus reintroduces into the last figurations of the emerging nationalist community an articulation of the male im-pulse to fully dispossess the beloved woman. This impulse tends to neutralize the men's inclination to free Nedjma, manifested for instance in Rachid's assertion that he "merely wanted to help her remain alone as she was, waiting for the result of the struggle" (184-85). And clearly, it works to negate the sole fantasy of Nedj-ma's articulated in the text:

Tout recommencer . . . Sans se confier à un homme, mais pas seule comme je le suis. (67)

A trip . . . Starting all over again . . . Not giving myself up to a man, but not alone the way I am. (89)

The "whirling blood" of the unsettled tribal order, then, not only holds the promise of a new, emancipatory social formation but also threatens to resurrect the familiar patriarchal line with its alternating—and ultimately deadly—male fantasies of impotence and omnipotence in relation to the mother/lover. The risk is not so much that the order of Keblout will again prevail, but that the woman who, in the liberating fantasy, "whirled somewhere" will be "chained to the bed" and enlisted to contain the nation's "fatal conflict" through a symbolic potency deriving from a psychic and social regression that renders her nearly impotent as a maker of so-cial meanings. The risk, in other words, is that woman will become a living symbol "linking [men] in friendship, uniting their rivalries the better to circumscribe her" (251). Since this is indeed an impor-tant feature of political life in postindependence Algeria, feminist readings of Nedjma should acknowledge the novel's disclosure of this historical possibility, rather than deny an important textual dynamic in *Nedjma* and, with it, the political situation of today's Algerian women.

Such a denial is clearly at work in the conclusion of Aurbakken's study of *Nedjma*, which maintains that

> at the end of the book, [Nedjma] emerges, freed from the yoke of the male imagination. The mediating metaphor being mediated in its turn—"adversity in the form of a woman," "the woman made adversity" [238, 239]—she too attains the status of historical subject, participating on an equal footing with men in the upheavals underway: "a revolution of the body that climaxed here under the masculine sun" [181]. And though the book, *Nedjma,* retains the spider's "trace" [the trace of Keblout's order of legitimacy], the protagonist, Nedjma, rejoins the Algerian woman—restored, like the Algerian man, to her active and engaged potential—on the stellar "road" of the nation being forged in the mold of "blurred origins" [128]. (176-77)

Aurbakken's interpretation places an unproblematic Algerian woman on a one-way street leading to liberation rather than taking seriously the repetitive and constrained character of the veiled Nedjma's travels, under guard, from Bône to Constantine, from Constantine to Bône. Similarly, it illuminates the text's celebratory articulations of the nation's blurred origins without accounting for the social and symbolic cost to Nedjma—Si Mokhtar's "problematic" daughter, Rachid's "problematic" possession—as bearer of those blurred origins. I have tried to show, on the other hand, that in terms of writing's engagement in Algeria's search for identity as a modern nation, *Nedjma* constitutes the most powerful articulation of the promise *and the perils* of that search with respect to women.

I believe my feminist reading of Kateb's novel is compatible with Antoine Raybaud's historical interpretation, to which I am indebted.[55] Raybaud writes:

> Granting Fanon's analyses [in *The Wretched of the Earth*] of the violent and alienating situation linked to colonial domination and its internalization, as well as the solutions he offers on the cultural plane (restoration of the past, paroxysmal literature, active engagement in the revolution with the people), Algerian novels are situated in an original way in this reclaiming of blurred or wounded identity. . . . [They are] a space in which the moments and elements of vertigo are put into perspective and combined; the novel "inscribes" the delirium born of the dismantling and

violation of identity in a movement of interrogation of identity, belonging, and order [55]. [This writing] effects the fusion of at least two functions of the literary work that we usually separate— the functions of founding subjectivity, and of founding the narrative of the world; and it may be that it also offers us an alternative to the neat realisms, always wavering nonetheless between didacticism and formalism (aestheticism?), a true realism of historical action in its modes of emergence and its impact. [62]

It is my contention that *Nedjma*'s "true realism of historical action" shows, more subtly than any other cultural intervention to date, what is at stake for women in the subjective and social transformations of the Algerian revolution.

Recasting the Colonial Gaze

The last text I want to consider in connection with feminism and Algerian nationalism, Malek Alloula's *The Colonial Harem*, is a relatively recent one that raises important questions for contemporary feminism and cultural studies.[56] Alloula's study analyzes the *scènes et types* postcards circulating widely in Algeria and France between 1900 and 1930. As their name suggests, the postcards are underwritten by the ethnographic alibi of surveying Algerian landscapes and customs. Alloula is concerned with the best-selling subgenre picturing Algerian women in various guises: traversing public space in billowing white veils; imprisoned in the dark recesses of the harem; modeling exotic headdresses and jewelry in various stages of native dress and undress; and finally, nude women surrounded by the props of the coffee ceremony, entwined in the coils of the hookah, or reclining in lascivious abandon on a divan in the manner of the odalisque. Evident in these photographs, Alloula argues convincingly, is the desire of the colonial photographer to render Algeria transparent: his fascination with veiled and unveiled Algerian women betrays his wish to strip Algeria of its cultural identity, deny the existence of its male population, and possess it through its women.

While I find Alloula's analysis compelling in many respects, I want to argue that it poses two major problems for feminists concerned with culture's political function. First, Alloula assumes that the colonial postcards merely reflect and reinforce a politics whose real basis lies elsewhere (in military conquest, economic exploita-

Femme des Ouled-Naïls   ND Phot

tion, colonial administrative policies, and so on), whereas in fact the postcards form part of a cultural network that actually produces the politics in question in conjunction with the other forces named above. And second, by assessing the pernicious effects of the postcard images almost exclusively from the standpoint of Algeria's male population, *The Colonial Harem* disavows—and thus obstructs efforts to resolve—conflicts between men and women in Algeria, conflicts that cannot be explained solely in terms of colonial exploitation.

Alloula demonstrates that a dream of transparency and possession places the early twentieth-century colonial photographer in solidarity with the colonial administration whose principled denunciation of the veil, the emblem of women's oppression, is belied by its policies. Its seizure of lands, for instance, disrupts the traditional family patterns of vast numbers of Algerians, forcing displaced rural women into the cities where they are either obliged to earn a living as prostitutes or, as we saw in the discussion of Tillion's work, subjected to stricter practices of seclusion and veiling.[57] One of the services performed by these displaced and impoverished women is to pose for photographers aiming to capitalize on the fantasies of Pieds-Noirs (French settlers in Algeria) and tourists. Clearly, although Alloula does not discuss the matter in any detail, the complicity between photographer and ad-

69 — LA BELLE "FATMAH" chez elle en costume de gala

ministrator extends to the intellectual as well. Mathéa Gaudry's *La Société féminine au Djebel Amour et au Ksel,* for instance, provides striking photographic, as well as textual, evidence of anthropology's ties to colonial exploitation.[58] Gaudry's book includes photographs in the style of the postcards that document many aspects of women's lives, for example, female dress in the Djebel Amour and Ksel regions. Plate 20 shows an anonymous veiled woman, presumably "typical" of these areas; but in plate 50, *in her place and in the same setting,* there appears an unveiled woman with hands on hips and a cigarette hanging from her lips, identified as "Khanoussa, a former courtesan, now a duenna." Seen side by side, these two plates at once shatter the sociologist's pretense of scientific objectivity in representing "authentic" native women, and implicate her in the exploitation of the very women whose lives she has written about with care and sympathy.

The postcard is thus embedded in a complex and extensive network of colonial power. As I indicated above, however, I disagree with Alloula that, as a "ventrilocal art, the postcard—even and especially when it pretends to be the mirror of the exotic—is *nothing other* than one of the forms of aesthetic justification of colonial violence" (76; my emphasis). Far from merely giving voice to a preexisting colonial ideology or justifying violence serving "real" economic and political interests, the postcards articulate a dream of ravishment, a colonizing desire that not only invests and orients administrative activity but helps to produce the interests it serves, for example by establishing a libidinally charged solidarity between *colons* of different classes and ethnic groups. And since the postcards form part of the growing tourist industry and the everyday correspondence between France and its colony, they also forge ideologically loaded bonds between the French in Algeria and those in the metropolitan center.[59] In short, they work to make "L'Algérie Française" a creditable proposition.

That a French Algeria is produced in and through culture as well as by military and administrative means is particularly evident from the fact that an International Colonial Exposition is organized in Paris in 1931 in order to arouse widespread public desire for the colony and, more generally, for colonialism. As one commentator in the *Bulletin du Comité de l'Afrique Française* puts it, "The public . . . must realize that the 'current miracle' of Greater France rests upon a persistent and longstanding colonizing tradition."[60] The

goals of the Exposition are presented in straightforwardly aggressive terms by its organizer, Marshall Pierre Lyautey, who wants
"to give the French public a punch in the eye so that it will finally
pay attention to the number and quality of our overseas posses-
sions."[61] Where Algeria is concerned, the centenary celebration of
the French conquest in 1830 is one of the most important cultural
forces at work. Charles-Robert Ageron shows, for example, that "a
committee was specifically assigned the task of 'creating a lasting
movement of opinion in metropolitan France in favor of African
France' "; "the French press was subsidized and received 2,075,971
francs to 'campaign in favor of Algeria' " despite natives' protests
at the prospect of such a humiliating spectacle (403-4).

The main intent of the Centenary is clearly to create an idealized
picture of Algeria as a desirable partner for France rather than to
garner support for concrete improvement of conditions in the colony. For instance, while there is a concerted effort to sell the centenary celebration in the French schools ("It is above all in the
schools that our propaganda must strike," declares the general secretary of the metropolitan committee on the Centenary), Ageron
observes that when the budget committee extends a credit of one
hundred million francs for social assistance and education (based
on its "intuition that France should at least make a charitable gesture in favor of the Muslims"), "the Financial Delegation [whose
members are mainly French Algerians] . . . refuses this important
credit on the pretext that the Chamber of Deputies has over-
stepped its powers by designating Algeria as the target of a sub-
sidy. The Financial Delegation reminds the Chamber that it alone
controls the granting of credits in Algeria's budget. This explains
why only five million francs are allocated, in the end, for the assistance of natives" (410).

In addition to an intensive press and education campaign, a radio station is set up to broadcast propaganda throughout Algeria
and the other French colonies; tourism is encouraged, museums
are opened, and art exhibits are organized to demonstrate that
"here [in Algeria] there is truly a new France . . . and that [its]
people have but one desire, one ambition: to be intimately fused
with the Mother Country."[62] The postcards analyzed by Alloula
must be set within the frame of this mass cultural picture. In this
context, it is worth considering Roland Barthes's observation,
quoted by Alloula, that "the age of photography corresponds ex-

actly to the irruption of the private in the public, or rather, to the creation of a new social value, which is the publicity of the private: the private is consumed as such, publicly."[63] The circulation of postcards placing the natives' private life on display for purposes of appropriation *is* a politics, one that complements a politics of the family that is seen as central to the colonizing project as outlined, for example, in the Congress on Rural Colonization held in Algiers in May 1930: "The creation of [centers of colonization] has entailed the assembly—I would even say mobilization—on the designated point, of many dozens of French families that are in general healthy, fully prolific, and whose conditions of existence encourage fecundity more than they limit it. 'A seminary of the French race': the center of colonization presents itself thus."[64]

At issue, then, in the circulation of the postcards, is not simply the fact that the figures of the harem inscribed on them are hypocritically justified, as Alloula points out, by legends identifying them as mere family portraits. As important as the use of European family ideology to veil sexual exploitation, as important as the postcards' function of putting formerly secluded and veiled Algerian women on public display, ensuring their symbolic availability to the conquerer, is the ideological work of implanting in Algeria the economy of the relation between public and private that is developing in Europe at the time. This comes to have decisive importance after independence in Algeria when conservative and progressive forces alike justify breaking their promises to grant women basic civil liberties by pointing to the degradation of Western women within the economy of mass culture, as if real or symbolic prostitution represented the only alternative to seclusion and veiling.[65]

Alloula suggests that the postcard photographer's dream of transparency and possession—his dream of unveiling Algerian women—places him in solidarity with the French colonizer not only in the early part of the twentieth century when the postcards are in widest circulation but also in mid-century at the time of the Algerian Revolution (1954-62). Here, I want to draw out some of the implications of Alloula's suggestion by pointing out that the French army's antinationalist strategy of dispersing village communities and resettling their inhabitants involves forcing female detainees to unveil before military photographers assigned the task of producing photos for the French national ID cards that these un-

willing Algerians are to be required to carry. One of the army photographers, Marc Garanger, denounces the army's policy—and the
role he is forced to play in carrying it out—by publishing and ex-
hibiting these photographs in various places during and after the
Algerian War, notably in the *Illustré Suisse* in 1961 (when Garanger
is still doing his military service in Algeria) and then some twenty
years later in a collection entitled *Femmes algériennes 1960*.[66] The
forced unveiling documented there at once parallels the unveiling
staged by the army officers' wives in May 1958 and, through its
critical reframing in Garanger's book, signals the coercion at work
in the production of the postcards analyzed by Alloula.

More starkly than the postcards, Garanger's photos disclose the
photographer's desire and its collusion with other forms of colonial
violence. However, they also mirror the postcards as inscriptions
of what Alloula terms the photographer's impotence. On the postcards, as Alloula notes, the haunting images of women in veils, re-
lentlessly opaque rather than transparent, floating rather than
fixed within the frame, and also the distracted or downright dis-
gusted look of many of the models, mark the photographer's incapacity to ravish his female subjects. Similarly, the dishevelment
and disarray of the women photographed thirty years later during
the war bespeak contempt and defiance as much as discouragement and defeat. In his introduction to *Femmes algériennes 1960*, Garanger remembers being "hit by their look at pointblank range" (3).
Leïla Sebbar attributes a similar interpretation of the Garanger photos to the Algerian teenage protagonist of *Shérazade:* "All of these
Algerian women had the same look—intense, ferocious, so savage
that the image would only be able to record it without ever control-
ling or dominating it."[67]

But here we encounter a problem regarding the relation between Alloula's critique of the colonial photographer's gaze and
the global political context in which his critique is generated, and
the relation of both to Algerian (and more generally, Arab) feminism. On the one hand, Alloula's analysis is effective in discerning
in the postcard images contradictions that are specific to the photographic medium in the colonial situation, contradictions that he
uses to reflect to the French photographer a critical image of the
gaze he casts on Algeria. By returning these postcards to their
sender, Alloula shows that the haunting figure of the Algerian
woman embodies a set of colonialist male fantasies, and in doing

Photos by Marc Garanger, from *Femmes algériennes.*
By permission.

so, he makes an important contribution to the body of feminist work on colonialism.

On the other hand, Alloula's analysis is itself haunted by a kind of spectral presence, that of an undivided Algeria—an emerging nation in which the conflicting interests of men and women appear only as the product of the conquerer's sexual fantasies and administrative policies. Despite occasional references to the postcards' effects on women—for instance, his remark in the final pages that the images represent "the deceitful expression of [their] symbolic dispossession" (76)—Alloula never really addresses the question of women's interests. Instead, he repeatedly invites readers to deplore the French imposter's efforts to insinuate himself into the closed space of the harem in order to take what he (the imposter) imagines to be the native man's place, and to destroy the forms of solidarity that make anticolonial struggle possible. What Alloula deplores is the rape of an Algeria in which women's differences with men remain veiled.[68] Implicitly, Alloula subscribes to the same view advanced by Fanon in "Algeria Unveiled," namely, that the affirmation of cultural traditions such as seclusion and veiling of women is necessary at a certain point in Algeria's history. But in suggesting this without revision nearly twenty years after independence, Alloula repeats the gesture of the colonizer by making of the veiled woman the screen on which he projects *his* fantasy (an idealization fueled, perhaps, by his exile in France)—that of an Algerian nation untroubled by questions of women's oppression.

The problem posed to feminism by Alloula's book resurfaces in Barbara Harlow's otherwise informative and nuanced introduction to it. For despite Harlow's lucid presentation of the colonial situation in Algeria and the range of responses to it, she sidesteps the key issue of feminism's conflicts with nationalism. Harlow's essay is particularly illuminating insofar as it sets Alloula's analysis in relation to the history of the French occupation of Algeria, including the intellectual and aesthetic strands of that history that extend through the revolutionary period, for instance in the writing of Camus. Equally helpful is the way it situates the book in relation to the critical rewriting of Maghrebian history and culture by influential figures such as Kateb, Khatibi, and feminists Assia Djebar, Fadela M'rabet, and Fatima Mernissi. Valuable as it is, though, it seems to me that Harlow's essay tries to cover over, rather than come to terms with, the contradiction between the demands of

Maghrebian feminists and the dominant (governmental and fundamentalist) means of affirming the Maghreb's Islamic identity. This
leads Harlow to give undue approval, for example, to "reforms" of
Muslim women's civil status that have been unequivocally denounced by the very feminists she cites.[69]

In her otherwise compelling account, in *Resistance Literature* (137-40), of the interconnections between writing, political
struggle, and imprisonment in the life of Egyptian feminist Nawal
al-Saadawi, Harlow likewise ignores basic conflicts between feminism and nationalism in Egypt and other Muslim countries, conflicts that sometimes result in what Ghoussoub calls "accommoda-
tion to obscurantism" by feminists engaged in the struggle against
Western imperialism. In the same essay I cited earlier, Ghoussoub
asks,

> How many times, over successive generations, as the tides of
> religious fundamentalism (or opportunism) ebbed and flowed,
> have we seen women who were once courageous in their rejection
> of mystification and oppression eventually bow before them and
> on occasion even end by defending them! Fear of being accused of
> the contagion of "Occidental values" all too easily leads to
> discovery of the superior virtues of the Harem, compared to
> Western marriage and adultery, as many examples show. Some of
> the most outstanding contemporary feminists, daunted by the
> scale of the task before them and the isolation in which they
> stand, have changed their tone recently.[70]

Of Nawal al-Saadawi, Ghoussoub writes with bitter irony, "She
too is now starting to claim . . . that Arab women really are more
politicized than their Western counterparts, because they are more
concerned to change the political system under which they live [a
system based on the exploitation of one class by another] than its
mere consequences, the superficial features of women's oppression" (18).

In situations where feminists in Muslim societies subordinate
women's struggles to the supposedly larger class struggle, or accept Islamic fundamentalism's antifeminist measures in the name
of nationalism or anti-imperialism, it is essential to analyze these
developments critically rather than ignore or rationalize them.
Nayereh Tohidi's "Gender and Islamic Fundamentalism: Feminist
Politics in Iran" is a good example of such analysis, for it explains
how women's varying class and regional affiliations fueled their

opposition to the Shah and to imperialism, motivating their provisional acceptance of fundamentalist rule during the revolution. Acknowledging the fundamentalists' betrayal of Iranian women in 1979 and emphasizing the interrelation of women's movements, national democratic, and anti-imperialist struggles in the third world, Tohidi writes:

> Alone, a women's movement can never transform the foundations of sexism and sexual oppression. Neither can a revolution which seeks to transform class relationships meet its goals if it does not incorporate the question of women's oppression. Specific demands of women must be incorporated into the national anti-imperialist movement and class struggle right from the beginning. The women's question should not be relegated to the days after the revolution.[71]

In the same passage she states unequivocally that "a call for separation of the state from religion as a democratic principle should be included in any progressive platform of political groups faced with the threat of fundamentalism. Women must insist on holding out for this principle more than ever." Tohidi's method of attending to the complex interrelation of feminism, nationalism, and anti-imperialism while simultaneously affirming Muslim women's status as historical subjects *and* insisting on the separation of religion and state is a productive one, I think, for feminist critics.

Today, the separation of the state from religion is the subject of important debates not only with respect to African and Near Eastern societies but also European and North American ones where Muslim, Christian, Jewish, and other religious and nonreligious groups are seeking to defend or change existing church-state relations. In the wake of the Rushdie affair, Women Against Fundamentalism in Britain committed itself to opposing all forms of fundamentalism, defined as "the mobilization of religious affiliation for political ends."[72] It organized demonstrations against Muslim fundamentalist demands for state-subsidized Muslim schools (especially girls' schools, whose main function was to police the students' sexuality), yet spoke out simultaneously against the state's long-standing investment in Anglican, Catholic, and a few Jewish schools. The group also mounted opposition to blasphemy laws that protect only the Christian denominations, and picketed the

Irish embassy in London in defense of Irish women's right to information on abortion.

In France, the demands of Muslims also sparked heated national debates about the church-state relation, particularly with respect to education. In the fall of 1989 high-school girls defending their right to wear the Muslim headscarf, the *hijeb*, in school met with intense opposition from many groups—groups that are often at odds with each other—despite support from civil rights advocates and antiracist liberals (including many Maghrebians) who refused to single out the *hijeb* (as opposed to the cross or the yarmulke) as an intolerable intrusion of religion into public education. Among their opponents were school administrators defending what they claimed was France's commitment to the separation of church and state. These administrators had a large public following that included both avowed racists and sectors of the liberal left. Other opponents included parts of the Maghrebian community favoring assimilation to French national norms and leftist feminists denouncing the equivalence posited by liberals between wearing the *hijeb* and exercising a "right." Gisèle Halimi went so far as to interpret France's tolerance of the *hijeb* in French schools as a feature of an international politics condoning increasingly reactionary and misogynistic state policies in the Maghreb.[73]

However, as Florence Assouline has shown, the main point about the *hijeb* affair—a point that was almost never addressed in public debates except by *Beurettes* (girls of Maghrebian descent) themselves—is that it signaled the degree to which these girls function as counters in a struggle between secularists and defenders of Islamic custom *without their concrete interests being taken into account at all*.[74] In the eyes of many French people, girls of Maghrebian descent are generally diligent students and compliant people—in short, the most assimilable element of the immigrant population; if they begin to defend their "right to difference," the whole project of integration seems to be jeopardized. As for conservative Muslim families, in their eyes control of the girls represents the power to preserve family honor and to resist assimilation by perpetuating tradition. But we should ask what it will mean for the adolescent girls if the school bans the *hijeb*. Will their parents simply take them out of school, with the result that they may marry sooner and have fewer professional opportunities than they might have had otherwise? Will the parents keep their daughters in school but be more steadfast in their refusal to allow them to participate in physical education and sex education classes, to go on class trips, or go to the movies with friends? Or will the ban have the opposite effect, reinforcing the legitimacy of the French school system so that the girls may continue their studies, participate fully in the curriculum, and so on? And on the other hand, would the absence of a ban on the *hijeb* merely encourage conservative Muslim families to restrict their daughter's activities while simultaneously legitimating an assimilationist French cultural politics?

Although the *hijeb* affair generally failed to address these fundamental questions, it did spark some reflection on racism in France, the function of human rights discourses in antiracist struggles, relations between national and sexual identities, and the effects of one powerful nation's public policy on global politics. One question it raises for feminists in Western countries is how we can best engage with the political and cultural work of feminists from Arab and other Muslim societies while at the same time taking account, self-critically, of the "boundary problems" cited by Mernissi in her enumeration of forces that are "tearing the Muslim world apart." These boundary problems include colonization, the "trespassing by a foreign power on Muslim community space and decision making"; contemporary human rights issues viewed in terms of "the political boundaries circumscribing the ruler's space and the freedoms of the government"; integration of technological information "without deluging our own Muslim heritage"; international economic dependency; and "the sovereignty of the Muslim state vis-à-vis voracious, aggressive transnational corporations."[75] It seems to me that, however we go about it, our efforts will be fruitful only on condition that we elude fascination by our own counter-ideologies, particularly if they work, paradoxically, to screen out the very voices and bodies they ostensibly address. Above all, this implies, at every moment, guarding against what Ghoussoub calls "the contemptuous anti-Arab racism of American society, and its hypocritical indignation at the fate of Arab women" (18).

Chapter 2

Wild Femininity and Historical Countermemory

Algerian Literary History in a Feminist Frame

Mohammed Dib's *Who Remembers the Sea* (1962) marks a turning point in the history of Algerian literature written in French, for like Pablo Picasso's *Guernica*, Dib's novel powerfully evokes the horror of war and its wrenching effects on subjectivities and the social body without relying on a realist aesthetic, which, in Dib's estimation, would probably render suffering and change banal.[1] Of course, Kateb's *Nedjma* had already revolutionized Algerian writing nearly a decade earlier, breaking with the ethnographic literature of Mouloud Feraoun, Mouloud Mammeri, and indeed Dib himself in *La Grande Maison* (1952), the first volume of the Algerian trilogy that would be completed with the publication of *L'Incendie* (1954) and *Le Métier à Tisser* (1957).[2] But although *Nedjma* and *Who Remembers the Sea* are formally innovative texts written before or during the war, Kateb, Dib, and other Algerian writers claim to feel freer to experiment with their writing once the liberation struggle has been won.[3] Along with Dib and Kateb, one can cite Rachid Boudjedra, Nabile Farès, and, more recently, Assia Djebar as writers whose reflections on the interrelation of gender, culture, and politics are inextricably entwined with the reworking of literary forms. What is more, these writers all use the French language in a doubly critical way. On the one hand, they give voice to experiences that, for a variety of reasons, are repressed or silenced in Algerian society. And on the other, they deterritorialize the language of colonialism and neocolonialism. In Ronnie Scharfman's words, theirs is a writing "in [and] of French."[4]

Dib's *Who Remembers the Sea* not only marks a major shift in Algerian literary history but also presages a change in the history of reading that literature in France. For if the texts of Feraoun, Mammeri, and the early Dib were read essentially for content, that is, as ethnographic documents or eloquent demonstrations of the justice and necessity of the anticolonial struggle, the "writerly" texts of the later Dib, Farès, and Boudjedra came to be read in the 1970s and 1980s not just as accounts of a particular cultural-political history but above all as instances of a liberatory "literariness." This literariness was recognized as being marked, to be sure, by the writers' cultural-political history, but was nonetheless seen primarily as subversive activity that, in and of itself, effected radical political change. In short, inspired by currents in French literary theory, critics freed Algerian literature from its traditional subservient role of reflecting reality only to idealize it as an autonomous force that almost single-handedly produced reality.

Of course, in the French context it was important to eschew the notion that all Maghrebian fiction is committed writing in which language is a transparent medium reflecting or expressing preexisting political realities and ideologies. So in a sense we should welcome the move of major critics like Charles Bonn and Anne Roche to make a case for reading Algerians as writers whose work acknowledges and carries forward literature's task of producing, rather than unproblematically representing, the social world.[5] I want to suggest, though, that in gradually abandoning historically grounded reading in order to resist the view of literature as realistic representation, critics like Roche and Bonn (Antoine Raybaud is the notable exception here) ended up throwing the baby out with the bath water: particularly in criticism of the 1980s, Algerian fiction retains only the weakest of ties to other forces that critically produce the social world, forces such as feminism and agricultural workers' movements that do inform Algerian writing, and without which progressive change is impossible.

If the subversive potential of Algerian writing as *writing* was emphasized in France at this time, it was not only because of changing critical currents and literary practices. It was also due to the fact that, until the 1988 riots against unemployment and corruption and the 1991 electoral successes of the fundamentalists, the Algerian government was successful in suppressing, or at least containing, most oppositional political activity within the nation's borders, including literary activity. Critical texts published in France were therefore an increasingly rare means of resisting authoritarian rule. Nor were the government elites the only repressive forces at work after independence, for many Algerian intellectuals berated writers of both the older and the younger generations for betraying the new nation on various counts. Writers like Mohammed Dib and Nabile Farès were criticized for writing in French rather than Arabic and for abdicating their responsibility as organic intellectuals. In the eyes of their detractors, they merely produced hermetic texts that relied on imported methods such as Freudian psychoanalysis, dramatizing their personal conflicts rather than helping to construct the new nation.[6] Thus, in a situation in which Algerian nationalism had hardened into a repressive ideology backed by the army and the elites, the view of textuality as subversive activity gained legitimacy as an alternative not only to ethnographic readings but to semiotically astute analyses of the quest for and interrogation of national identity, analyses that had figured centrally in criticism of the early 1970s.

Today, however, when the power of fundamentalists and conservative supporters of various stripes rivals that of the ruling military regime, it seems especially inappropriate to read Algerian writing in terms of the supposed autonomy of aesthetic practices, particularly since that writing explicitly engages political debates in Algeria, challenging the reduction of national identity to a unity defined by religion or culture. Without naively assuming a continuity between literary contestation and challenges issuing from social movements, we should recognize and affirm literature's ties to the oppositional forces that have acquired new life in Algeria since 1988, forces that obliged President Chadli Bendjedid to allow the formation of new political parties that were to participate in what turned out to be an ill-fated electoral process. Since Algerian feminism is one of the most significant oppositional movements in Algeria today, I want to stress the importance of reading Algerian fiction by attending to its subtle and fluid articulations of women as agents of social transformation, and of gendered social relations as both targets and forces of progressive change.

What are the main concerns in Algerian feminism at present, and how do they relate to problems of literary analysis? Clearly, attention is now focused on the powerful fundamentalist movement that, in the estimation of many feminists, threatens to return women to "the veil and the night"[7] and "to force Algeria back into the Middle Ages."[8] It is claimed that, by exploiting justifiable anger with the Front de Libération Nationale (FLN), fundamentalists are succeeding in forcing women into complicity with their "jailers."[9] Naturally, feminists are alarmed at women's electoral support for the fundamentalists, support that had already been manifested publicly in a December 1989 demonstration in which, for the first time in the nation's history, several hundred thousand veiled women marched and chanted. The mass demonstration, organized by the Islamic League in celebration of the "Islamic woman," came in response to feminist protests against the family laws in meetings and demonstrations on several occasions during 1989. On March 8 of that year, International Women's Day, and again on July 2, Algeria's Independence Day, several hundred women had assembled in front of the Parliament and the headquarters of the Human Rights Commission. On November 30 and December 1, three Algerian women's organizations had met with independent feminist activists, including Assia Djebar and Egyptian feminist Nawal al-Saadawi, to discuss ways of challenging the family laws, for instance by showing that they were in conflict not only with the national constitution but with international conventions ratified by the Algerian government. The women also aimed to put pressure on the government to ratify the Copenhagen Convention on Women's Rights and put a stop to the fundamentalists' harassment and intimidation of feminists. (To cite one incident among many, fundamentalists were blamed for physically assaulting and setting fire to the house of a member of the Organization for the Promotion of Women in the city of Annaba at this time.)[10]

In the Algerian context, where fundamentalism and other conservative currents have acquired great force and where feminist activists are often perceived to be out of touch with the masses of Algerian women, it is crucial to develop cultural analyses that, like Homa Hoodfar's study of reveiling in Cairo (discussed in chapter 1), affirm democratic principles and women's civil rights without focusing exclusively on campaigns against state-sanctioned family laws, waged mostly by educated middle- and upper-class urban women. One feminist journalist, Aissa Khelladi, recently appealed to progressive groups in Algeria to respond with something other than stunned silence to Algerian women's support for the fundamentalists, and to seriously ask why large numbers of women are taking this position today.[11] Khelladi speculates that many women joined the 1989 demonstration in favor of "Islamic" womanhood not because they were mystified or backward but because the Islamic movement's call for social justice struck a chord in them, whereas, for various reasons, they were unmoved by progressives' appeals for women's rights or women's liberation. That fundamentalists and other conservatives have capitalized on Islam's commitment to social justice is hardly a new idea. But in the context of Maghrebian feminism, it suggests a need to investigate the multiple and conflicting meanings of social justice for particular groups of women who presently support the religious right or, for whatever reason, remain untouched by the Algerian feminist discourses that have been circulating since independence. Without such an investigation, feminists can only follow Florence Assouline in citing partial explanations that, by Assouline's own account, are as familiar as they are unsatisfactory: women are being coerced, their fear and ignorance are being exploited (of eight million Algerian women, 57 percent are still illiterate), they are victims of the colonial legacy and of the nation's refusal to make women's liberation a priority in the face of disastrous economic conditions. Although she rejects essentialist explanations, declaring with bitter irony that "there is no question of believing [Muslim] women to be carriers of the gene of obedience," Assouline is nonetheless at a loss to account for what appears "from the outside" (and, it would seem, to Assouline herself) as a "will to servitude," particularly in the case of Algerian women whose anticolonial struggle had given the world reason to expect that their next battle would be waged against patriarchy.[12]

It seems to me that the feminist analyses of scholars like Hoodfar cut through this dilemma by showing that women in Muslim societies are conscious of the problems they face and actively seek solutions to them by the means at their disposal. Another example of such work is Fatima Mernissi's interviews with Moroccan women of different social classes and generations.[13] The interviews emphasize the fact that urban and rural Moroccan women, whether educated or uneducated, cast a critical eye on gender relations in their society as they struggle to secure a better life for themselves and those they love. In Algeria, where feminist politics is generally regarded as a modern movement pitted against a traditional culture most forcefully expressed today by fundamentalist men, it is essential to avoid entrapment in the traditional/modern binary and to affirm the critical potential of women's historical agency even in "traditional" spheres of everyday life. Where women's parareligious practices are concerned, for example, Mernissi argues convincingly that in Morocco visits to shrines constitute a "power operation" in which women elude the medical, legal, and religious experts who disqualify them as agents capable of defining and proposing solutions to their problems.[14] While acknowledging that visits to shrines constitute "the best ally of unresponsive national bureaucracies" insofar as they reinvest "alienating institutions which strive to absorb [women], lower their explosive effect, neutralize them" (112), Mernissi nonetheless affirms the importance of such cultural manifestations of women's "collective energies" (112), which must be shaped into effective motors of social change.

A related and equally important strategy, proposed by Mernissi in another context, is to historicize "tradition" as it is articulated by conservative Muslim men.[15] Mernissi urges us to view the fundamentalist wave not merely as an anachronistic demand for a return to the feudal past but rather as a response to bewildering social changes of the present that threaten—or, from her point of view, promise—to radically reshape the future. She cites, for instance, the widespread tendency among both women and men in the Maghreb and the Middle East to postpone marriage, and the large numbers of young, unmarried women in secondary and postsecondary educational institutions as developments that mark a veritable revolution in the traditional Muslim family system, according to which young women must be married as soon as they begin menstruating in order to safeguard family honor. She also signals the competition for jobs between newly urbanized, conservative lower-middle-class men and more progressive urban middle-class women, arguing that conflicts of class and political orientation are often expressed by fundamentalist men in sexual terms, that is, in a call for their female rivals to reveil. By aligning fundamentalism with modernization, Mernissi emphasizes the contradiction between supposedly timeless Islamic traditions and the particular uses to which specific groups of conservative men are putting those traditions in the course of their own radical transformation by the modern forces of urbanization, mass education, and new forms of employment. In short, she historicizes Islamic tradition in the context of men's, as well as women's, lives. At the same time, in challenging Western stereotypes of Islamic backwardness, Mernissi enhances her credibility as a critic of Muslim societies; she affirms her own Islamic cultural heritage and her solidarity with Arab peoples, all of whom, she says, are undergoing a "painful but necessary reshuffling of identity" (8) in the face of irreversible historical change. Mernissi adopts a similar strategy in her reexamination of early Islam in *Sultanes oubliées: Femmes chefs d'état en islam* and *Le Harem politique: Le Prophète et les femmes,* as does Assia Djebar in *Loin de Médine.*[16]

It is important to note that Mernissi relies on a neat distinction between fundamentalist ideology on the one hand and material reality on the other, mistakenly assuming that ideology shapes the understanding of concrete social relations but not the relations themselves. So, for example, in claiming that "class conflicts do sometimes express themselves in acute sex-focused dissent" (9), as they do in relations between newly urbanized lower-middle-class men and urban middle-class women, Mernissi suggests that such conflicts are not really of a sexual order but rather are class conflicts disguised as sexual ones. This approach misses the fact that fundamentalist ideologies are articulating new gendered social identities—not just familiar class identities in disguise—that work to women's disadvantage. Moreover, like many commentators today both in the West and in Algeria, Mernissi uses the term *fundamentalist* to refer to a wide range of groups whose positions need to be specified according to particular regional, national, and cultural contexts. Despite these shortcomings, however, Mernissi's approach serves the threefold purpose of developing a more differentiated analysis of fundamentalist ideologies, defusing fundamentalism as a political force, and articulating the feminist or protofeminist dimensions of Arab women's interests, desires, and everyday life practices. It also suggests productive ways to reread Algerian literary texts, many of which are centrally concerned both with women's historical agency and with the gendered character of social relations between colonizer and colonized, elites and masses, and Arabs, Kabyles, and Berbers in independent Algeria.

La Femme Sauvage as Female Agent and Gendered Social Body

In Algerian literature in French, *la femme sauvage* is a complex figure embodying volatile forces that resist incorporation into any fixed configuration of gender, nation, or culture. As the ogress in Kabyle folktales, she represents what Camille Lacoste-Dujardin calls "negative, wild femininity," which is by turns fertile and sterile, nourishing and devouring, domesticated and untame, economically productive and ruinous.[17] She is associated, too, with wildfire that can be used to rekindle the flame of the domestic hearth, although it may also devastate the countryside or be used by the male hero Mquides to destroy the ogress herself. Both Nabile Farès and Kateb Yacine explicitly invoke the figure of the ogress in their volatile articulations of Algeria's cultural complexity and the contradictory forces at work in the emerging nation. In Farès's *Le Champ des oliviers* the ogress is both the full body of indigenous (Kabyle) cultural meaning and an indecipherable enigma disclosing the exclusions that both found and haunt every identity. Verbally voracious, the ogress is "she who devours all prohibitions . . . / . . . she who demands all permissions . . . / . . . [and] animates popular intelligence."[18] Similarly, as we saw in the last chapter, Kateb's Nedjma, the "ogress of obscure blood," is "capable of electrifying public opinion," although she also functions to reinvest atavistic tribal identifications and strife.[19] And as *femme sauvage*, Nedjma is able to gather the disparate peoples who comprise Algeria while simultaneously opening the national configuration to ever-renewable forms and meanings:

> Souvent, ils s'enfonçaient dans la fôret, en suivant le Rhummel,
> Nedjma en tête, rare femme qui se fût risquée dans ces lieux,
> suivie par cette légion de parias qui avaient l'air de marcher sans
> se soucier d'elle, bruyants et patibulaires; mais dès qu'ils
> s'arrêtaient quelque part et qu'elle se mettait à accorder le luth, ils
> se rapprochaient, accroupis ou couchés autour d'elle, et ils ne
> bougeaient plus. . . . Elle seule savait laisser tomber sa voix
> comme une pierre fracassée jusqu'à l'intensité proche du silence,
> et remonter par une cascade verticale, avec des hiatus
> prolongés,oubliant enfin l'instrument ou le faisant taire aux mains
> d'un autre pour ne plus être que la cantatrice des nuits blanches
> dispensant cette seconde respiration qui l'avait à jamais incorporée
> à la horde, car elle était, elle aussi . . . plurielle en son féminin, et
> faite pour l'impérieuse affection du clan matriarchal éploré sous
> son aile, et tous les habitués du fondouk, éclats de son propre
> sang, ou rayons lointains et aveuglants de tribus croisées de
> désastre en désastre, tous ils venaient boire à son eau troublée,

flairer son parfum andalou, provoquer sa violence africaine,
reconnaître son épaisseur sémitique et s'embruner dans sa
fraîcheur d'Europe, avec le sentiment que cette femme sauvage,
terre en friche pour les hautes herbes de la liberté, steppe
immense et Sahara réservant son essence, était la gardienne de
leur orphelinat famélique dont elle avait réussi à maintenir
ouvertes portes et fenêtres, vers les fôrets pleines de génies
attentifs. . . . [20]

[Often they went deep into the forest, following the Rhummel,
Nedjma taking the lead, a rare woman who would risk a foray
into these parts, followed by this legion of pariahs who seemed to
be walking without taking any notice of her, noisy and sinister;
but the moment they stopped somewhere and she began tuning
her lute, they gathered, stooping or lying around her, and then
kept still. . . . She alone knew how to let her voice fall like a
shattered stone as far as the near intensity of silence and climb
back up along a vertical cascade, with prolonged hiatuses, finally
forgetting the instrument or letting it fall silent in the hands of
another in order to be only the singer of sleepless nights
dispensing this second wind that had forever incorporated her
into the horde, for she too was . . . plural in her feminine and
made for the imperious affection of the matriarchal clan weeping
under her wing, and all the regulars at the hashish den, gleams of
her own blood or distant and blinding rays of tribes crossed from
disaster to disaster, they all came to drink at her troubled waters,
smell her Andalusian perfume, provoke her African violence,
recognize her Semitic depth, and cover themselves in the mist of
her European coolness, with the feeling that this *femme sauvage*,
fallow land for the tall grasses of liberty, immense steppe, and
Sahara reserving her essence, was the guardian of their half-
starved orphanage, whose doors and windows she had managed
to keep open onto the forests filled with attentive spirits. . . .]

Here, Nedjma's song and her mixed origins enable those around
her to identify not only with her similarities to them—"gleams of
her own blood"—but with her differences as well: "plural in her
feminine," she forges bonds with "distant and blinding rays of
tribes crossed from disaster to disaster." This mode of bonding
through the articulation of differences extends spatially beyond the
colonial "orphanage" to an "immense steppe" and "the forests
filled with attentive spirits," which presage the continual reforging
of political identities within and across national boundaries.

In its reference to *la femme sauvage* as "the guardian of their half-starved orphanage, whose doors and windows she had managed to keep open onto the forests filled with attentive spirits," Kateb's 1959 text echoes Dib's *Who Remembers the Sea*, in which another figure for wild femininity, Nafissa, is a maternal guardian who at once protects and keeps open the social spaces that she and others inhabit. The anxious narrator, Nafissa's husband, tells us that her "voice covered me with its water, cradled me" (19), just as the voices of women as a group cover and protect the male collectivity:

Sans la mer, sans les femmes, nous serions restés définitivement des orphelins; elles nous couvrirent du sel de leur langue et cela, heureusement, préserva maints d'entre nous! Il faudra le proclamer un jour publiquement. (20-21)

Without the sea, without the women, we would have remained orphans permanently; they covered us with the salt of their tongue and that, fortunately, preserved many a man among us! It'll have to be recognized publicly someday. (10)

At the same time, however, the light associated with Nafissa, "light that grows in proportion to the opening of the space" (114), forces the narrator to question everything that is happening around him.

Before looking more closely at Nafissa as an embodiment of wild femininity, let me suggest briefly what *is* going on around the narrator. The text is structured partly by an opposition between the "underground city" and the "new constructions" that seem to correspond to the Algerian revolutionary movement on the one hand, and the colonial machinery on the other; however, the text provides no specific historical or geographical reference points that allow us to determine these correspondences with any certainty. The narrator and, with him, the reader are most often wandering in the maze of the city itself, a space that disorients us not only because there is no straight path from one point to another, but also because there is often no fixed path at all insofar as the walls shift positions and even slither, continually changing form and substance. We are disoriented, too, because the characters who inhabit the labyrinthine space of the city also change form and substance: they turn to rocks, to water, to black holes, and to objects of revilement as they fall prey to the spitting and sarcasms of the bird-like "iriaces," strange, foreboding creatures for which Dib has invented a myth-ical name.

Through all of this, Nafissa seems to navigate confidently and even happily. The narrator says:

> Quelque chose me dit qu'elle est contente: horrible pensée, si l'on considère les circonstances où nous nous trouvons placés. Bénit-elle ces intruses parce que venues à point nommé pour pousser les hommes hors d'eux-mêmes? Ce n'est pas impossible. . . . Beaucoup de choses passent encore qui demeurent hors de mon atteinte tandis que, la regardant, j'ignore qui je vois. (66, 69)

> Something tells me that she's happy: a horrible thought if you consider the circumstances in which we find ourselves. Does she give her blessing to these intruding presences because they come just at the appointed moment to push men beyond themselves? It's not impossible. . . . Much is happening that lies beyond my reach while, watching her, I don't know who I am seeing. (38, 40)

If the narrator, in watching Nafissa, does not know who he is see-ing, it is not only because Nafissa is an irreducibly ambiguous fig-ure, but also because he is not yet able clearly to discern the change wrought by the war, change of which Nafissa is both a confident agent and an embodiment. Nafissa's sudden and unexplained dis-appearances and reappearances, her association with "the mes-sage [taken] from out of the hands of the strangers" (90) and with the explosion of a new construction during one of her absences (104) all suggest her militant involvement in the war. And as a re-sult of her involvement, her social significance changes as well: she is no longer defined by her name, Nafissa, which "equally refers to the place of residence and to the soul that resides and acts in that place, [and] also designates our line of descent and the learning that has been passed on to us" (80). For although she comforts and shelters her beleaguered husband, she is not a refuge of traditional values, but rather an agent and symbolic bearer of the historical transformation figured in the "embryonic cities [that] have formed beneath our feet" (39). In this she resembles the sea, which is com-pared to "a pregnant woman" "preparing the coming of another world" (106).

The change in Nafissa is staged with particular clarity in the scene where she encounters her husband in a street filled with "mummies" (103). When he presents her with two stone figurines

he has found, effigies of Nafissa and himself, Nafissa forbids him
to bring them home, thereby causing him great distress:

> Je lui lance des regards traqués. Ravalant mes remords, j'obéis à
> sa demande. . . . Bientôt elle me devance pendant que je traîne
> encore les pieds. (162)

> I look back at her with a haggard expression. Swallowing my
> remorse, I obey her. . . . Soon she passes me while I drag my
> feet. (104)

Pointing gently but critically to her husband's nostalgia for paired
gender identities that have no place in their new situation—"You
wanted me to give them life again, warm them at my breast, with
my breath. Did you know it at least?" (104)—Nafissa appears as a
vanguard figure who brings her husband to consciousness of social
change that renders the old public/private distinctions, and thus
the old order of gender relations, untenable. Far from enshrining
the married couple as refuge of traditional values in the inviolable
space of the home, Nafissa functions here to reconfigure the conjugal relation as rubble encumbering the public space of the streets
where "the air smells of the carnage of decomposed rock, an odor
that seeps into everything" (102).[21]

If Nafissa is a vanguard figure marking engagement in and historical consciousness of the transformations being wrought during
the war, however, she also marks the end of an era in which
certainty—the source of Nafissa's serenity—is still possible. For
Nafissa, there is no disputing the fact that the war is necessary and
must be won—hence the narrator's repeated claim that Nafissa
"knew everything already" (85) despite doubts as to the fate of particular combatants who have disappeared and possibly been imprisoned, tortured, or killed. But Nafissa's certainty and indeed her
existence as social agent are contained by the temporal and spatial
frame of the war itself. Beyond that frame are the uncertain dimensions of the underground city where the future will unfold, and although Nafissa *figures* that space and time, especially in the fantas-
tic forms she assumes in the narrator's imagination after her final
disappearance—she is a "constellation that dreams . . . now flame,
now woman" (114)—she never assumes the "superhuman task
[of] . . . undertaking the exploration and charting of the underground city" (120). Granted, the male narrator-writer underlines
the fact that all people must chart their own course and find the

"path" by which "the sea will bring them their message"; and as he designates those around him only as "strangers" or "neighbors" (108) with no determinate identity, he does not rule out the possiblity that women as well as men, and perhaps people of variable genders, will participate in this process. Nonetheless, the narrator clearly replaces Nafissa as the principal social agent in the last sequences of the book, which elaborate his efforts to chart the unbounded territory of the underground city, that is, to "spell out all the names of Nafissa" (108) and "remember the sea" (120):[22]

> La ville du sous-sol ne connaît pas de limites . . . ses derniers retranchements ne sauraient être atteints par l'un quelconque de ses habitants ou par un moyen d'investigation, si puissant soit-il; et son domaine s'étendrait encore plus loin. Pour tout dire, selon moi, elle plonge ses racines non pas dans le sol, au sens restreint du terme, mais d'une façon générale, dans le monde, avec lequel, par une infinité de conduits, d'antennes, elle entre en communication comme jamais ne l'a fait la ville de l'air. (185)

> The underground city knows no limits . . . its outermost boundaries cannot be reached by any of its inhabitants or by any means of investigation, however powerful. And its domain extends even further. In fact, I believe, it sinks its roots not just into the ground, in the narrow sense of the term, but more generally speaking, into the world, with which, by an infinite number of channels, of antennae, it enters into communication as the open-air city never did. (119)

Once a social agent, Nafissa is by the end no more than a "light" (85) guiding the narrator in his effort without offering a fixed point of reference. Here is a passage foreshadowing the disembodiment of Nafissa as agent and her transformation into a figure of the city's postmodern condition:

> Nul n'aurait la force de vivre sans croire à quelque chose, même si cette chose n'existe pas: je me trouve dans une disposition d'esprit semblable vis-à-vis de Nafissa, sans savoir toutefois ce à quoi, en elle, je crois. Je chante avec force dans l'intention de ramener Nafissa des rives incertaines d'où elle me fait face. (136)

> No one has the strength to live without believing in something, even if that thing doesn't exist: I find myself in just such a mental stance with regard to Nafissa, but without knowing what, in her, I believe in. I sing loudly to bring Nafissa back from the uncertain shores where she stands and faces me. (85)

Although Nafissa's "bright gleam" is also capable of administering "an electric shock" (117) associated with the star-bombs exploding around the narrator, there is no sign that it will usher women onto the historical stage after the war, when Algerians will grapple with the "problem of identity" (120) posed and then figured by Nafissa. Nafissa's wild femininity—fused, like Nedjma's, with the stars astir in other worlds—provides a "transfusion of energy" (63) to a collectivity that "enters into communication as the open-air city never did," blurring the boundaries between tribes, nations, and environments, and possibly between genders as well. New possibilities arise for the articulation of political identities, and yet while the underground city of the future is gendered female by virtue of its figuration by Nafissa, it is far from certain that women, as well as men, will participate in spelling out all its names.

Gender, Writing, and Historical Countermemory

In *Un Passager de l'occident* Nabile Farès's narrator Brandy Fax faces the prospect of interviewing James Baldwin in Paris and mistakenly attributes to the African-American writer a phrase that in fact appears in Albert Memmi's introduction to the French translation of *The Fire Next Time*: "The United States must accept the fact that it is a [racially and culturally] mixed nation."[23] What interests Brandy Fax about the phrase is that it "belongs to the impossible discourses, discourses that will only rarely be heard, discourses that will never be understood" (20), although they clearly suggest the need to theorize and politicize the relations between postcolonial struggles in North America, in Europe, and in Africa. Farès's "impossible discourses" in *Un Passager de l'occident* and in his trilogy *La Découverte du nouveau monde* establish his affinity with Dib as a writer concerned to articulate the irreducible ambiguities and contradictions of Algerian national and cultural identity. Like Dib, Farès often figures these contradictions and ambiguities as negative, wild femininity, embodied in *La Découverte du nouveau monde* by the ogress and by many female characters who share her creative-destructive potency. But although Farès shares Dib's commitment to exploring the new cultural-political spaces opened by Algeria's anticolonial struggle, his texts, written a decade or more after *Who Remembers the Sea*, continually remind us that his explorations are now circumscribed by both a repressive Algerian state and by first-world economic and military interests, emblematized in *Le Champ des oliviers* by an "American boat (an aircraft carrier or patrol boat)" off the shore of Barcelona "awaiting some anti-imperialist movement" (204).

Farès's trilogy *La Découverte du nouveau monde,* originally entitled *En Marge des pays en guerre,* is a writing of the history of the Algerian War and its aftermath. The first two volumes, *Le Champ des oliviers* and *Mémoire de l'absent,* deal with the rending of Algerian society by the war of independence, whereas the third, *L'Exil et le désarroi,* grapples with social inequalities that are reinforced rather than overcome after independence.[24] The violent clash of cultures under colonialism, the loss of Algeria's precolonial cultural past, and the tension between the desire for and the impossibility of a coherent cultural identity in the independent nation are materialized in Farès's trilogy by means of a discontinuous narrative comprising what Antoine Raybaud calls an "epic inscription . . . [incorporating] not only the multiple dimensions of history (combat, popular accounts of the war, an agonic account of the [culture's] origins), but also the incessant interrogation of the meaning of this history."[25] As Raybaud and Anne Roche have shown, the narrative is interrupted by the insertion of poems, traditional Kabyle songs and myths, dramatic scenes, and drawings; there are abrupt changes in rhythm, typography, and page layout, as well as startling uses of punctuation. Often the pronouns do not clearly identify the locutors, and scenes can be extraordinarily contracted or expanded: for instance, the entire text of *Mémoire de l'absent* unfolds within the frame of a taxi ride and can be viewed as an amplification of chapters 8 and 9 of *Le Champ des oliviers,* just as the text of *L'Exil et le désarroi* can be considered an amplification of pages 221-23 of that same volume. The texts' figurations of murder and rending suggest that violence not only comes to Algerian society from the outside—that is, from the forces of imperialism or French colonialism—but also inheres in that society and is unleashed by the war in such a way as to shatter the fantasy of a return to a supposedly authentic Algerian culture once the anticolonial struggle has been won. The interpenetration of love and murder, plenitude and rending, joyful life and wrongful death is presented through a series of figures of immolation and communion—arrests, imprisonment, torture, and murder, as well as lovers' yielding bodies suddenly wounded and sundered.[26]

The impossibility of a unitary Algeria stems from conflicts between rich and poor, urban and rural populations, Arab, Berber,
and Kabyle communities, and men and women. It stems, too, from
the contradictory, heterogeneous character of each of the terms of
these oppositions. And yet through figures like that of the water
skin (or wineskin, which is obviously foreign to Muslim Algeria),
the text articulates a provisional political identity for Algeria that
ties the modern independent nation to its colonial and even its pre-
Islamic past. In *Mémoire de l'absent* the water skin is said to provide
a reassuring enclosure for all the elements of the human and natural world while simultaneously threatening to destroy them
through engulfment or violent expulsion; it emblematizes not only
the ambiguous maternal character of the protective/destructive
ogress but also the "cracking skin" (10) of the young Abdenouar's
sense of belonging to his family and his Kabyle community. Within
family and community, the water skin designates the reversibility
and mutability of masculine and feminine positions: "The enigma
is in us. On us. On you. Like a skin. Your own skin" (68). The water skin also names the "danger" of inventing life anew—the "risk
of nascent earth" (12)—and at the same time offers hope of reconciling antagonistic forces inside and across Algeria's borders:

> Autour de toutes les dislocations ou pertes, autour de tous les
> éloignements et migrations, il y avait cette enveloppe, cette
> première donnée de l'outre, ce premier pas, cette enveloppe qui
> réunissait tout le monde. (113)

> [Around all the dislocations and losses, around all the separations
> and migrations, there was this envelope, this first given of the
> water skin, this first step forward, this envelope uniting
> everyone.]

Similarly, the contradictions and ambiguities of cultural identity
are figured in the notebook of the young revolutionary Ali-Saïd,
which occupies the center of *L'Exil et le désarroi*. Ali-Saïd's writing is
metaphorized as a life-giving tree that is also a tomb, and as a fire
that both generates and consumes human life, love, and struggle:

> La parole/existe/nouée à l'arbre. . . . Le corps/même/est parole/
> jusque/dans/sa brûlure. (65, 66)

> [The word/exists/knotted to the tree. . . . The body/itself/is word/
> in/its very burning.]

But the most compelling and recurrent figure for the ambiguities of Algerian cultural identity is the ogress Yemma Jidda, to whom the first part of *Le Champ des oliviers* is devoted. At once loving and murderous, nurturing and devouring, the ogress is always nearby, both "above and below the world" (27):

> Je . . . Voyage. Bien. Oui . . . Juste au-dessus . . . Ou au-dessous . . . Dans le dégel . . . Oui . . . Le dégel de ce monde . . . Celui que tu habites (habitais) dans l'ignorance de ton monde . . . Après les glaces . . . A ce lieu de surgissement . . . Dans la montée des mondes. . . . (27)

> [I . . . Travel. Well. . . . Yes . . . Just above . . . Or below . . . In the thaw . . . Yes . . . The thaw of this world . . . The one you live in (lived in) in ignorance of your world . . . After the ice . . . In this place where things suddenly appear . . . Where worlds arise. . . .]

Many female characters in Farès's trilogy display characteristics of the ogress, for example, in *L'Exil et le Désarroi*, Ali-Saïd's mother Aloula, who hangs herself on a branch of the tree where her son's ashes are buried, not simply out of madness or despair, but as a way of restoring the connection to her children, "as if the tree . . . would preserve her from all the anxieties, or, losses" (99). There is also Rachida, Ali-Saïd's lover, who tries in vain to reconcile one of the young man's comrades, Mokrane, to the wrenching quality of life in independent Algeria, a world of "silence and arrests" (13) where the fields of the agricultural workers are "barred to self-management" (14) and where women remain "caught in the ine-quality of laws and powers" (80). Unwilling to endure and con-tinue struggling against the internal exile imposed by government forces that "issued from us/and/against Us" (16), Mokrane, who has just returned to his native Kabyle village from France, emi-grates once again.

In *Mémoire de l'absent*, figures recalling the ogress include Jidda, the grandmother of the male protagonist Abdenouar. Like Aloula, Jidda is mad with grief and loss, as her son, Abdenouar's father, is imprisoned in France and her grandson has been killed in the war. But Jidda produces enigmatic drawings that figure the plenitude of family, village, and culture while simultaneously articulating the loss of that plenitude and holding out to Abdenouar the promise of its recovery:

Elle traçait les lignes qui ouvraient l'Outre ou les différents
ventres de l'Outre. (67)

[She traced the lines that opened the water skin or the different
bellies of the water skin.]

In this same volume of the trilogy we find another embodiment of
the ogress in Abdenouar's lover Malika, whose bite on the boy's lip
inflicts an irreparable wound even as it initiates him into love. It is
at the point where Abdenouar is bitten by Malika that the text
opens onto the epic poem of Kahena, the legendary Berber queen
of the Aures who, like the ogress, powerfully bodies forth the ambiguities and contradictions of the culture.

Renowned for her defense of the Berber kingdom against Arab
invaders in the seventh century, Kahena nonetheless embodies the
realm's "slow agony and death" in "the impossible place of love"
(147), as she forsakes her Berber consort Koceïla for an Arab,
Khaled, thus extinguishing "the fire of unity" (146), "the unity of
the cedars and fig trees" (145).[27] Kahena's "strange force," which
had formerly "made the Blue Man [of the desert] cross the sands,
against the advance of the Bedouin" (154), introduces the foreigner
into the heart of the now "impossible Berber kingdom" (166), with
the result that the country "becomes many" (166). Issuing from the
sacrificial death of Kahena is a world remade: "the earth has encountered a new meaning" (149). Through Kahena and other figures of the ogress, through the transformations they work in male
characters like Abdenouar, and through the consuming and regenerative writing of Ali-Saïd that figures the writing of Farès's own
text, La Découverte du nouveau monde gives voice to Algeria's social,
cultural, and subjective upheaval: it explores both the problem of
"no longer knowing one's place in the murderous course of the
world" (Passager, 50) and the possibility of constituting provisional
meanings without disavowing the exclusions that necessarily result from that process—without, that is, forgetting Kahena's death.
Antoine Raybaud and Anne Roche argued eloquently and persuasively in 1977 that Farès's work is mythic not in the sense of providing "an answer more or less marked by cultural origins [as related in] folktale and legend" but in the sense of "an active and
risky interrogation of the possibility that an unbearable or incom-
prehensible situation has a meaning."[28]

I suggested at the beginning of this chapter that historically grounded readings such as those of Roche and Raybaud in the 1970s were gradually overshadowed by readings that focused less on Algerian literature's ability to articulate "the possibility that an unbearable . . . situation has a meaning" than on its capacity to destabilize meaning as a way of resisting the repressive force of power lodged in fixed structures of signification. I want to argue here that this critical shift obscures Farès's textual engagement with the oppositional meanings—the counter-ideologies—of progressive political movements such as feminism in Algeria. By assimilating Farès's writing to a culturally and historically undifferentiated notion of *écriture* whose function is to give voice to supposedly prediscursive forces that resist, without ever altering, a fundamentally immutable paternal Law, criticism of the 1980s discourages attention to the relation between Farès's writing and other social forces that are resisting particular configurations of power in a specified time and place and, in the process, are necessarily producing power configurations and ideologies of their own.

What are the practical consequences of reading Farès in terms of literariness as an autonomous form of cultural politics? Charles Bonn's reading of *L'Exil et le désarroi* provides some examples of the more troubling ones. First, despite his insistence on polysemousness, ambiguity, and contradiction in the text, Bonn's account of the evolution of Farès's oeuvre is itself organized by a very unambiguous narrative in which the text moves from a fairly conventional representation of reality in *Yahia, pas de chance* to the explosion of every reality, including its own—an explosion whose manifestations, however multiple, always stand in the same relation to a static, immutable instance of power.[29] According to Bonn, the last book in Farès's trilogy is the most polysemous of the author's five novels to date, and the only one to deconstruct meaning and place (the univocal, repressive meaning of the nation, the capital city as the site of centralized governmental power) to the point of being consumed by its own activity and reduced to silence: "Deprived of meaning, the movement of the text of *L'Exil et le désarroi* annihilates itself in its own 'internal fissure'."[30] In order to place Farès's writing on this one-way street to ecstatic self-destruction, Bonn has to construct a rigid interpretive frame aligning power, place, and univocal meaning on one side against subversion, non-place, and polysemy on the other—as if meaning, place, and power had no role to play in subversive social movements. This goes against the grain of Farès's writing, in which many tropes—not just that of wild femininity—function now to destabilize meaning, now to bring a new, liberatory one into being. For instance, the "fields" and the "hills" figure not only division, conflict, and groundlessness but also the provisional ground of liberation and reconciliation, as in the chapter on women's dream of emancipation from the constraints of traditional Algerian society:

> Nous implorons/:le village/ou la vallée/les collines/ou les champs/ *car:* Nous n'avons pas d'autre manière de dire notre monde, ou, délaissement, situé là dans le désir de l'homme, et, sa prépondérance. (80-81)

> [We implore/:the village/or the valley/the hills/or the fields/*for:* We have no other way of speaking our world, or, abandonment, situated in the desire of man, and, his preponderance.]

In order to read Farès as he does, Bonn thus has to deny the obvious ideological function of lengthy narrative passages explicitly denouncing the repression of feminist and other democratic movements. Rather than acknowledging the disruptive force of counter-ideology production, he claims instead that Farès's novelistic discourse is not ideological except insofar as it is "inscribed" (286) in the ideological discourse of the novel's epigraph, which reads:

> Les destructions causées par les bourgeoisismes révolutionnaires et nationalistes de l'époque actuelle n'épargnent aucun des champs développés et inscrits par le travail humain. Valeur d'échange et, comme le reste, valeur de réalité, le travail d'écriture n'échappe pas aux conditions politiques de cette inhumanité. (7)

> [The destruction caused by today's revolutionary and nationalist middle-class opportunism spare none of the fields developed and inscribed by human work. As exchange value and, like the rest, reality value, the work of writing does not escape the political conditions of this inhumanity.]

Like many critics of the 1980s, Bonn wants to assign writing a value whose "efficacy" (286) consists in its ability not only to produce new realities that subvert exchange values, but to escape existing realities altogether. Clearly, this view of writing is contested by Farès's text, which insistently and purposefully links the dismantling of meanings and identities to their ongoing reconstitution not only in texts but in progressive social formations.

Bonn's idealization of writing is most apparent in his treatment of Ali-Saïd's notebook. He not only underscores the fact that it occupies the center of *L'Exil et le désarroi* but, more importantly, claims that it subsumes all the other subversive discourses in the text, notably those of women and agricultural workers, giving them their most radical expression. Whereas "Power" (that is, the Algerian state) is castigated for imposing a single voice that suppresses the multiplicity of popular discourses arising from what Bonn calls the "collective voice of the 'waiting country' " (292), Bonn unself-consciously unites these counterdiscourses under the banner of the dead male revolutionary's writing so that, as in many power configurations I can think of, the discourse of the educated, spiritualized male individual takes precedence over and ultimately functions to silence the discourses of corporealized women and illiterate men.

In order to privilege Ali-Saïd's writing as he does, Bonn has to bracket several key points that he himself has raised about *L'Exil et le désarroi*, notably the fact that Ali-Saïd's writing is not given directly but is presented by Rachida. The text lovingly folds Rachida's discourse into Ali-Saïd's (and vice versa) in such a way that at certain points it is impossible to know which of the two is speaking. A voice says, "The mother cries/against/the death/of the son/while/the father/lives/in the force/of the son" (70), but when Rachida resumes the refrain, "I'll tell you a story," how can we know if it is only there that she is speaking again in her own voice or if she has already been doing so for several lines? Boundaries are blurred between male and female identities as well as between the dead and the living, the past and the present, the human and the natural world. It seems to me that this technique invites us to ask what the explosion of identities and meanings means for Rachida, as well as for Mokrane, whom she is addressing, and for the writing of Ali-Saïd (the hero of Charles Bonn's epic).

For readers of Farès, to focus on writing as the most important contestatory practice is to ignore the very explicit references to other practices from which Ali-Saïd's writing arises — not only his passionate bond with Rachida, but also his bond with the old woman Nouria, whose eccentric relation to the community recalls that of *la femme sauvage*. Nouria is an illegitimate daughter who goes to live in the desert to the South, then returns to Kabylia to live alone on the hill as a "stranger" (61), unguarded, unsecluded, her dress "torn in many places, like her flesh and her heart" (56), procuring for herself both "food and knowledge" (57). Like Ali-Saïd, Nouria is situated "between the revealed truth of the Book [the Koran] and the pure animation of fire" (61). Parallel to the fire of the young man's writing—indeed fueling his writing in the sequences dealing with Nouria—is the fire set by Nouria every night in the hills as she "addresses supplications and praise to the Spirits of Revolt and Sacrifice" (62) in order to ignite the revolutionary passions of those around her:

> La mise en condition commença à déborder le cadre étroit et silencieux de la nuit, pour atteindre, bien que timidement, certains moments du jour. Entre les travaux, les habitants des vallées et collines environnantes réapprenaient à tirer. (62)

> [The conditioning began to exceed the narrow and silent frame of the night, to attain, though only timidly, certain moments of the day. Between daily tasks, the inhabitants of the surrounding valleys and hills learned to shoot once again.]

And just as Malika had wounded and transformed Abdenouar by biting him in love, so Nouria, in her seduction of Ali-Saïd, becomes "savage" (67) and "opens his skin" with her "slender, moving hands," moving him "to lose his body . . . in order to transform space and the hill" (69). Nouria's fire not only figures the material base of Ali-Saïd's writing but also interpellates him in a specific way:

> Je peux voir ma chair/nommée à vif/dans les mains du feu. (69)

> [I can see my flesh/named alive/in the hands of the fire.]

Just as her fire had prompted the inhabitants of the hills and valleys to "learn to shoot once again," it moves Ali-Saïd to "learn to read" differently, to "read between the lines of the sky, and the tree" (66). Nouria's fire, then, like Nedjma's and Nafissa's, is to be read not merely as raw material for the young man's writing, but as a symbolic force that is already transfiguring Algerian culture.

It is true that Farès, like Dib and Kateb, often uses female figures like Nouria, Malika, and Jidda as means to an end that does not necessarily serve them—most often, the painful but liberatory transformation of their male lovers and kin. Farès frequently implies that women always already possess and are possessed by the transformative powers of the ogress, for instance when he has Abdenouar say of his grandmother, Jidda:

> Le simple frôlement de [sa] voile me redonnait la vie. C'est ainsi que je la surprenais ou plutôt: qu'elle me ravissait, qu'elle jetait au loin l'impossible existence coloniale, m'enfonçait dans les replis de ses croyances et maîtrises, me parlait, et m'initiait au langage autre, celui qui devait faire déborder l'Outre. (*Mémoire*, 66)

> The mere rustling of [her] veil gave me new life. It is thus that I surprised her, or rather: that she ravished me, cast afar the impossible colonial existence, enveloped me in the folds of her beliefs and knowledges, and initiated me into the other language, the one that was to make the Water Skin overflow. (66)

Similarly, Jidda is presented as belonging to a shadowy world that Abdenouar can only vaguely discern, a world to which Malika and Kahena belong as well. Just as Abdenouar addresses Kahena as the "veiled shadow of my delirium" (*Mémoire*, 54), he likens the shadowy aspects of his own subjectivity to the "gigantic shadow of [Jidda's] face on the streets" (*Mémoire*, 48). A related point is that even though Farès's text underscores the racial and sexual ambiguity of human beings whose identities are always unstable and "mixed" (*Mémoire*, 79), it often uses female energy to drive itself forward, as in the scene where Malika's bite generates the staging of Kahena's sacrifice, which in turn produces a "new meaning" for Farès's "new world."[31]

Nevertheless, like *Nedjma* and *Who Remembers the Sea*, *La Découverte du nouveau monde* takes the relatively unusual step of placing women's history in history.[32] It not only presents women as agents of social transformation, asserting, for instance, that "Malika . . . will splash you with history and presence" (*Mémoire*, 101); it also explores the potential consequences, for women, of the ogress's work of making and unmaking identities. Farès writes:

> Dans leurs vêtements de Ciel et d'Etoiles, les Femmes rêvent de transgresser leurs soumissions séculaires. D'agir. Selon leurs hardiesses. Profusions. Sensibilités./Contre les hommes./Ou: leurs prétentions de puissance. (*L'Exil*, 79-80)

> [In their clothes of Sky and Stars, Women dream of transgressing their age-old submission. Of acting. In accordance with their

boldness. Profusions. Sensibilities./Against men./Or: their
pretensions to power.]

More than Charles Bonn suggests, certainly, Farès's "impossible
discourses" continually reformulate the question of the relation between writing and other material practices. Far from subsuming
Algeria's multiple voices in Ali-Saïd's spiritualized word, Farès invites us to consider what that word means for women's struggles
and for the struggles of the dispossessed in a nation that does not
and cannot have a unitary identity. And through his references to
James Baldwin and to the United States as a "mixed society," he
invites us to ask, too, what his "impossible discourses" mean for
readers in Europe and North America, whose knowledge of and
political relation to Algeria require critical scrutiny.

Gender Trouble in Boudjedra

If I have so far left Rachid Boudjedra out of my discussion of gender in Algerian literature of the 1960s and 1970s, it is because, unlike Dib and Farès, he is basically uninterested in women's history
at this time, even though he shares Farès's commitment to breaking "Algeria's patriarchal spine" (*Passager*, 75). Although Boudjedra passionately denounces women's exploitation in Algeria in his
first two novels, *La Répudiation* and *L'Insolation*, both texts are elaborated in the form of a male monologue that makes no attempt to
give voice to women's subjectivity or historical agency.[33] In these
early novels, the female characters function pychologically to "ad-
ulate" the male narrator (*Répudiation*, 11, 141, 216, etc.), but their
main purpose is a formal one. On the one hand, they provide a
pretext for the narrator's discourse, as when Samia disappears after
being seduced by Rachid, the narrator-protagonist of *L'Insolation*,
who then wonders what has become of her. And on the other, the
female characters actively elicit the narrator's speech and writing:
in *La Répudiation*, the narrator's lover Céline "presses" (9) him to
speak of his mother, just as in *L'Insolation*, Nadia, the repressive
head nurse in the psychiatric ward where Rachid is confined, has
"set her mind to making [him] talk" (217).

The narrators' purely instrumental relation to the female characters is tacitly legitimated by the incompetence attributed to "stupid
exploited women" (233) in general and, in particular, by the sys-

tematic association of Céline and Nadia with repressive social forces. Céline, a French woman working in Algeria as a teacher, is a product of neocolonial power relations in which "foreigners end up getting rich and despising [the native] population" (198), and Nadia is aligned with the "Secret Members of the Clan" who "lynch" (47) their victims, whether they be women subjected to confinement and, sometimes, rape; landless peasants forced to live on the edge of starvation; or boys whose foreskin is sacrificed in the circumcision ritual recounted obsessively by the narrator. In short, Boudjedra's texts banish wild femininity, focusing instead on an Oedipal drama in which the (often feminized) forces of castration and repression control a country deemed so backward that "the tall tale of *la femme sauvage* invented by smokers of kif" still has purchase among the "large landowners of the high plateaus . . . and the immense cohort of starving men whom they manipulated for the municipal elections" (*Insolation*, 41).[34] In *L'Insolation*, then, Rachid seems justified in entertaining fantasies of raping Nadia or "cutting off her breast" (11), for her power is excessive and abusive like that of the Secret Members of the Clan. What is more, Nadia wields the powers of horror. Her genitals and especially her menstrual blood inspire in the narrator a terror to which fantasies of aggression and self-glorification seem a natural response: Rachid wants to excite Nadia sexually to the point that she will "take God to be a very hard stick" (218). Because female identity is cast as either a double of male identity or a horrifying inverted image of it, it can function, at best, as the instrument of men who, like Boudjedra's male narrators, manage to usurp it and turn it to their own purposes, namely, the generation of subversive texts. It is no surprise to find this process figured in *La Répudiation*, in the narrator's fantasy of a "poem written on the wide white [or blank] back of a lover busy brushing her hair before a mirror that I end up breaking" (199-200).[35]

Hafid Gafaiti argues that in Boudjedra's later texts, especially *La Pluie*, there emerges a critical female voice and an articulation of women as subjects of history.[36] Yet he also notes (53) that in *Le Démantèlement*, Boudjedra's attention to women as perpetrators of subversive violence is accompanied by an exploration and vindication of male homosexuality, and it seems to me that this is where the main interest of Boudjedra's work lies, at least in terms of sexual politics.[37] Putting a perverse spin on Lacoste-Dujardin's characterization of *la femme sauvage*, I would say that a kind of "negative, wild masculinity," articulated in terms of male homosexuality, is already at issue in *La Répudiation*. It is manifested not in the "pillaging" (218) of male childhood by patriarchal molesters (241), which merely mimics abusive aspects of heterosexual relations, but rather in the pleasurable clandestine homosexual activity of the narrator's brother Zahir, particularly his relationship with his Jewish lover, whom the narrator dubs Heimatlos (Homeless). Male homosexuality is at issue, too, in *L'Insolation*, in the narrator's fantasy of castrating (blinding) his male persecutors by means of a suicide in which the blood spurting from a self-inflicted gunshot wound to the head doubles as ejaculated semen: "I'll explode in their faces, just when they least expect it. Splatch! Flower of blood. So violent that they'll be blinded by it for several minutes" (219). This fantasy has heterosexual counterparts in the violent fantasies I mentioned a moment ago, that is, fantasies of raping, mutilating, and forcing pleasure on Nadia. It is worth noting in this connection that Rachid often places himself in a "feminine" position in his fantasies, for instance, when he becomes the object of his own penetration (the act of shooting) in the suicide fantasy, or when he associates the blood of his newly circumcised penis with that of Samia's defloration or with the blood shed in the black man's sacrifice of the she-goat as a means of purifying Samia.

Evident in Rachid's vacillation between "masculine" and "feminine" positions is Boudjedra's concern to disclose the instability of the sexual binary and other social oppositions intersected by it. This concern manifests itself as well in the trope of dissymmetry that appears again and again in the male narrators' monologues. I am thinking, for instance, of the "dissymmetry" in the narrator's face and in that of Céline, his "double" (16), in *La Répudiation*, where the man/woman opposition is bound up with that of colonizer and colonized. Similarly, in *L'Insolation*, the dissymmetry in Nadia's breasts (10) and in the moustaches of the circumcisor (28) render grotesque, or even comical, the hierarchies between men and women, men and boys, rulers and ruled, the sane and the insane, and heterosexuality and homosexuality. Although I am unable to do so here, it would be interesting to investigate the possibility that Boudjedra's oft-cited preoccupation with the abject, articulated in his male narrators' parodic discourse, elaborates a wild masculinity that dislodges the association between homosexuality and abjection.[38]

In *L'Insolation*, the trope of dissymmetry is doubled by that of disarticulation, evoked in connection with Djoha, the cunning figure from Maghrebian popular culture who is forced to pose as Rachid's father by Siomar, a powerful businessman who has raped and impregnated his young sister-in-law, who will give birth to Rachid. Described as a "grotesque and disarticulated puppet" (225) threatened with arrest "for his activities as a notorious political agitator and for trafficking narcotics" (85), Djoha eludes confinement by the structures in which Rachid is trapped: the hospital and prison, to be sure, but also home and family, religion, class, language, and nationality. Ruse and "politico-poetical rhetoric" (232) enable Djoha to put pressure on the authorities and radicalize the masses while also pursuing forbidden pleasures. An irreducibly contradictory figure, Djoha always "has a rosary at hand" in case it's needed (70), "recites Lenin in Arabic" (70), contends that "theory should not necessarily coincide with practice" (70), and is usually "full of kif and wine" (229). He is a "terribly lucid, terribly rebellious clown, alone capable of fanning the flames of the people's hatred for all the fat cats who exploit them and all the muftis who demagogically take them for a ride" (232).

Rachid's "nebulous filiation" (228) with Djoha suggests that the young man's writing and storytelling should be read as instances of disarticulation as well. As I indicated above, Rachid's stories scramble the codes organizing sexual, generational, and national relations in terms of fixed binaries. Occasionally, his subterfuge enables him to seduce the authority figure Nadia, short-circuiting her resistance to his subversive discourse:

> Pouvait-elle dire qu'il n'y eut jamais de vieillard nègre, ni de chat blanc? Là, elle hésitait et je la surprenais. Vite! Il fallait l'amener à de meilleurs sentiments avant que le jour fît irruption. (*Insolation*, 23)

> [Could she say there had never been an old black man or a white cat? There she hesitated and I was catching her by surprise.
> Quick! I had to make her more kindly disposed before day broke.]

If Rachid's writing promises to undermine Nadia's authority, it is in part because he will eventually "read [it] to those who are sleeping at the moment" (23), that is, to the other patients in the psychiatric ward with whom he wants to establish a network. He writes from a variety of contradictory positions, and although there is no effort to consolidate these positions or resolve the contradictions between them, there is an attempt to find a way to link them by means of "politico-poetical rhetoric" so that he and others may leave the hospital and reshape the social spaces of independent Algeria. In the end, however, Rachid's suicidal depression causes him to abandon the search for a subversive language, and his inertia casts a long shadow over Djoha's inexhaustible energy. Already in 1972, Boudjedra's *L'Insolation* displays a pessimism that will permeate writing by Algerian women of the 1970s and 1980s.

Women's Voices

The novels published in French by Algerian women in recent years convey a sense of discouragement, if not desperation, with respect to women's situation in Algeria. For example, Fettouma Touati's *Le Printemps désespéré*, Hafsa Zinaï-Koudil's *Le Pari perdu*, and Myriam Ben's *Sabrina, ils t'ont volé ta vie* all deal with the constraints women negotiate daily in the workplace, in the nuclear family, in marriage, and in child-rearing arrangements.[39] Touati's narrator says of the protagonist Malika at the age of ten: "She was so negated by the life she led and had built up such a wall inside her that she lived in the most appalling solitude" (37). Years later, when Malika has returned to Algeria to work as a secretary after living and studying in France, she is a "liberated woman" with very limited prospects in her intimate relations with men. "Either she was a personal prostitute or she was confined. Many women accepted one or the other out of fear of loneliness. . . . Every hour Algeria became more and more unbearable to her" (131). A similar view of the constraints placed on women, and pessimism about the possibility of lifting them, pervades the recent work of Algeria's foremost woman writer, Assia Djebar. Yet, without underestimating the formidable threat posed to Algerian feminism by fundamentalists today, and without idealizing the feminist or protofeminist aspects of Algerian women's everyday lives, I want to caution against reading the pessimistic texts of the 1980s as the only possible responses to the current situation in Algeria. For as I suggested earlier, the work of feminist scholars like Fatima Mernissi and Homa Hoodfar proposes ways to affirm women's desires, interests, and agency.

Before turning to a consideration of Assia Djebar's writing, I want to point out that, generally speaking, when the women writers of Algeria are not discussed solely in terms of their attention to the conjugal couple, they are nonetheless treated with a certain condescension because their writing is considered to be trite and to serve, at best, to demonstrate pregiven ideologies, especially anticolonial, democratic, and feminist ideologies. While it may be acknowledged that women's demonstrations of feminist ideologies are necessary and valuable, it is assumed that they are only marginally pertinent to literary activity per se, that is, the process of interrogating the conditions of possibility of meaning and disrupting the fixed meanings that underwrite the existing social order.[40] Tacitly, it is assumed that women's writing is trite because women have not yet had time to develop as writers in the brief forty-year period in which Algerians have been writing novels in French.

Rejecting this explanation, Simone Rezzoug argues that because women are generally perceived to be transgressing in taking up the pen and making women's interests the subject of public debate, they have developed a writing strategy adapted to this social context: they parade hackneyed discourses as a way of gaining acceptance by readers and "soliciting the recognition of the female voice within and not against the male community. Indeed, the frequency of marks of sociability in the texts signifies the desire for participation and not, for the moment at least, a declaration of difference."[41] Hence the "hypercorrectness" (88) of their discourse, which rarely strays from the forms dictated in school manuals, and their highly readable linear narration: far from striving for the baroque effects cultivated by Boudjedra or the hermetic writing of Dib and Farès, most women writers steer clear of la parole sauvage (88), opting instead for prose that conveys the reasonableness and comprehensibility of their positions. Hence, too, the strategy, evident in Yamina Mechakra's La Grotte éclatée, of setting the account of a woman's physical and moral dispossession in the frame of the Algerian War—a period in which Mechakra herself was too young to have had the experiences of her protagonist.[42] As Rezzoug points out (87, 89), the war setting, which recalls a privileged moment in the nation's and Algerian women's history, invites readers to take women's dispossession seriously. Thus, at the same time that Mechakra's figure of the exploded cave marks the devastating effects of French napalm bombs on the male and female Algerian combatants who have taken shelter there, it implicitly criticizes the traditional practice of "burying women alive between four walls" (51). In the same way, the "invented border" (24) separating the Algerian freedom fighters from the French doubles as a border simultaneously dividing and uniting Algerian men and women who, by working together, might ensure that "a deracinated land be reborn" (24).

If it is true that Mechakra experiments more with literary form than most other women writing in French in Algeria, no woman writer has done more than Assia Djebar to give new life to her deracinated land through writing. Trained as a historian, Djebar began publishing fiction as a young woman during the Algerian War and in the first years of independence. Two of the novels from that period, *Les Enfants du nouveau monde* and *Les Alouettes naïves*, are continually reissued in Algeria and are regularly taught in high school and university courses.[43] However, some of Djebar's more recent work is looked upon less favorably by those who control the media. For example, her prizewinning feature film *La Nouba des femmes du Mont Chenoua* (1978), which was supposed to have been shown on Algerian television, was never aired because officials deemed it disrespectful of Algerian manhood, among other things because the only man to appear in it is handicapped and confined to a wheelchair. (Djebar cheerfully explains that he was the only man she could find occupying interior space, which was the space she was interested in exploring.)[44] And if none of her novels has been translated into Arabic in Algeria, it is because, in the eyes of government officials, she is a "Westernized" expatriate who writes feminist books in French that distort the supposed realities of the women of Algeria.

Without question, Djebar's novels are feminist and are highly critical of women's situation in Algeria. Here, I want to discuss two novels of the mid-1980s, *Fantasia, an Algerian Cavalcade* (1985) and *A Sister to Sheherazade* (1987), which challenge the domination of women by giving voice to them in fiction while also registering a profound pessimism about feminism's power to change social relations in contemporary Algeria.[45] The first of these novels—in my estimation, Djebar's best book—interweaves autobiographical sequences and short, lyrical prose poems with histories of the French conquest of Algeria culled from the reports, memoirs, and correspondence of military officers, aristocrats, and publicists who engaged in the conquest or came to Algeria with the aim of capitalizing on it. Djebar's novel also mentions accounts of the conquest recorded by Algerians, most of which are lost and are attested only in the Europeans' records. In the last section of the text, autobiographical sequences and prose poems alternate with voices of Algerian women, whose accounts of their experiences during the war of liberation are transcribed or adapted from interviews Djebar conducted in the mountainous area near her hometown of Cherchell on the Mediterranean coast west of Algiers—the same interviews that provided much material for the film *La Nouba des femmes*. Djebar thus establishes a dialogue between texts written in French (the colonizers' as well as her own) and different oratures—that of the author and her mother's family, city dwellers who speak an Arabic dialect, and that of the women in the nearby countryside who speak a Berber dialect.

The overall formal alternation between written and oral texts and individual and collective histories recalls an element of the text's title, *fantasia*, which refers to a method of musical composition in which fancy takes precedence over formal conventions. Indeed, the third section of the novel, which is divided into five movements followed by a coda, is arranged as a musical fantasia. The term *fantasia* also gestures toward the sonorous quality of Djebar's prose, which mediates between the voice and writing, making the sounds and rhythms of her native Arabic resonate in the French of her own text, itself a "palimpsest" (79) imbricated not only in the texts written by the French conquerers, but also in those read by the pupils in the French colonial schools where the author/narrator was educated.[46]

Fantasia has another meaning as well, however, for as the translator points out in her introduction to Djebar's text, the Arabic *fantaziya* refers to "a set of virtuoso movements on horseback executed at a gallop, accompanied by loud cries and culminating in rifle shots . . . [a cavalcade] associated with ceremonial occasions and military triumphs." This term thus brings together the fanciful elaborations binding different, sometimes violently conflicting elements of Algerian life with acts of aggression, whether real (as on the battlefield), ritualized (as in the *fantaziya*), or grimly textualized and aestheticized (as in Baron Barchou's recollection of the Algerian woman who "lay dead beside the corpse of a French soldier whose heart she had torn out . . . an image that prefigures many a future 'mater dolorosa' who, carrion beetles of the harem, will give birth to generations of faceless orphans during Algeria's thraldom a century later" [18-19]).

Djebar's novel is a work of painstaking and often unspeakably painful excavation. It ventures into spaces such as the caves near her birthplace where in 1845 resistant Berber tribes—men, women, and children, together with their animals—took refuge from and refused to surrender to the troops of the master strategist Pélissier. Pélissier resolved to smoke the resisters out, and nearly all—fifteen hundred of them—died of asphyxiation. In relating this somber event in Algeria's history—an event that is repeated just two months later, twenty leagues away, by another officer, Colonel Saint-Arnaud—Djebar's text echoes the report of a European observer, a distressed Spanish officer who noted that after the violent blaze "at the summit of El-Kantara," which "rose to a height of more than two hundred feet" (69), Pélissier ordered his men to bring some six hundred corpses out of the dark caves into the sunlight. In its emotion, her text also echoes Pélissier's own report, "which he intends to compose in official terms" but is unable to do, for his "promiscuous contact with the fumigated victims" has made him "the quasi-fraternal embalmer of this tribe" (79):

> Pélissier, l'intercesseur de cette mort longue, pour mille cinq cents cadavres sous El Kantara, avec leurs troupeaux bêlant indéfiniment au trépas, me tend son rapport et je reçois ce palimpseste pour y inscrire à mon tour la passion calcinée des ancêtres. (93)

> Pélissier, speaking on behalf of this long-drawn-out agony, on behalf of fifteen hundred corpses buried beneath El-Kantara, with their flocks unceasingly bleating at death, hands me his report and I accept this palimpsest on which I now inscribe the charred passion of my ancestors. (79)

It is thus by means of the "father tongue"—a language of liberation to which the narrator had access by virtue of being sent to French schools by her father, but also "the language of yesterday's enemy" to which she feels bound by a "forced marriage" (213)—that she composes a fantasia. The fantasia, in turn, gives voice to her mother tongue, tying her ancestors' history of resistance and deadly defeat to the different but related histories of the narrator, the women in her mother's urban community, and the peasant women of the nearby mountains. One significant effect of Djebar's textual strategy is to enable literate Algerian women to reclaim their buried histories, often available only through the accounts of the enemy that Djebar critically resignifies, venturing deep into the caves beneath El-Kantara without, however, "restoring" a voice that never was to the women and men who were asphyxiated there: it is the history of asphyxiation itself that is presented in Djebar's text. She writes:

> L'amour, si je parvenais à l'écrire, s'approcherait d'un point nodal: là gît le risque d'exhumer des cris, ceux d'hier comme ceux du siècle dernier. Mais je n'aspire qu'à une écriture de transhumance, tandis que, voyageuse, je remplis mes outres d'un silence inépuisable. (76)

> Love, if I managed to write it down, would approach a critical point: there where lies the risk of exhuming buried cries, those of yesterday as well as those of a hundred years ago. But my sole ambition in writing is constantly to travel to fresh pastures and replenish my water skins with an inexhaustible silence. (63)

In counterpoint to Pélissier's macabre act of carrying the Berber corpses out of the caves into the sunshine, Djebar brings to light, both in her text and in her conversations with the women of Mount Chenoua whose oral histories she records, elements of colonial history that can be construed as having a liberatory dimension for women. For example, Djebar speaks and writes of Pauline Rolland, a Saint-Simonian republican, a feminist, and a pacifist who was deported to Algeria by Napolean after the 1848 Revolution. While it is somewhat troubling that Djebar elides the cultural-imperialist ambitions of the Saint-Simonians, who saw in the supposed mysticism of the orient fertile ground for their ideologies, her effort to construct a history linking feminist impulses in two warring nations is still a worthy one. In *Fantasia,* she cites a letter of July 1852 in which Rolland writes:

> En Kabylie . . . j'ai vu la femme bête de somme et l'odalisque de harem d'un riche. J'ai dormi près des premières sur la terre nue, et près des secondes dans l'or et la soie. (250-51)

> In Kabylia . . . I have seen women treated as beasts of burden, and others odalisques in a rich man's harem. I have slept at the side of the former on the bare ground, and beside the latter amid gold and silk. (223)

In the narrator's interpretation these are "affectionate words from a woman, pregnant with the future: they give off light before my eyes and finally set me free" (223). The narrator quotes a shepherd-girl from Mount Chenoua as saying that Pauline "fights for her faith and her principles" (222); it is as if she had bequeathed her revolutionary past to Algerian women. Although the forty-eight-year-old schoolteacher is allowed to return to France four months after her deportation due to extreme illness, she is delirious upon arriving home and dies soon afterward without having been able to communicate with her three children. In the narrator's eyes, "our country became her grave":

> Ses véritables héritières—Chérifa de l'arbre, Lla Zohra errante
> dans les incendies de campagne, le choeur des veuves anonymes
> d'aujourd'hui—pourraient pousser, en son honneur, le cri de
> triomphe ancestral, ce hululement de sororité convulsive! (250)

> Her true heirs—Cherifa hiding in her tree, Lla Zohra wandering
> among the fires that ravaged the countryside, the chorus of
> anonymous women of today—could pay homage to her with that
> ancestral cry of triumph, the ululation of convulsive sisterhood!
> (223)

In *Fantasia*, Pauline Rolland's grave, marked by her revolutionary feminist legacy, both mirrors the funeral ancestral caves of El-Kantara and holds the promise of Algerian women's collective emergence into the light and the open air. The women's hypothetical homage to Pauline in the form of an "ancestral cry of triumph," which traditionally accompanies the *fantaziya*, counters colonial and neocolonial forms of domination with the transnational material and symbolic work of feminism that, in Djebar's estimation, could free the "anonymous women of today." It is important to note, though, that in Djebar's text the women of today rarely appear as the heirs of Pauline Rolland, Lla Zohra, or the nineteenth-century female captives who "smear their faces with mud and excrement when they are paraded in front of the conquerer" (56). More often, they are presented as anonymous "wraiths," the heirs of the silent women asphyxiated not only by the deadly fires of the French army but by their own countrymen:

> Les femmes se meuvent fantômes blancs, formes ensevelies à la
> verticale, justement pour ne pas faire ce que je fais là maintenant,

pour ne pas hurler ainsi continûment: son de barbare, son de
sauvage, résidu macabre d'un autre siècle! (131-32)

Women are walking white wraiths, shrouded figures buried
upright, precisely to prevent what I am doing now, to prevent
them uttering such a constant howl: such a wild, barbaric cry,
macabre residue of a former century! (115)

Only the narrator and her analogues—women exiled from their
mother tongue, from the women's communities of their mothers'
generation, and often from their country as well—escape the fate
of silence and confinement in Djebar, the fate of being buried alive.

Her text movingly presents itself as a "cluster of strangled cries"
written by another (a lover) in a letter addressed "to all the other
women whom no word has ever reached, those of past generations
who bequeathed me the places of their confinement . . . [whose]
only path to freedom was intoning their obsessional chants" (59-
60). Written in "the language formerly used to entomb my people"
(215), it seeks to enable other Algerian women to leave their places
of confinement and enter the symbolic realm of writing: it seizes on
a severed woman's hand—the hand that Eugène Fromentin had
found in his path in Laghouat and inscribed in a text that has come
into the narrator's hands—attempting "to bring it the *qalam*" (226),
or stylus, the instrument of Koranic writing. Yet even as it offers
itself as an instrument of Algerian women's liberation, Djebar's text
reinscribes a pessimistic view of her Maghrebian sisters that many
feminists, such as Fatima Mernissi, contest, emphasizing not their
mutilation and dispossession but rather their capacity to speak and
act on their own behalf today. Whereas Djebar's narrator says her
writing enters a public space that, at present, is empty—it is
"washed up on the deserted seashores of today" (215)—Mernissi
insists on the entry of her writing into a public space already occupied by large numbers of women who will not, under any circumstances, return to confinement.

This same issue arises in Djebar's *A Sister to Sheherazade*, which,
like *Fantasia*, is narrated by an urban woman who is educated and
has lived abroad, in this case with her husband and daughter. The
narrator, Isma, who has left her husband, speaks alternately in the
first person about her own life and in the second person (in the familiar form) to Hajila, the woman her husband has just wed. In the
sequences addressed to Hajila, Isma narrates Hajila's emergence

from the domestic space in which her husband has confined her, a modern apartment with a "new kitchen that is like a tomb" (85). This text doubles the earlier novel in deploying female space as a tomb from which women must emerge. Like the descendants of the resistant Berbers in *Fantasia*, the masses of Algerian women in *Sheherazade* are "anonymous women buried alive" (79; translation modified),[47] disempowered women whose cries, shouts, and capacity for action and self-fulfillment need to be "unearthed" (139). In fact, in the latter text much of the narrative is organized by an opposition between spaces of confinement and spaces of liberation, with Isma's narration moving Hajila from the house to the streets, from the shelter/prison of the veil into the sunlight, and from a "maternal cocoon" (152) to the wide world, "[her] body . . . radiating solar light as [she] traverses the spaces of the town" (62; translation modified). As was the case in *Fantasia*, the narrator's discourse provides the instrument of liberation, at one moment metaphorized as a key that Isma literally hands Hajila so that she may escape her domestic prison.

Of course, Djebar is careful to show that her narrator, too, is unfree in numerous ways, and that her discourse is not meant to speak for Hajila. If Isma "weaves a story to free the concubine" (139), she also says, "I neither invent you nor pursue you. I can scarcely even testify; I simply stand here in your presence" (157). Moreover, the inequality between Isma and Hajila in the frame narrative is offset by the reciprocity of the relations in the secondary narrative between the characters of Sheherazade and her sister/servant, who love and give pleasure to each other as well as offering mutual protection from mortal danger. Indeed, even in the Isma-Hajila narrative, mutuality is unexpectedly ensured by the man who has been husband to them both. Although he forms an "ambiguous border" (160) between them, he is nonetheless designated a "common wall" (91) linking inside and outside, protection and vulnerability, imprisonment and freedom. Djebar's text transforms the co-wife—in Arabic the *Derra*, she who hurts—into a sister and friend, and makes of the silent, passive Hajila a woman who "tells herself she too has a history" (41). For Hajila as for Sheherazade, the "bed of love and death" becomes a "storyteller's throne" (143).

It is interesting to note that Hajila's transformation takes place in the ambiguous space of the Turkish bath. A "liquid prison," the bath at night becomes space in which hierarchies between men and women, and between urban and rural populations, are unsettled: the bath presents itself as "a harem in reverse" where transient peasant men seek shelter (148). For the women inside who communicate as Isma does with Hajila, it becomes a "place of nocturnal rebirth . . . [and] secret collusion" (148), and not surprisingly, it is here that Isma hands Hajila the key that will open her domestic prison onto the outside world. From the ambiguous space of the bath, the reader is transported to an uncertain "shore" where the "sandal of liberty leaves its dancing footprints," a border between land and sea, a "threshold" between inside and outside (159), where it seems possible that those who, like Hajila and Isma, "were mutilated in their adolescence, their happiness excised," may retrieve the "exuberant disorder" of their childhood (160; translation modified). Yet the text ends on a somber note, as the narrator of the last sequence voices her fear that women's self-affirmation will be crushed. Echoing the narrator of *Fantasia*, who fears that a countryman's horse will trample "every woman who dares to stand freely, all life that comes out into the sunlight to dance" (227), she says:

> O ma soeur, j'ai peur. . . . J'ai peur que . . . nous nous
> retrouvions entravées là, dans "cet occident de l'Orient", ce lieu
> de la terre où si lentement l'aurore a brillé pour nous que déjà, de
> toutes parts, le crépuscule vient nous cerner. (171-72)

> Oh my sister . . . I'm afraid for all women. . . . I fear lest we all
> find ourselves in chains again, in "this West in the Orient," this
> corner of the earth where day dawned so slowly for us that
> twilight is already closing in around us everywhere. (160)

Clearly, in light of religious conservatives' recent victories in Algeria, the fears expressed in Djebar's texts are well founded. And yet precisely because the situation is so difficult and the stakes are so high, it is especially important today to continue to affirm Algerian women as subjects in their own right, as Rabia Abdelkrim-Chikh does when she points to the resistance of believers who reject "Islamism" and of Muslim Sisters who refuse to let their Muslim Brothers censor their activities.[48] Needless to say, this effort has nothing to do—pace Julia Kristeva—with "making feminism a new religion, an enterprise, or a sect,"[49] but rather involves the construction of international networks in which feminism's relation to other progressive struggles can be defined within specific historical, geopolitical, and cultural contexts, and in which languages of revolt can challenge hegemonic discourses, including those of first-world feminism.

Chapter 3

Exile

Ni un état ni un fait ni une morale ni
une condition être immigré
c'est être
histoire & Et vous en savez quelque chose

[Neither a state nor a fact nor a moral nor
a condition to be an immigrant
is to be
history & And you know something about that]
—Nabile Farès, *Discours pratique de l'immigré*

Expatriates, Immigrants, and Other "Nomads"

In French studies, the term *exile*, like its companion *nomadism*, refers to an array of political and cultural concerns whose interconnections need to be rethought in relation to the tensions that have developed, particularly in the last decade, within an ethnically diverse French nation. The conflicts within and between racial, ethnic, and national groups in France call for a critical reexamination of the uses to which tropes of exile and nomadism have been put in poststructuralist theories, and suggest ways to revise the reading of texts by and about France's cultural others.

It is instructive in this regard to consider the recent work of critics who, in addressing the postcolonial situation in Britain and its former colonies, have underscored the need to differentiate various groups of cultural others living in exile. At the most basic level, this means distinguishing expatriate intellectuals, writers, and artists from what Edward Said calls "the uncountable masses for whom UN agencies have been created, or refugees without urbanity, with only ration cards and agency numbers."[1] In the French context, as in the British one, it also means distinguishing expatriates from immigrants, for while members of both groups may undergo forced emigration and engage in struggles for social equality and cultural integration in the metropolitan country, the economic and cultural marginality of immigrants makes the stakes of their struggles quite different.

Along these same lines, it is essential to draw distinctions within and between groups of expatriate intellectuals who have come to France at different times and in various circumstances: those from other Western European countries, or from the United States and Canada, who have come mainly for reasons of intellectual or cultural affinity (such as Nancy Huston), and those for whom oppression in their native land is a central factor (as for James Baldwin); those who have come from Eastern European countries as political and intellectual dissidents (Julia Kristeva, Tzvetan Todorov), and those who have come from third-world countries, particularly former colonies (Abdelkebir Khatibi, Nabile Farès), to take up residence in France permanently or intermittently for political, cultural, or intellectual reasons. Exile means something different in each case, and figures in the work of these individuals and groups in very different ways.

Where the related question of nomadism is concerned, the French context requires that we distinguish its significance in the lives of literal nomads, such as migrant workers, from its meanings in the life and work of expatriate writers on the one hand, and in the work of French theorists on the other. In their nomadic texts, Tahar Ben Jelloun and Leïla Sebbar, for example, directly address problems of cultural hybridity and the processes by which they are negotiated in various postcolonial situations both in France and in the Maghreb. In the case of Ben Jelloun and other Maghrebian writers such as Khatibi and Rachid Boudjedra, textual nomadism stands in relation to real changes in the writers' geographical location—their movement between France and the Maghreb. For theorists like Gilles Deleuze and Michel Foucault on the other hand, nomadism is a trope for nondialectical modes of thought and "wild" modes of social affiliation that do not necessarily have anything to do with minority groups' experiences of cultural hybridity and exploitation, even though they stem in part from Algeria's successful challenge to French political, intellectual, and cultural hegemony in colonial regimes as well as from the Gulag, from Auschwitz, and from Hiroshima—events that unsettled the first world's pretension to epitomize cultural achievement and enlightened thought. What I propose to do, then, before examining Leïla Sebbar's treatment of exile in its various guises, is to consider some of the ways real and symbolic exile and nomadism have figured in poststructuralist theories in order to show what relation this bears to issues of cultural hybridity confronting Maghrebian expatriates and immigrants in France.

In the early 1980s, Julia Kristeva begins to pose avant-garde textuality as an exemplary form of political dissidence—in Paul Smith's words,

> the only kind of linguistic and thence political dissidence possible in relation to the symbolic. This happens as Kristeva turns her attention away from the mutually constraining dialectic between the semiotic and the symbolic, and toward a revindication of a putative priority and primacy of the semiotic. . . . This move is designed to foreground the resistant quality of the semiotic, but at the same time it "individualizes" that force, makes it transhistorical and largely removes it from the closely worked historical and material dialectic of the earlier work.[2]

Pointing out that "Kristeva's political path seems to have led her most recently to the United States," Smith cites the following remark as evidence of the shift in her political allegiances:

> Now that the Latin American and Arab Marxist revolutions groan at the gates of the United States, I feel myself closer to truth and liberty when I am working in the space of this embattled giant which is perhaps on the point of becoming a David confronted with the growing Goliath of the third world. I dreamt that, to the camp of this David, even with all his faults and difficulties, our children will go.[3]

Kristeva's remark suggests that fear of the third-world Goliath has undermined the critique of imperialism that condemns, among other things, the destruction of Palestinian villages by Israeli tanks. It suggests, further, that despite increasing ethnic and racial tension in France in the eighties, the question of exile is to be posed in terms of a newly individualized notion of political dissidence rather than in terms of the collective plight of immigrants. Although Maghrebian writers in France such as Tahar Ben Jelloun have for some years been drawing attention to the importance and interrelatedness of first-and third-world postcolonial struggles, these questions have aroused only marginal interest until recently. The social desert that Paris constitutes for Maghrebian factory workers, the "modernization" of the Sahara by the oil cartels, the distribution of residence cards to Palestinians by the forces occupying their land, "the metallic hand [of the Israeli tanks] erasing the writings on our bodies"—these matters, which Ben Jelloun brings together in his poetry, are obscured rather than illuminated by the notion of dissidence in Kristeva's work.[4]

When Kristeva turns her attention to the problem of foreigners and foreignness some five years later in *Strangers to Ourselves*, she does so by attending, in particular, to the transformation of subjectivity that she posits as the indispensable underpinning to a progressive national and international politics. "As a still and perhaps ever utopic matter, the question is again before us today as we confront an economic and political integration on the scale of the planet: shall we be, intimately and subjectively, able to live with others, to live *as others*, without ostracism but also without leveling?"[5] Particularly in the parts of the book dealing with modern France, Kristeva analyzes relations with foreigners in terms of the foreignness within, that is, in terms of Freud's notion of the uncanny—*das Unheimliche* or *l'inquiétante étrangeté*. She notes that in the essay on the uncanny Freud focuses on "death, the female sex, and the 'baleful' unbridled drive" (191), never mentioning foreigners in connection with the feelings of unease and fascination associated with the uncanny. Freud's "distraction" or "discretion" in this regard embodies an ideal advanced throughout Kristeva's study, that is, a world in which there would be no reificaton of foreigners, no fixation of our own subjectivity, no impulse to reject disturbing feelings arising from within, no need to project our own alterity onto others (192).

The problem is that Kristeva's own distraction or discretion with respect to foreigners has the effect of leveling differences between foreigners and other groups, as well as effacing inequalities within and between groups of foreigners on the one hand, and between foreigners and French people on the other. To cite two of the more startling examples: "Whether a Maghrebian street sweeper riveted to his broom or an Asiatic princess writing her memoirs in a borrowed tongue, as soon as foreigners have an action or a passion, they take root" (9). And regarding Camus's stranger, Meursault, as he is shooting the Arab, she writes: "Meursault is just as, if not more, distant from his conationals as he is from the Arabs. At whom does he shoot during the imporous hallucination that overcomes him? At shadows, whether French or Maghrebian, it matters little—they displace a condensed and mute anguish in front of him, and it grips him inside" (26). By virtue of focusing on the foreignness within and systematically dissociating it from social inequalities, Kristeva ends by ignoring the foreigners whose foreignness, unlike her own, sparks hostility and violence in France.

In Kristeva's study, the rationale for canceling out social differences in analyzing the foreignness within is that the recent preoccupation with the sociological analysis of relations to foreigners has prevented the public from giving due attention to the universal psychic dynamics and the universalizing ethical thought that shape those relations in fundamental and potentially liberating ways. Writing of certain Renaissance men, Kristeva protests, for example, that "the brutality of colonizers has been emphasized to such an extent that one should point out . . . this other design of universalist explorers who, on the contrary, balanced their own culture with the thought of a 'concord of the terrestrial globe'— such a person was Guillaume Postel (1510-1581), the 'cosmopolitan Gaul,' as he liked to call himself" (124). However, even if one accepts the dubious view that colonizers' brutality has been given undue emphasis by postwar critics, and that universalizing European ethical thought has had too little influence in recent years, it seems counterproductive to promote the acceptance of difference by refusing to distinguish between differences that should be respected and protected, such as those of ethnicity, gender, and sexuality, and differences that mark continuing economic and social injustice, such as those of class and status, which are inevitably bound up with sexuality, gender, and ethnicity. The need to distinguish these two types of differences is obvious, given the context that motivated Kristeva's study in the first place, that is, violent ethnic and racial conflict fueled by economic recession in France. Despite her desire to avoid ostracism and leveling in her treatment of foreigners, Kristeva unfortunately relies on both to plead the worthy cause of learning to live alterity differently. Perhaps because her book privileges the foreigner within over the foreigners without, it loses sight of the fact that the stakes of defining and coming to terms with difference vary, depending whether one is a Maghrebian streetsweeper, an Asian princess, or a European intellectual.

The inappropriateness of downplaying differences of sex, class, ethnicity, and nationality becomes especially apparent in light of recent events in Eastern Europe. For as the glow faded after the fall of communism, it became increasingly clear that anti-Semitism, as well as virulent revindications of ethnic and national identity, would result in violent conflicts with potentially global repercussions. Moreover, within Germany and, more generally, within the wider European community, economic divisions between East and West became more obvious and more offensive as the old political barriers crumbled. Following Kristeva's logic, one could say that Eastern Europe now constitutes a Goliath whose groans have drowned out the victory cries of the West.

It was the combination of ethnic conflict and economic difficulties in France, on the one hand, and the resurgence of European nationalisms, on the other, that prompted Kristeva's February 1990 "Open Letter to Harlem Désir," the leader of the liberal antiracist group SOS Racisme.[6] Here, as in *Strangers to Ourselves*, she argues in favor of attending to psychic dynamics of identity and alterity in order to forestall further violent conflict. In the "Letter," however, she makes concrete proposals for changes at the symbolic level—in education, politics, and the media—that could foster the subjective transformations she is calling for. The French, she claims, must undergo treatment for their national "depression" (21), a condition resulting from the economic and political humiliations they have suffered in the twentieth century: the Nazi occupation and the loss of Empire, followed by large-scale immigration and imminent incorporation into a European community. The French must have their "good narcissistic image" restored in order to be capable of embracing Montesquieu's notion of a "general spirit" as the guiding principle of national unity. Following Montesquieu, Kristeva proposes, first, that the national unity be conceived as an identity that changes historically; accordingly, the teaching of French history should be revised in such as way as to take account critically of its relation to the histories of all the groups that now constitute France's population. Second, the national unity is to be understood as an amalgam of concrete and heterogeneous particularities whose singularity is to be respected. Third, the national unity implies a possibility of moving beyond the nation state by forming larger entities, such as the European Community, based on a spirit of cooperation and economic development (24-25). There is no mention of the relation between the economic development of the European Community and the development of other, especially poorer, parts of the world.

Not surprisingly, there is no suggestion in Kristeva's text that a French person should lose citizenship rights for failing to be cured of the "national depression," or for espousing the overtly racist and nationalistic ideologies that transform defeatism into aggression. Immigrants, on the other hand, should be denied citizenship rights under certain conditions, in her view. While it is true that exclusion is not explicitly recommended for those who fail to be cured of the humiliation of colonialism and the economic dependence imposed by transnational capitalism, this is so because these ills are not taken into account at all; although they are mentioned, no treatment is prescribed for them because, for Kristeva (now a French citizen herself), they are not France's problem. She wants immigrants—and her readers—to regard France as a "host" whose hospitality immigrants must acknowledge (31). Chiding the French left for the misguided third worldism that leads it to dismiss proposals that immigrants be held accountable for their choice of host country, Kristeva advances the idea that in order to enjoy citizenship, immigrants must explain how they can enrich the French general spirit and how they see it responding to their concrete needs. In other words, as a condition of citizenship, immigrants must accept as an established fact the very general spirit that, just a moment before, was said to have been long forgotten or devalued by the French, and that needed to be restored to the national memory and "revalorized" by means of massive campaigns in politics, education, and the media (29). Immigrants, in short, are to be required to enrich a national unity that is pregiven only for them; they are to play no role in reconfiguring that unity.

Kristeva's intellectual and political trajectory is indicative, in a limited but telling way, of the drift in French poststructuralism away from the collective political struggles in which its various strands were initially embedded. Generally speaking, this shift manifests itself—with varying implications—in the recasting of debates about representation and its political effects. Kristeva's elaboration and subsequent restructuring of the semiotic/symbolic relation is one version of the change that takes place in the critique of representation. As Paul Smith shows, in prioritizing the semiotic, especially in her work on the abject, Kristeva

> clings to a version of the "subject in process," but it is now imbued with a kind of pessimism and deprived of its theoretical connection to real political struggle. This change in Kristeva's theory has been accompanied by her disillusionment with various kinds of political discourses, and also by an increased emphasis on the value of individuality and its inappropriateness to concerted political effort.[7]

It has been accompanied, too, as we saw above, by an affirmation of the "truth and liberty" supposedly safeguarded by Western societies, especially the United States, where Kristeva, a Bulgarian exile living in France, frequently lectures.

In contrast to Kristeva's drift away from political struggle in her critique of representation is Jean Baudrillard's dizzying leap from a semiotically informed post-Marxist cultural politics (for example, in *The Mirror of Production* and *Pour une critique de l'économie politique du signe*) to the triumphant declaration of the end of both representation *and* politics, based in no small part on his interpretation of developments in the United States (read: Disneyland), where all systems of representation have supposedly collapsed. Indeed for Baudrillard, social relations themselves have vanished, due to the "retotalization in a homogeneous space-time of all the dispersed functions of the body and social life (work, leisure, the media, culture), the retranscription of all contradictory flows in terms of integrated circuits."[8] Oppositional relations between rulers and ruled, representatives and represented, are said to have dissolved in the "circular Moebian compulsion" of today's world where "all referentials mix their discourses."[9] In formulations such as these, Baudrillard is caricaturing Derrida and the later Barthes in using the materiality of language to dematerialize its referent and abolish the distinction between the two; his giddy proclamations of the end of politics are but a burlesque articulation of the break, in certain versions of semiotics and deconstruction, between the critique of representation and real political struggle.[10]

It is no accident, of course, that Baudrillard's pronouncements are haunted by specters of sexual, racial, and ethnic differences,

differences whose politicization he attempts to dismiss as "naive" (in the case of feminists against pornography), "folkloric," or even "autistic" (as regards ethnic identity). In the order of the simulation, where there is ostensibly no stage, no scene, but only the obscene, even racial differences can be dismissed as a mere instance of "promiscuity."[11] For what collapses along with the representation/reality opposition, according to Baudrillard, is the concept and experience of alienation and the struggles they fueled. Whereas Kristeva poses the internal differentiation of subjects as the only remaining site of effective political (that is, semiotic and psychoanalytic) intervention, Baudrillard dismisses the critical force of even this division, claiming that subjects are internally differentiated only insofar as they are hooked up to their bodies through their Walkmans and connected to their brains by their word processors; in his account, they are capable of producing no interference either inside themselves or among themselves. Since all subjects now remain enclosed in their sterile bubbles, they can neither organize oppositional activity nor experience any form of collectivity except when driving on freeways, where they find "something of the freedom of movement in the deserts"; they are nomads in the desert of contemporary sociality.[12]

However, far from attesting to the end of representation, politics, and even history (by collapsing the distinctions between "primitive" and modern societies), the tropes of the desert and the "nomadic" in Baudrillard's work signal the failure of his attempt to purge his own culture of the differences that are presently dividing it in violent but also, in some cases, productive ways. Not surprisingly, Baudrillard tries to banish racial difference from France and deport it to Los Angeles or to New York City where, as we have seen, it becomes a mere instance of "promiscuity." But in the figure of the nomad—albeit a nomad roaming the California freeways—France's Arab population along with the peoples of its former colonies return to haunt Baudrillard's discourse. Baudrillard's rather desperate assertions that political movements have been replaced by "panic" or "chain reactions" are merely his own reaction to the successes of women and minority groups in widening and deepening democratic struggles in the seventies and eighties.[13] In their articulations of collective demands and desires, these groups have marginalized intellectuals *like him*—that is, intellectuals who, in spite of everything, are nostalgic for the days when it seemed necessary and possible to speak for the masses. This is why Baudrillard now enjoins them to "forget Foucault" and his notion of genealogy, "the union of erudite knowledge and local memories which allows us to establish a historical knowledge of struggles and to make use of this knowledge tactically today."[14] The gist of Baudrillard's recent writing is: If I can't speak for the masses, no one can speak for them; in fact, no one can speak effectively—whether globally or locally—under any circumstances whatsoever.

In Britain and the United States, Baudrillard's exhortation to forget Foucault has been ignored by Marxist scholars intent on remembering him and using his concept of genealogy to criticize his position on representation—for Foucault, too, affirms, with Gilles Deleuze in their famous conversation on intellectuals and power, that "representation no longer exists."[15] For Foucault and Deleuze, the end of representation is clearly tied to the events of May '68 when the masses showed they were perfectly capable of articulating and acting on their demands and desires spontaneously without the intervention of theorists, who could only distort what the masses were saying and doing and usurp their power. After the concentration camps and the Gulag, after Algeria's successful challenge to French intellectual, cultural, and political hegemony, the role of the intellectual can no longer be to articulate the will of the collectivity (as it was for Gramsci), but rather, as Rhada Rhadakrishnan puts it, "to struggle against the forms of power that transform him into its object and instrument in the sphere of 'knowledge,' 'truth,' 'consciousness,' and 'discourse,' " by means of a micropolitics attentive to specificity and contingency.[16] While acknowledging the importance of Deleuze's notion of micropolitics and Foucault's analysis of the power/knowledge nexus in demonstrating the futility (and the danger) of trying to account for social conflicts within the frame of a single narrative, scholars such as Edward Said, Gayatri Chakravorty Spivak, and Rhada Rhadakrishnan challenge their claims about the end of representation. Said shows, for example, how the claim that "the great narratives of emancipation are over," however valid at a certain level of abstraction, works to discourage any possible response from subordinate groups whose collective, emancipatory discourses can, from this point of view, only play into the hands of power.[17]

Spivak makes a related point when she argues in "Can the Subaltern Speak?" that the prioritization of concrete experience by Foucault and Deleuze forecloses

> the necessity of the difficult task of counterhegemonic ideological production. . . . It has helped positivist empiricism—the justifying foundation of advanced capitalist neocolonialism—to define its own arena as "concrete experience," "what actually happens." Indeed, the concrete experience that is the guarantor of the political appeal of prisoners, soldiers, and schoolchildren is disclosed through the concrete experience of the intellectual, the one who diagnoses the episteme.[18]

Drawing on Spivak's claim (275) that Foucault and Deleuze run together two senses of representation—"representation as 'speaking for,' as in politics, and representation as 're-presentation,' as in art or philosophy," Rhadakrishnan shows that Foucault's

> universal and unsituated delegitimation of "representation" does away with distinctions between "who" is saying and "what" is being said, and also between forms of representation that are organic and coercive. . . . Since "representation as such" is a "speaking for," and since "speaking for" is an act of violence, all representations are inauthentic and/or culpable. At a rarefied structural level, a feminist speaking on behalf of women, the African National Congress representing black South Africans, and Foucault speaking on behalf of the masses are all one and the same. (75)

The alternative to the violence of representation proposed by Foucault is the "freeing of difference [which] requires thought without contradiction, without dialectics, without negation; thought that accepts divergence; affirmative thought whose instrument is disjunction; thought of the multiple—of the nomadic and dispersed multiplicity that is not limited or confined by constraints of similarity."[19] Rhadakrishnan takes issue with this notion, pointing out that the dismantling of representation, like "the quarrel with the individual and the unified self, eventuates not in a more complex understanding of the dialectically mediated relationship between individuality and collectivity but rather in the apotheosis of multiplicities or 'groupuscules' that are *intraindividual*. . . . It is still a world where 'liberation' is a banner that the 'individual as multiple' waves against society" (76-77).

The stance presented in the Foucault-Deleuze conversation on intellectuals and power manifests a departure, then, from Foucault's earlier claims about the stakes of genealogical research in relation to political struggles. It marks something of a departure, too, from Deleuze's work, with Félix Guattari, in *Kafka: Pour une littérature mineure*, where, despite insistence on the necessarily oppressive effects of "extensive or representative" uses of language (in which language "ceases to be a sense organ, and becomes an instrument of Sense"); despite a corresponding affirmation of Kafka's "intensive, a-signifying use of language" (in which "there is no longer a subject of the utterance, nor a subject of the statement . . . but rather a circuit of states that forms a mutual becoming"), questions of subjective deterritorialization in and through language are connected to the production of an oppositional "national consciousness" and a "collective utterance":[20]

> A minor literature is not that of a minor language, but rather a literature that a minority produces in a major language. But the first characteristic is, in any case, that the language is affected by a strong coefficient of deterritorialization. . . . The impossibility of not writing is due to the fact that an uncertain or oppressed national consciousness necessarily passes through literature. . . . The impossibility of writing in a language other than German is for the Jews of Prague the impression of an irreducible distance from primal Czech territoriality. And the impossibility of writing in German is the deterritorialization of the German population itself; an oppressive minority that speaks a language cut off from the masses' collective or national consciousness is [in Kafka's words] "often inactive in outer life and always in the process of disintegrating." It is literature that finds itself positively charged with this role and this function of collective and even revolutionary utterance; it is literature that produces an active solidarity, in spite of skepticism. (30-31)

Although Deleuze and Guattari point out that "the German of Prague is a deterritorialized language, susceptible to strange minor usages," the issue of deterritorializing French is scrupulously avoided except in connection with Godard's avant-garde cinema and the regionalist movements of French people (43-45). As we saw in the case of Kristeva, the problem of language in its relation to political dissidence is situated principally in foreign territories and worked out in analyses of writings by European men, presumably because of what they see as the "sparsity of talent" in the context of minor literature. And while the authors mention that Kafka's use of German is comparable, in today's context, to "what Blacks can do with American English" (30), racial difference as a deterritorializing force is reassuringly deported to a distant continent as it was in Baudrillard's *Amérique*.

If we make France the target of deterritorializing strategies, however, the notion of minor literature—and with it, the tropes of exile and nomadism—implies investigating the relation between the nomadic quality of poststructuralist and avant-garde practices of writing and the hybrid, unstable identity not only of writers and intellectuals, but also of immigrants who continually negotiate between conflicting traditions—linguistic, social, ideological—in order to make a life for themselves in the metropolitan country. Where immigrants in the modern French nation are concerned, it is necessary, no doubt, to employ deconstructive strategies to dismantle fixed identities (whether of oppressor or oppressed) that work to ensure their subordination. But at the same time, while attending to intraindividual differences, as well as to the scattering of peoples and languages across times and spaces in an effort to open restrictive national and narrative frontiers, it is essential to affirm the liberatory aspects of the *gatherings* of dispersed identities, peoples, and histories, rather than immediately dismissing them as "extensive and representative"—and therefore oppressive—formations.

As Homi Bhabha has suggested, liberatory formations may include

> gatherings of exiles and emigrés and refugees, gathering on the edge of "foreign" cultures; gathering at the frontiers; gatherings in the ghettos or cafés of city centres; gathering in the half-life, half-light of foreign tongues, or in the uncanny fluency of another's language; gathering the signs of approval and acceptance, degrees, discourses, disciplines; gathering the memories of underdevelopment, or other worlds lived retroactively; gathering the past in a ritual of revival; gathering the present. Also the gathering of the people in the diaspora: indentured, migrant, interned; the gathering of incriminatory statistics, educational performance, legal statutes, immigration status.[21]

To attend to these gatherings is to question more effectively the metropolitan identity that certain poststructuralist theories have paradoxically worked to consolidate. To do so is also to affirm the symbolic status of immigrants—and, for that matter, of expatriates—as *effective speakers and actors on a particular social scene*—which is quite different, I think, from speaking for them.

Of course, as Alain Boureau reminds us, it is important for critics of Maghrebian literature and cultural politics to avoid essentializing the literary object on the one hand, and the identity of the Maghreb on the other; we must beware of both "the mythic halo of 'writing' and the transcendence of the 'Maghrebian soul.' "[22] For Boureau, the best strategy is to give full play to the tension in Maghrebian texts between French and Maghrebian culture, exile and national belonging, literary and political concerns. I want to argue that it is necessary, at the same time, to relate that literature's nomadic staging of these tensions to a context that is distinctly post*colonial* (and not the other way around) in order to keep in view France's present relation to its former colonies as well as the ways in which both expatriates *and* immigrants are challenging France's constructions of its own identity. In this connection, it is instructive to consider an observation made in 1983 by Michel de Certeau, speaking at a colloquium on cultural diversity:

> The reality of sociocultural mixing and ethnic difference in France is still largely occulted. . . . [The presence of immigrants] is the indicator and the strategic site of all problems concerning social communication, so much so that in a general report on communication, we have been led to consider the immigrant as its central figure. To express this in the form of a program, one would have to adopt the slogan "we are all immigrants," that is, sociocultural voyagers caught in situations of transit in which real immigrants are the first victims, the most lucid witnesses, the experimenters and inventors of solutions. From this point of view, immigrants are the pioneers of a civilization founded on the mixing of cultures.[23]

Here, de Certeau points to the exemplary status of the immigrant as the "central figure" of a modernity that deprives everyone of familiar landmarks, forces everyone to adapt to new codes. I want to insist that in interpreting de Certeau's somewhat ambiguous formulation of the problem, it is essential to underline what is specific to the situation of "real immigrants," "the first victims, the most lucid witnesses" of sweeping historical and cultural change. In this way, the slogan "we are all immigrants" can bring together real and figurative immigrants *without collapsing the differences between them*, and can thus figure an effective collectivity rather than a monolithic subject of history. While the subjects in this "immigrant" collectivity are divided internally and differentiated from each other, they nonetheless enjoy agency as "inventors of solutions." The solutions are found by means of "systems of translation" (between languages, between cultural practices) that enable people living in exile both to adapt to their surroundings and to reshape the environment for their own purposes.[24]

Insofar as they connect work on language and high culture to popular culture and everyday routines, de Certeau's "systems of translation" make it possible to forge links between the immigrants, expatriate writers, and other postcolonial subjects; the nomads of modernity share not just the shifting sands of real or symbolic exile, but a set of practices that mediate various levels of social experience. If the writing of Maghrebians is considered in relation to the model of "plural culture" proposed by de Certeau, it can be read not just as the staging of one paradox after the next in the situation of postcolonial subjects, but as an articulation of the conflicts and means of negotiation within and between central and marginal racial, ethnic, and national groups. As de Certeau shows, analysis of the means of translation avoids enclosing exiled peoples in a static identity based on language, place of origin, belief systems, and the like. And equally important, by focusing on the processes by which immigrants continually invent their existence, this type of analysis works ideologically (albeit in a restricted sphere) to legitimate their status as subjects of their own history.

The Exile of Leïla Sebbar and the Migrant Territory of France

At first glance, one might wonder about the relevance of these concerns to a writer like Leïla Sebbar, at least in terms of her self-understanding. Born of a French mother and an Algerian father and raised in Algeria, Sebbar has resided in France for over twenty years. Although she writes about immigrants from Africa, Asia, and the Caribbean as well as Eastern and Southern Europe, she states emphatically in *Lettres Parisiennes: Autopsie de l'exil:*

Je ne suis pas immigrée, ni enfant de l'immigration. . . . Je ne suis
pas un écrivain maghrébin d'expression française. . . . Je ne suis
pas une Française de souche. Désormais je sais qu'il faut que je
puisse dire, déclarer, affirmer sans ambiguïté, sans culpabilité, en
me réservant le temps de développer les subtilités de cette
position particulière qui est la mienne: je suis Française.[25]

[I am not an immigrant, nor a child of immigration. . . . I am not
a Maghrebian writer of French expression. . . . I am not a native
Frenchwoman. From now on, I know I must be able to say,
declare, affirm without ambiguity, without guilt—while
simultaneously reserving time to develop the subtleties of the
particular position that is mine—I am French.]

Why does Sebbar want to identify herself as a French writer, despite her refusal to take a "neutral, universalizing" French pen
name (126)? Why does she insist on her Frenchness when much of
her readership regards her as Maghrebian? Is she simply disavowing the otherness assigned to her willy-nilly by French book reviewers who assume she is Maghrebian? No doubt there is an element of disavowal at work, not because Sebbar sees herself as
French, but because she appears to feel immune to racism despite
her keen awareness of increasing racial conflict in France. While
she observes with alarm that "the right and the far right are winning their fight against the immigrants; together, they are stronger
than the left with its good intentions and its ineffectual righteous-
ness" (59), she alludes only once to "xenophobia" (42) directed at
her, not in Paris but in a resort town in Corsica. Where her own life
is concerned, in other words, she relegates to the geographic and
cultural margins the racial tensions of the urban center, disavowing the fact that racism affects not just Maghrebian immigrant
workers but also people of her social class who, despite their mixed
origins and French ID cards, are regarded as unwelcome Arabs by
many sectors of the population.

Sebbar is clearly troubled by the difficulty, and the necessity, of
articulating her contradictory identity in the present situation. For
at the same time that many readers and reviewers identify her,
without qualification, as Maghrebian, certain Arab intellectuals (especially male intellectuals) denounce her for presuming to write
about Arab immigrants when she does not speak Arabic and is not
an immigrant. She writes:

> Si je parle d'exil, et c'est le seul lieu d'où je puisse dire les
> contradictions, la division . . . , c'est tellement complexe que je
> m'en veux chaque fois d'avoir simplifié. Si je parle d'exil, je parle
> aussi de croisements culturels; c'est à ces points de jonction et de
> disjonction où je suis que je vis, que j'écris, alors comment
> décliner une identité simple? (126)

> [If I speak of exile—and it is the only place from which I can
> speak of the contradictions, the division—it's so complex that,
> each time, I reproach myself for having simplified things. If I
> speak of exile, I speak also of cultural intersections; it is at the
> points of juncture and disjuncture where I am that I live and
> write, so how is it possible to decline a simple identity?]

Sebbar's formulation of this question, in which she implies the impossibility of *declining* a noncontradictory identity (as one *declines* a
noun), points to another, equally compelling, problem: How is it
possible to flatly refuse (*decline*) a simple identity in a culture in
which the desire for one is still authorized, and in which concrete
benefits accrue to those native French people who can plausibly lay
claim to one? Sebbar ends this letter saying that she is writing "in a
state of slight distress," which her correspondent Nancy Huston
understands as "despondency"—a state quite antithetical to Sebbar's amused detachment in the passages dealing with the "xenophobia" she encountered in Corsica and attributed to the Corsi-
cans' anxiety about lacking a single cultural or national identity.

In certain respects, Sebbar's claim that she is not a Maghrebian
writer is analogous to that of the French women writers interviewed by Alice Jardine and Anne Menke, writers who still maintain, as they have been doing for some fifteen years, that they are
not "women writers," or that they write as women but not as feminists.[26] The explanation is by now familiar, namely, the importance of poststructuralism's critique of identity, including sexual
identity, as a basic support of oppression, and its related critique of
ideology, including feminist ideology, as a totalizing fixation that is
politically regressive when it is not downright dangerous. In the
political climate of the seventies, especially, women's insistence on
being simply "writers" had the double advantage (although this
was rarely acknowledged) of resisting enclosure within a devalued, or even a revalued, gender identity *and* winning for women
the prestige and legitimacy of the *writer*, whether in its traditional,
sexually "unmarked"—that is, male—guise (Marguerite Yource-

nar) or its sexually ambiguous, disruptive, postmodern incarnation (Hélène Cixous). Sebbar's refusal to enclose herself within a "simple" and devalued cultural identity follows the same logic insofar as a French writer is considered either culturally "unmarked" or free to float between cultural identities, provided the textual strategies employed have purchase in French intellectual circles.

The writers' refusal of any fixed sexual or national identity stems in part from the conviction that the writing process gives us access to psychic, somatic, and social territories that are, almost by definition, excluded by academic literary criticism and other French cultural institutions. Writing is also considered an activity that safeguards social heterogeneity and a nuanced mode of thought in the face of increasing homogenization of all thought and experience by the mass media—as if the media's homogenizing effects were inherent in the technology and were uniformly negative, regardless of the social position of producers and consumers. In both cases, the writers assume that the writing process works against, if not outside of, repressive social institutions; they assume, wrongly, that this way of understanding writing has eluded institutionalization, and therefore has no harmful effects of its own; they ignore the political implications of dismissing as nostalgic, or condescendingly approving as humanistic but necessary, the gathering of identities by displaced and/or disempowered individuals and peoples.

Evident, too, in the refusal of sexual and national identities are vestiges of the conviction, prevalent in France in the seventies, that first-world writing is produced in societies basically committed to egalitarian principles, societies in which feminists, Marxists, opponents of racism, and other leftist activists are preserving and expanding the spheres in which equality is ensured, so that the question for writers and intellectuals becomes how to go "beyond" liberal and socialist humanism. At this juncture, however, it is unwise to assume that France is or is necessarily on its way to becoming an egalitarian nation. As François Furet points out: "Like other [countries], France has ended up taming the formidable power of the people's will in regularly elected institutions, making it compatible with a strong executive power. . . . Its citizens argue about the distribution of the nation's wealth, but no longer about the legacy of the nation's history. Along with its revolutionary stakes, French politics has lost its theatrical dimension."[27] A telling symptom of this development, according to Furet, is that in the place formerly occupied by a Marxist critique of the abstract and formal character of the rights of man is a discourse of human rights taken up with equal enthusiasm by liberal-left groups such as SOS Racisme and right-wing extremists of the National Front—a discourse firmly rooted in liberal individualism and almost completely divorced from political action.[28] Furet argues persuasively that "the universality of rights brandished by good souls, generally in good neighborhoods, is of little help to the small businessman in a poor neighborhood who has been robbed three times in the past month. If one doesn't want him to find a ready-made scapegoat in the immigrant, a concrete politics of housing and urban planning is more effective than the reiteration of moral principles" (62).

In short, the political climate in France has changed significantly over the past two decades; the waning of Marxist contestation and political action—dubbed an "opening" by Giscard, a "consensus" by his socialist successors—has to be reckoned with. I would suggest that, given a context in which the so-called political consensus is shot through with racism and xenophobia, it is worth reconsidering Sebbar's claim to be French. Particularly in light of critiques of the "right to difference" that have emerged in recent years, this claim and others like it productively alter the terms of debates about Frenchness—what it is, whose voices and experience count in determining its contours, and the means by which it may be revised.

In a book addressing many of the same issues that concern Furet, Jacques Donzelot argues convincingly that since the mid-seventies a "discourse of change" has been working to mobilize racial, ethnic, sexual, regional, and class differences in support of the status quo by interweaving the languages of neoliberalism and socialism and eluding the goals of both:

> The demand for autonomy, affirmed against the effects of the social control produced by the state's strong-armed solicitude, finds itself coupled with the denunciation of the miscalculations engendered by the statutory form of social protection. The blossoming of the individual will come by way of his renunciation of the chilly withdrawal to secure positions to which he has become too accustomed. And likewise, the will to include him in economic dynamics will require that his demand for self-fulfillment be taken into account. The redeployment of differences

in society, against the homogenizing language of welfare-state policies, is connected in the same way to the critique of the tutelary conception of the state, and its propensity to fabricate a society of dependents.[29]

In response to this dynamic, Maghrebian critics engaged in antiracist struggles have begun to counter the rhetoric of difference with that of integration. As Tahar Ben Jelloun observes, the right to difference is now a "hollow and dangerous gimmick [which has been] prostituted and . . . appropriated by the opportunism of advertising to the point that it will have to be left to unimaginative politicians and the peddlers of cigarette lighters."[30] This is not to say, however, that Maghrebian intellectuals and activists agree to integrate themselves into a nation fashioned for them by others. Adil Jazouli has recently argued that although immigrant youths are "as well and as badly assimilated" to French society as French youths are, their mode of integration will necessarily differ radically from that of their French counterparts. The same is true of youths who have French citizenship but are nonetheless regarded as "foreigners," such as the Beurs or blacks from Martinique. For them, integration "becomes a collective stake and a stake of conflict through the marches they began to organize a few years ago [marches for equality and against racism]. It is a conflict imposed by racism, but also a conflict borne by them in the face of racism."[31]

The double articulation of young people's identity—for integration, but against an assimilation that would obliterate their difference—is evident not only in their marches against racism but in a range of activity including protests against unemployment (in the form of wildcat strikes, or student demonstrations against restricted access to the university on the one hand, and the uselessness of the diplomas obtained on the other), voter registration drives, tenants' strikes, the production of rock music by groups like Carte de Séjour who sing in Arabic and in French, and the publication of novels by young Beurs. All of this activity stems from and attempts to politicize the ambiguous position occupied by youths, especially Maghrebian youths, who have run up against the limits of their identity—Maghrebians who (to echo Ernesto Laclau and Chantal Mouffe) cannot *be* Maghrebians; it confronts and challenges the inadequacy of existing forms of political and cultural representation while keeping in view the ways institutions fix the identity of immigrants and others who are considered foreigners regardless of the national ID card they carry.

The conflictual process by which immigrant youths such as the Beurs are integrating themselves into French society and at the same time transforming that society is analogous to Sebbar's contradictory move to claim French identity while simultaneously retaining her father's Arab name and identifying herself in certain situations as a "Maghrebian intellectual"—for instance, in signing a collective letter to a liberal-left magazine denouncing the Algerian government's complicity with fundamentalists and its repressive measures against women, the poor, and others who oppose its policies.[32] It is this "system of translation" that links her activity as a writer to that of the people she writes about.

If in her *Autopsie de l'exil* Sebbar's concerns are often writerly, there are no grounds for reading exile merely as the enabling condition of the writing itself; even in these *Lettres parisiennes*, exile retains its link to social movements as well as to a social void of which Sebbar is often painfully aware. Each moment of writing, each social terrain is divided, contested, *and* purposefully reconstituted in the movement of Sebbar's text. Granted, in the first letters, exile is principally embodied in the paper and pen with which she writes (she is too "underdeveloped" to write at the typewriter) and works to motivate lyrical meditations on "the necessary, vital division" it imposes, "an imbalance that, today, after changes, political and amorous initiations, makes me live, makes me write" (30). And indeed, once exile has fulfilled its function as pre-text for Sebbar's correspondence with Huston, it becomes in some sense a dead letter: the published book presents itself as an "autopsy."

Later, though, the "imbalance" of which Sebbar has written so gaily in the first letters returns as a source of "distress" expressed in the urgent question, "Who are my peers?" (124). The absence of peers, of fellow travelers, has become a personal—and also a political—problem:

> Je me sens privée de la complicité, de la solidarité, de toute la force qui se transmet dans l'appartenance à un groupe, à un réseau, à un courant (je ne parle pas de parti politique). . . . Nos intransigeances, notre horreur des tuteurs . . . ces attitudes de rigueur nous renvoient non pas à la marge mais à la solitude. (122)

[I feel deprived of the complicity, the solidarity, all the force that
is transmitted in belonging to a group, a network, a movement
(I'm not talking about a political party). . . . Our intransigence,
our horror of tutors . . . these hard-line attitudes relegate us not
to the margin but to solitude.]

The defection of Sebbar and her friends from leftist and feminist
movements in defense of critical thought ("a return to the private,
against dogmatism" [122]) is negatively mirrored by the self-
interested defection of middle-class leftists from a movement that
linked them to poor people of color: "my former companions . . .
from '68 and afterward, who scatter in pursuit of the State's favors
and sell out the third-world people in their own country" (123).

If in the opening letters Sebbar enjoys her impersonal immer-
sion in the crowd at *La Coupole*, the upscale restaurant where she
writes to Huston, she later complains of her isolation. Although
she initially feels little more than nostalgia for spaces where
women might gather—a nostalgia tempered by her enthusiasm for
"anonymous places . . . where I can see and hear differences,
where I precisely don't meet the same [people]," Sebbar is subsequently overcome by a sense of loss that is explicitly tied to a well-
defined political territory on the one hand and to a weakening of
feminism's oppositional force on the other:

Terre symbolique des femmes en rupture, terre nourricière
d'élans, de désirs, de projets. . . . Mais il me semble que nous,
nous avons perdu notre terre et un peu de ces forces de
subversion qui nous faisaient bouger et qui ont à un moment
ébranlé le terrain social. (122)

[The symbolic land of women in revolt, land that nourishes
impulses, desires, projects. . . . It seems to me that we have lost
our land and some of the subversive force that both impelled us
to act and, at a certain moment, unsettled the social terrain.]

The swing from easy detachment to anguish is equally evident
in Sebbar's reflections on immigrants, whose exclusion from the
French mainstream is no longer offset, as it was in the opening
pages, by a form of community arising, among other things, from
confinement within certain Parisian neighborhoods—neighborhoods into which Sebbar can venture only as a "tourist." Here is
Sebbar's anguished figuration of immigrant groups:

Ne parlons pas des immigrés. . . . Ils ne forment pas une
communauté. Ils sont divisés, faibles dans l'incapacité de protéger
leurs propres enfants. Ils vivent en déportation analphabète. . . .
Auront-ils un jour les forces et les armes spécifiques qui ont
donné à la communauté juive de France sa puissance? (123)

[Let's not even talk about the immigrants. . . . They don't form a
community. They are divided and weak to the point of being
incapable of protecting their own children. They live in a state of
illiterate deportation. . . . Will they one day have the particular
strengths and weapons that have given the French Jewish
community its power?]

As these passages make clear, the trope of exile forges links between the unbounded, pleasantly anonymous scene of writing, the
lost "symbolic land" of feminist solidarity, the "social terrain" of
the French nation, and the "illiterate deportation" of immigrant
populations. Exile also works to relate these public scenes to the
domestic one where, for Sebbar, motherhood is at once a reassuring ground of existence and a constraint that often prevents her
from writing. "Without children," she writes, "I would have had
no ground. . . . I mean they have been necessary to me in order to
mark out a territory, even a hypothetical and mythic one" (135).
And yet her children also restrict her access to what she calls an
"autonomous zone in which one isn't exiled from oneself" (41). In
her *Lettres Parisiennes* Sebbar maintains the tension between several
conflicting figures of exile: between the open and anonymous subjective and social space of the cafés and the autonomous zone she
marks off for a less ambiguous self; between feminism's lost
ground and its imaginary recovery in her published correspondence with Huston; between the terrain of political struggle in
France and the political "void" with which she feels confronted;
and finally, between that void and the space of fiction where Sebbar protects herself from exile by engaging in a process of gathering reminiscent of the "gatherings" evoked by Bhabha: "To place
myself at the heart . . . of fiction writing is to place myself in a unitary place, to reassemble divisions, murderous schisms, explosions
of memory and of History, always with the temptation to flee, to
run away in solitary adventure" (138). In what follows, I hope to
show that this tension is maintained in Sebbar's fiction as well.

The Space of Fiction: Postcolonial Orientalism

In her fictional mapping of the postcolonial territory, Sebbar gives full play to the contradictions, continuities, and disjunctures that mark the history of colonialism for women of the Maghreb, for Maghrebian women who have emigrated to France, and for European women as well. An important feature of that history is the orientalist tradition that, however multiform and contradictory it may have been, worked both to prepare the symbolic ground for and to legitimate the military and administrative arms of colonialism.[33] The social function of that tradition in present-day France is a central concern in *Shérazade, brune, frisée, les yeux verts*, where an Algerian girl living in Paris becomes the object of fascination for a modern orientalist, Julien, because of her resemblance to the green-eyed woman in Delacroix's *Femmes d'Alger*.

Julien is the son of French *colons* who fought with, not against, the Algerians in their war of independence. An aesthete who devotes as much attention to Egyptian cinema and the music of Oum Kalthoum as to the French new wave and the operas of Verdi, he is well versed in many forms and periods of cultural production. An eager student of Arabic and Maghrebian history, he is committed not only to genealogical work on the past, but also to his friend Enrico's project of publishing and distributing contemporary Maghrebian writing. Julien is more forward-looking than nostalgic, more critical than he is complacent in his study of the Maghreb and France's imperialist ventures there. Yet his passion for Delacroix's *Femmes d'Alger* and other paintings of that genre, transferred to the seventeen-year-old runaway, is shown, at certain junctures, to converge with and fuel sexist and racist ideologies circulating in France in the 1980s.

Shérazade shows that Julien's obsession with figures of Algerian women stems from one of the colonialist fantasies enacted in paintings such as the *Femmes d'Alger*, which position the European spectator as the privileged observer of a forbidden scene, placing the harem entirely at his disposal. That Julien is taken with this fantasy of a woman—indeed, a group of women and, through them, an entire culture—being "taken" by surprise is abruptly disclosed in an exchange between Shérazade and the young Frenchman, who has just communicated his distress at being unable to procure a certain painting at the flea market:

> J'étais très malheureux et je me sentais prêt à acheter n'importe quoi, pourvu qu'il y ait une femme algérienne . . . Une femme arabe. — Mais qu'est-ce que tu as avec ces femmes-là? — Je les aime. — Tu les aimes en peinture? — Oui, c'est ca.[34]

> [I was very unhappy and was on the verge of buying just anything, provided it had an Algerian woman in it . . . an Arab woman. — What is this thing you've got about those women? — I like them. — You like them in paintings? — Yes, that's right.]

The fabric of Sebbar's text makes clear that, in France, Shérazade's identity and her relation to others — even the most "sympathetic" Frenchmen — is informed by the orientalist tradition and the history within which it is inscribed. Julien's obsession with Arab women in paintings is doubled by his preoccupation with images of the elusive Shérazade, photographic images that he himself produces (and endlessly reproduces), displaying them on the walls of his apartment. Just as she resists Julien's effort to assimilate her to the Delacroix figure by writing in lipstick on his mirror, "I am not an odalisque," Shérazade foils his attempt to capture her on film by tearing all the pictures off the walls:

> J'en ai marre de voir ma gueule partout, tu comprends . . . tu as pas besoin de moi vivante, finalement. (158)[35]

> [I'm sick of seeing my mug everywhere, do you understand? . . . You don't even need me alive.]

Julien's dream of possession, fueled by orientalism, is shown to be subject to sudden reversal, not just in his love relationship with Shérazade, who, he believes, has "conquered" him, but in his view of relations between his culture and hers. The metaphor of a specifically colonial conquest is extended across the map of France in a remark of Julien's: "I've heard, from certain Pieds-Noirs, that in a very short time France will be colonized by the Arabs of the Maghreb, the Mashreq, and the Gulf" (191). The Pieds-Noirs, however, are clearly invested in seeing the world upside down by virtue of their own history of conquest and *its* reversal. Their version of the story is inscribed in the history of orientalism and colonialism by means of its juxtaposition to an excerpt from Théophile Gautier's *Voyage pittoresque en Algérie* of 1843:

Nous croyons avoir conquis Alger, et c'est Alger qui nous a
conquis. Nos femmes portent déjà des écharpes tramées d'or,
bariolées de mille couleurs qui ont servi aux esclaves du harem.
(190-91)

[We think we have conquered Algiers, but it is Algiers that has
conquered us. Our women are already wearing gold-threaded
scarves of a thousand colors that were used by the slaves of the
harem.]

Gautier's technique of reversing the colonial relation of domination
and feminizing it (as fashion) is adopted by Julien in his effort to
persuade Shérazade to abandon her claim that "the Pieds-Noirs are
crazy"; he presents the supposed immigrant invasion—which now
includes Russians and Eastern and Southern Europeans along with
Arabs—as a population explosion effected by immigrant women:
"In a few decades, people of French stock will be the new minorities, . . . Julien said laughingly, and all because of girls like you"
(191).[36]

Against Julien's powerful and oppressive translations of colonialism, Sebbar mobilizes countertranslations that productively alter Shérazade's position in contemporary France. Through the motif of fashion, and specifically, the exotic scarf alluded to in
Gautier's *Voyage,* for example, Sebbar challenges Julien's xenopho-
bic and misogynistic reading of the relation between the French
and immigrant populations. Shérazade is wearing a version of the
exotic scarf when Julien (and the reader) first encounter her in a
fast-food restaurant:

Shérazade, dans ses mains en coquille saisit les écouteurs du
walkman . . . et les replaça exactement sur ses oreilles, après avoir
cassé le fil de rayonne rouge et jaune du foulard à franges
brillantes, comme les aiment les Arabes de Barbès et les femmes
du bled, lorsqu'elles n'ont pas encore été éblouies par les foulards
Monoprix qui imitent, dans la couleur fondue et le motif abstrait,
les foulards de marque. (8)

[With her cupped hands, Shérazade grasped the headphones of
her Walkman . . . and placed them carefully back on her ears,
after breaking the red and yellow rayon thread of the scarf,
brightly fringed the way the Arabs of Barbès and the village
women liked them, when they hadn't yet been dazzled by the
cheap Monoprix scarves whose soft colors and abstract designs
imitate brand-name scarves.]

In this passage, Shérazade's bright scarf links her to the Arab women Julien remembers from the Algerian village where he lived as the child of *colons*, and to the immigrant women whose tastes and sense of social location are transformed through their entry into French consumer culture. It also works to establish a contrast between hip teenagers who want to "seduce and spit on *Babylon—* the corrupting and moribund Occident of the whites" (119)—and the Arab women of their mothers' generation who admiringly imitate, but remain socially and economically subordinate to, the wealthy Parisian women who wear designer scarves.

Thus, insofar as the scarf motif reinscribes colonial occupation and the economic domination that follows Algerian independence, it counters Julien's (and Gautier's) observations regarding Algeria's "conquest" of France. In the same way, the textual thread tying Shérazade's scarf to the Palestinian keffia counters Julien's contention that France is being conquered by foreigners. As a mark of the girl's solidarity with an Arab nation presently subject to imperial violence, the *keffia* signals her status as an object, rather than an agent, of domination. Moreover, in the French context, the *keffia* is taken to be a sign of subversiveness in immigrant youths, who are routinely rounded up by the police; because of this, Shérazade has been forced to abandon her *keffia* in favor of a traditional scarf that connotes submissiveness. Within this metaphorical matrix, Shérazade's gesture of breaking the rayon thread of her scarf serves to discredit Julien's move to assign her a position of dominance in the cultural web he is weaving. The fact that Shérazade performs this gesture before tuning into contemporary France through her Walkman suggests that she is nonetheless integrating herself into French cultural networks, networks that are now inextricably bound up with both multinational corporations (Sony) and with the alternative media, such as Radio-Beurs, that interest the teenage girl.

It is worth noting that, in her treatment of the scarf motif, Sebbar contests the ideology that informs Julien's translations of colonialism, not at the level of individual or collective consciousness, but at the level of social practices where ideology is also at work— practices such as patterns of production and consumption, fashion, the policing of identity, and disguise. At other moments, however, Shérazade becomes a translator whose readings of cultural artifacts, especially orientalist paintings, deliberately and effectively challenge Julien's neocolonialism at the level of consciousness (both Shérazade's and ours) and transform our sense of the girl's identity. Like Julien, Shérazade is fascinated by the figure of the odalisque; however, rather than fixing her within an oppressive frame, the seductive power of the odalisque moves her to reinvent her ties to both Algeria and France. On the eve of the trip she has planned to take with her friend Pierrot, Shérazade spends the night in the museum at Beaubourg, viewing nineteenth- and twentieth-century odalisques and copying information from the accompanying plaques into her notebook. It is true that she is momentarily arrested by one figure in particular, Matisse's *Odalisque à la culotte rouge:* "She doesn't understand why it moves her. . . . Shérazade stares at her until noon." But then, a few lines later: "Her decision is made. Shérazade will go to Algeria" (245). She buys all the postcards picturing the odalisque and sends one to her friends Zouzou and France saying, "I'm leaving because of her" (252).

The painting that initially captivates Shérazade thus ends by moving her to explore Algeria. Since throughout the novel her relation to her native land is conspicuously mediated through memory, family relations, relics such as her brother's burnoose, and encounters with other Algerian immigrants in Paris, Shérazade's proposed voyage, which is never realized in the frame of the novel, must be seen not as a search for a bounded, "authentic" identity, but rather as a project to recover her past in order to reinscribe it in today's Paris, where Shérazade intends to resume her relationship with Julien. The nomadic quality of her existence is tied at every moment to the evasion of various forms of confinement evoked in and through the figure of the odalisque: the practices of veiling and seclusion in Algeria; Shérazade's father's attempt to translate those practices, in the Parisian context, by strictly (and violently) regulating her movement in public space; the collusion between her father and the French police who, despite their mutual mistrust, together devise a description of the runaway girl to be tracked down; and a modern orientalism that at once exoticizes the girl as an object of fascination and embodies in her the supposed conquest of France by foreign invaders.

Significantly, while acknowledging the disturbing and seductive power of the odalisque from Delacroix to Matisse, Sebbar's reinscription of this figure emphasizes the female spectator's active engagement with it as a means to effect change in her own life. Sebbar's way of connecting orientalist painting to a feminist project thus differs from Assia Djebar's, where, despite the political importance granted women's *speech* throughout Algerian history, the genius of the masters holds sway over women's *gaze* and directs their future efforts to free themselves. Djebar writes in her essay on the *Femmes d'Alger:* "The fragments of ancient murmurings are the only means I can see of restoring conversation, the very one that Delacroix froze in his painting. The door flung wide open to let in the sunlight, the one Picasso later imposed, is the only hope I see for a concrete liberation of women in everyday life."[37]

Like Djebar, Sebbar insistently ties her reflection on the high cultural orientalist tradition to the "concrete liberation of women in everyday life," whether by detailing the effects of one teenage girl's encounter with that tradition or by drawing our attention to the mass-cultural circuits into which the paintings of Delacroix and Matisse are now integrated. If cultural institutions such as the Beaubourg museum and postcard reproductions of the odalisque serve neocolonial interests, *Shérazade* shows that they are also capable of fueling anticolonial activity. More broadly, Sebbar's novel demonstrates the need to link reflection on orientalist art to an analysis of other cultural forms, such as fashion, film, and advertising—in short, "the representation business" (118), which plays a fundamental role in mediating relations between central and marginal populations in France.

The Representation Business and the Put-On

In negotiating their relation to the representation business, Shérazade and her two girlfriends, France (a mulatto from Martinique who is and is not from "France") and Zouzou (a Tunisian), assume an active, if often equivocal, stance. Salesclerks in the shops of the Forum des Halles, the girls and their male companions display an immigrant chic that occasionally wins them invitations to posh parties given by their bosses:

> Cette nouvelle bourgeoisie cultivée et esthète se laissait volontiers, pour un soir, maltraiter par ces jeunes excentriques, insolents et séducteurs, nés pour la plupart dans le béton des blocs de banlieue. (116)

[This new bourgeoisie, at once cultured and aesthetic, gladly
subjected itself, for an evening, to abuse by these young
eccentrics who were both insolent and seductive, born for the
most part in the concrete high-rises of the working-class suburbs.]

Middle-class opportunism furnishes another motive for cultural
mixing at parties, however, because designers and photographers
are eager to capitalize on the latest fashion trends developing
within minority youth culture. "The designers spotted them immediately at these parties, and the fashion photographers never
missed a chance to court them for photos that would generate a
line of ready-to-wear clothes that would sell well" (117).

Yet the young people are looking for opportunities, too:

Ils paradaient et frimaient pour rire, mais pas seulement. . . . [Ils]
souhaitaient provoquer au moins une fois une telle émotion,
qu'un cinéaste, un photographe, ou un publiciste leur proposerait
à titre d'essai un rôle, une série de photos de mode, une place de
mannequin. . . . C'était déjà arrivé. Pourquoi pas eux? (118)

[They paraded about and put on airs for a laugh, but not only for
that reason. [They] hoped to cause such a stir that, at least once, a
filmmaker, a photographer, or an advertiser might suggest they
try out for a role, a series of fashion photos, a modeling job; it
had happened before, so why not to them?]

And for them, the attraction of the private parties lies not just in
the chance to conquer "Babylon," but in the sumptuousness of the
surroundings, which "made them forget the hours of waiting in
line at the employment office, the hours standing up in the Forum
shops, the hours spent in the sickening odor of hot croissants and
little tarts sold hand over fist to the suburban commuters" (118).
Their self-presentation at parties, then, is at once a put-on and a
way of making satisfying, if fleeting, changes in their daily life.

Through the motif of the put-on, Sebbar's novel stages a series
of struggles over the means of representation in French culture, indicating how immigrant youths move to position themselves as
subjects, rather than objects, in the production and circulation of
images that shape their cultural identity. One move, which recurs
in various guises throughout the text, involves refusing the status
of "exotic" object assigned to them by the French, particularly the
media barons, even and especially in situations where the youths
have opted to make an exotic spectacle of themselves. This is the

case, for example, when Shérazade, France, and Zouzou indulge "their own narcissism" (122) by dancing before a crowd in a "Moorish" setting at the party I alluded to earlier. Infuriated by one onlooker's attempt to translate *her* self-display into the realization of *his* fantasy of finding "the daughter of the Grand Vizier under a palm tree" (124), Shérazade makes an abrupt exit from the scene. When the same onlooker tries to photograph her a moment later, she smashes his camera and becomes the object of verbal abuse that discloses the stakes of this struggle over the representation of immigrant girls. In and through image production, the photographer enacts his fantasy of *possessing* the daughter of the powerful vizier sexually, while *dispossessing* her as a maker of cultural meanings. The flip side of this fantasy is the violent impulse to expel Shérazade and her "lesbian" friends from France once his "equipment" is "mutilated": "Those little whores should go back where they came from" (124-25).

Shérazade's move to block this impulse results in the photographer's abandonment by his "clan"—"artistic directors, fashion photographers, editors of women's magazines" (124). Sebbar's handling of this episode shows, however, that there is no question of a collective ethical decision to ostracize the racist and sexist aggressor; indeed, it turns out that his clan is composed of people who had been only tenuously attached to him in the first place, "his friends, for the evening." In short, Shérazade's gesture doesn't raise anybody's consciousness, but rather works to dissolve the apparent unity of the group associated with the photographer and thus break down the stark opposition between the French "clan" and the immigrants.

A related dynamic is staged two pages earlier when the Parisian guests watching the girls dance suddenly disperse upon recognizing their resemblance to the "tourists or provincials" who form a tight circle around "African or Moroccan drums" on the esplanade at Beaubourg (123). Here, however, the text keeps more clearly in view the conflicting forces at work in dissolving and refashioning the category of Frenchness. True, the contours of one version of French national identity fade with the dispersion of the guests who, as in the passage examined above, do not align themselves, in any sustained way, *against* the young immigrants. However, another, "Parisian" version of Frenchness is the very force that motivates the dispersion; the guests scatter to avoid the embarrassment of resembling tourists or provincials. Moreover, in the figure of the crowd at Beaubourg to which the guests are compared, the problematic assembly of tourists and provincials—all of whom are in some sense foreigners in the French capital—nonetheless forms a bounded unit (a "tight circle") organized around the focal point furnished by France's cultural others, represented in terms of their cultural equipment, the "African or Moroccan drums." The effect of this comparison, then, is to underscore the relative stability of the hierarchized opposition first world/third world underlying the unstable category of Frenchness, which assumes different shapes, depending on the significance accorded regional identities, multinational economic and political arrangements, and so forth. My point here is that in *Shérazade* the shifting representations (and self-presentations) of immigrants, like the struggles over the means of representation, do not simply body forth a liberating dissolution of cultural boundaries; they also show how cultural frontiers are continually redrawn in contemporary France, usually to the detriment of minority populations.

In the sequences of *Shérazade* I have discussed so far, the immigrants' role in the representation business has been restricted to accepting or refusing the place reserved for them as objects of representation. Shérazade's refusal to be photographed at the party has many analogues in the novel, such as Omar's refusal to pose for pornographic photos in his leather motorcycle gear (125) and France's principled rejection of offers for modeling jobs, which, in her opinion, are a form of "prostitution" (121). Although the youths do have some room to maneuver even here—they are by turns provocative and insolent, they dress "so that people will notice them" (118) and then "spit on" their admirers—they are eventually obliged to say either "yes" or "no" to Babylon.

In other parts of the novel, however, Sebbar explores the youths' means of effectively taking up and inflecting the languages of the representation business. In a scene reminiscent of the party, Shérazade is once again before the eye of a camera, this time in the company of Zouzou and France in a pornographer's studio. Here, however, they neither accept nor reject the role they have been given—that of kinky jungle guerrillas whose assignment is to terrify and turn on the film's spectators.[38] Instead, they put the pornographer on by turning to their own advantage the very techniques he enjoins them to use. Far from enhancing the filmmaker's power of direction and simultaneously titillating him as spectator by using the "savage" dress and fake machine guns as he orders them to do, the girls simulate violence by their own means and for their own purposes, training on the pornographer plastic pistols that he mistakes for the real thing, that is, the .38s used by another breed of guerrilla, the Red Brigade.

In warning the pornographer that they're "not putting him on" (C'est pas du cinéma [155]), the girls are at once lying and telling a cultural truth, namely that, given the right material conditions, representations such as their put-on have very real effects, indeed are themselves "real." In the porn studio, conditions are such that Shérazade and her friends really are empowered by seizing fake pistols in place of fake machine guns, and assuming the role of urban rather than jungle guerrillas. They have constructed meanings in a language that is and is not the pornographer's, in order to interrupt his command and force him to listen to them. In this scene, the girls use their power to trash the studio, rather than to seize the equipment and make their own films. In other sequences, however, the text underscores the oppositional force of alternative media produced by and for cultural minorities (such as the African magazine in which Shérazade will publish some poems), although not without signaling their inevitable complicity with, or absorption into, mainstream cultural forms.

In the latter connection, it is interesting to note the contradictory positions Shérazade occupies in making an "independent" film with Julien and one of his friends, a film about an all-girl band of urban guerrillas led by the formidable Zina. In this venture, more than at the party or in the porn studio, Shérazade engages actively and critically in the process of producing representations of immigrant girls. For instance, she gives Julien permission to incorporate her account of the "jungle" adventure into the scenario he is writing, but reads and criticizes the text he comes up with: "he changed the scenario, taking account of what she had said" (160).

Because she is pleased with the final scenario, Shérazade agrees to play the role of Zina, but despite the director's enthusiasm ("That's her! She *is* Zina!"), she is increasingly put off by the production process and finally abandons the film project. In the first place, the director's passionate endorsement of Shérazade stems from his unwitting seduction by the same orientalist figure that fascinates Julien; he congratulates himself for having found, at last, an actress "with green eyes" who, he says with unintentional irony, "eludes every stereotype" (216-17). The filmmaker's project involves translating nineteenth-century exoticism into a contemporary urban context by transforming the silent, passive woman of the harem into a terrifying but seductive public enemy, a *femme sauvage* whose wild femininity is made to serve the culture industry:

> Une chef de bande, une rebelle et poète, une insoumise habile au couteau, efficace en karaté . . . intrépide et farouche, une mutante des Z. U. P., une vagabonde des blocs, des caves, des parkings et des rues, imprenable et redoutable comme un chef de guerre. . . . Zina—ça voulait dire jolie en arabe. (218-19)

> [A gang leader, a rebel and a poet, a wild woman who was handy with a knife, adept at karate . . . intrepid and ferocious, a mutant from the urban renewal zone, a vagrant combing the low-income high-rises, the basements, the parking lots, and the streets, impregnable and redoubtable as a war commander. . . . Zina— that meant "pretty" in Arabic.]

The director's orientalism, and the similarity of "his" Zina to the jungle guerrilla of the porn film, have the effect of disqualifying Shérazade's interpretation of the part.

Another factor in her alienation is the director's appropriation of the counterculture in naming the film "The Suburbs Are Beautiful." Shérazade protests that her friend Pierrot intends to give that title to his newspaper (or his radio show—she can't remember which), to which the director replies curtly, "That paper doesn't exist, and neither does the radio show. . . . I'm going to get the copyright for the title and the scenario. I don't want anyone to steal them from me" (218). But it is her estrangement from the filmed images themselves that is decisive for Shérazade, on two counts. First, whereas the director is more convinced than ever that Shérazade "is" Zina, she sees herself on the video monitor "as if it weren't her" (219). And second, as an Algerian girl being filmed by a French director, she occupies a position analogous to that of the Algerian women mentioned a page later, women who were forcibly unveiled during the revolution and placed before a French soldier's camera as if before a "machine gun." The war photos, in which the women's look is "intense, ferocious, so savage that the images could only record it, without ever mastering it," at once recall the director's modern orientalist fantasy and violently negate it. What is more, they induce Shérazade to abandon the film project, not because they inspire in her the same violent resistance attributed to the women in the photographs—women with whom she feels a cultural affinity since they all "spoke the same language, her mother's language"—but because the critical documentation of their subjection to the army's will moves her to tears and stifles her interest in playing Zina (220).[39]

Sebbar's treatment of the disjuncture between Shérazade and her image on film works less to denounce all representation as repressive than to signal the need to use representations by and of cultural minorities to bring the history of colonialism into the present in critical and productive ways. Sebbar does this not only by staging struggles over representation such as those we have just examined, but by structuring her novel as she does, that is, dividing it into sequences whose titles link orientalist writers and painters (Delacroix, Chassériau, Fromentin) to Algerian writers (Feraoun) and exiled cultural workers (Esther, a magazine editor) as well as to historical figures such as Zingha, the Angolan queen reputed to have terrified the Portuguese colonizers—figures now celebrated by politically aware immigrant youths. The titles also tie cultural production to the geography of colonial Algeria and of postcolonial France: Algerian villages such as Nédroma and Bouzaréa and Parisian suburbs such as Vanves, where the flea markets support a variety of overlapping and interdependent economies, such as Julien's purchase of orientalist paintings and Shérazade's sale of stolen goods (which is one way the runaway teenager makes her living). Finally, the titles in *Shérazade* interweave with this matrix the names of the immigrant youths (Zouzou and France, Driss, Basile, Pierrot—descendants of Maghrebians, Caribbean peoples, or Eastern Europeans) who are attempting both to invent new social relationships with each other— avoiding traditional family ties as well as bonds determined by rigidly defined class, sexual, ethnic, or racial identities—and, more broadly, to redraw the cultural map of France in the eighties. Taken together, and considered in relation to the narrative sequences they designate, the proper names that mark off the divisions in the text signal the shifting, "nomadic" character of the meanings attached to them in varying historical and cultural contexts. Yet the struggles over meanings, as well as struggles over the processes by

which meanings are raveled and unraveled, are clearly situated
within a national territory still deeply marked by the legacy of colonialism, a legacy still legible in Sebbar's tropes of exile.[40]

Women, Writing, and Postcolonial Politics

Leïla Sebbar is the only French writer to have interwoven highly
nuanced interrogations of female identity with every strand of her
inquiry into the problem of exile, the plight of immigrants, and the
vacillation of modern political movements between a void that
marks the absence of a collectivity and an embodiment of "the
people" that attempts to represent them fully, finally, and thus, co-
ercively. Her attention to women—and not just to "the feminine"
as a trope for the making and unmaking of identities—encourages
the rethinking of colonialism and its aftermath in terms of the ways
gender operates to establish and maintain social hierarchies within
and between cultures.

In her *Lettres Parisiennes* Sebbar writes:

> La colonisation a donné lieu à des déplacements hallucinants. Je
> ne suis pas sûre que ces déplacements aient toujours été négatifs;
> ils ont bouleversé des traditions archaïques et oppressives, ils ont
> permis des avancées par croisements de cultures. (119)

> [Colonization gave place to mind-boggling historic displacements.
> I'm not sure all of these displacements have always been negative;
> they disrupted archaic and oppressive traditions, and enabled
> advances through the mixing of cultures.]

In Sebbar's fiction, the positive displacements brought about by
colonization almost always concern women's situation. Where the
Maghreb is concerned, the "oppressive traditions" that are dis-
rupted include veiling and seclusion, forced marriage, domestic violence, and illiteracy. Sebbar's novel *Fatima ou les Algériennes au
square* stages not the "original" displacements themselves, but
rather their reverberations in the lives of Maghrebians living in
France.

The book begins and ends with figures of a young girl's exclusion, first from social networks outside her family, then from the
family itself. In the opening pages the girl, Dalila, has "shut herself
in the bedroom" where she will stay for nearly a week, until the
cuts and bruises she has sustained from her father's beating have

had time to heal.[41] She has been beaten not only because she has transgressed the code that requires her to remain secluded whenever she is not in school or doing errands for her mother, but above all because of her father's frustration with the social situation in France, which delegitimates the code, makes its enforcement impossible, and undermines his authority in the family. In the closing pages, there is one last evocation of Dalila "secluded in her room"—this time, as her mother Fatima tenderly touches her cheek, saying "my daughter"—before the girl's definitive departure is recalled: "When Dalila left, Fatima cried for a long time, sitting like an old woman on the Aflou rug" (233-34).

At first glance, then, it seems that Dalila is forced to choose between two painful forms of exclusion: exclusion from the family she loves, or from the peer group she needs in order to function socially in France. On closer inspection, though, it is clear that Sebbar's text complicates the inclusion/exclusion duality so as to show that both Dalila's identity and that of her family are crossed from the start by French identities (identities that are themselves heterogeneous and contradictory), so that there is no question of Dalila or any other family member being simply inside an ethnically "pure" family circle or outside it, although much of the domestic violence stems from a wish to preserve or restore ethnic purity. Dalila's "inclusion" in the family depends on a seclusion that is as impracticable as it is intolerable; her self-imposed seclusion in the bedroom, far from simply repeating and confirming the seclusion imposed by her father, marks a fissure in Dalila's identity as well as in that of her family. The disjuncture between the two modes or moments of seclusion divides the domestic space internally and discloses the effects of this division on the young girl, who refuses to do the symbolic work of covering it over by accepting her confinement or taking responsibility for it by accepting her expulsion as a just punishment.

In the same way, Dalila's departure marks her difference from the daughter her parents wish to have without identifying her simply as the nondaughter, the one who is excluded by virtue of transgressing the family code of honor. Far from restoring the family's integrity, her departure reopens the wound and moves Fatima to tears. Between these two moments of rending, the text interweaves stories of Dalila's childhood (at home) and adolescence (on the streets of Paris) with those of the Arab women her mother meets at the square in their housing complex. The crisscrossing of story lines, the sudden interruptions, detours, repetitions, and returns in the narrative constitute a symbolic network that bind the mother to her daughter, tie the girls of Dalila's generation to Fatima and her friends, set the father's nostalgia for the homeland in relation to the children's view of Algeria as a "reform school" for the disobedient, and link Maghrebian immigrants to other ethnic groups and to the working-class French people who live among them in the Paris suburbs. Although Sebbar's text doesn't reconcile the parties who stand opposed in the fiction by incorporating them into a new communal whole (Dalila has finally been forced to leave home, ethnic strife continues, and so forth), it does body forth some of the processes by which anxieties about identity can erupt into racial and sexual violence, or can be appeased in order that people reconcile themselves with the differences that both inhabit them and distinguish them from others. In this respect, Sebbar's *Fatima* exhibits the same ingenuousness that Daniel Sibony attributes to his *Ecrits sur le racisme*, which he introduces in these terms: "This book . . . is intended to contribute to the art of rendering these walls [of racism] inoffensive, or less lethal—not by accumulating many 'truths' about racism, for accumulated truths choke each other and end up rotting, which in no way prevents their waste from fertilizing other lands. But in this sort of affair, ideas that are just, just ideas, are not enough. It is a matter of making an experience possible, the experience of a tension and an overcoming, and of giving place to it in words; as if it were for lack of words, for lack of place in words, that one acted out in the racist outburst."[42]

In laying bare and defusing the force of racism and sexual domination, Sebbar's narrative foregrounds the stakes of this process for immigrant women—women who, like Fatima, tell each other their stories knowing that "there really wasn't any story, but she went ahead as if what had happened . . . was worthy of being reported faithfully to her friends, like a historical event rather than a mere anecdote devoid of meaning" (64). The novel itself operates in this "as if" mode, gently mocking the inflated rhetoric of the Maghrebian women, reinstating (rather than resolving) conflicts between generations of immigrants, but nonetheless affirming the symbolic processes by which they continually renegotiate the terms of their integration into French culture. For example, in relating Dalila's role in a brawl that takes place in their housing complex, Fatima presents her little daughter as an epic hero who, pained and angered by the realization that the slur *bicots* designates her and her clan, declares that she will "fight like an African tigress":

> Les femmes . . . voyaient dans cette scène dont Dalila était l'héroïne, une grandeur, une noblesse qui en faisaient une scène exemplaire dont chacune pourrait se servir à l'occasion pour souligner une fois de plus que l'exil n'enlevait rien à la fierté et à l'orgueil de la race. (64-65)

> [The women . . . saw in this scene, of which Dalila was the heroine, a grandeur, a nobility that made of it an exemplary scene that every one of them could use to drive home the point once again that exile in no way diminished the pride and self-respect of the race.]

Sebbar ironizes this "epic" grandeur not only through her use of hyperbole, but also by underscoring the fact that the Maghrebian women's cultural hybridity infiltrates even their most ardent articulations of ethnic pride: "the friends punctuated the story with exclamations in Arabic and in French . . . '*Mesquina*' . . . the poor little thing" (64). One woman, who has had extensive dealings with the psychological services available to immigrants, observes that the slur *bicots* "traumatized" Dalila, and thus introduces into Fatima's narrative a specialized vocabulary whose "barbarism" rends the storytelling process ("Dalila didn't understand, the other women and her mother had gotten the gist") without arresting it (64).

The women's cultural hybridity, and the instability of the meanings they generate through their storytelling, are evident, too, in the divergent and even conflicting meanings assigned Dalila's ferocity. Before Fatima transforms it into an exemplum of ethnic pride in the epic tale she spins at the square, she regards Dalila's vehemence as simultaneously moving and comical, a mark of her daughter's childishness:

> "Tu vas te battre pour ça, tu es petite, tu sais.—Oui, je me battrai . . . jusqu'à la mort. . . . Sa mère se mit à rire. Elle embrassa encore son héroïque petite fille avant de lui servir un chocolat chaud. (63)

["You're going to fight over that? You're little, you know.—Yes, I'll fight—to the death." Her mother smiled. She kissed her heroic little daughter again before serving her some hot chocolate.]

Later, in a move characteristic of Sebbar's narrative technique, the collective mirth inspired by Dalila's verve changes almost imperceptibly to disapproval when the image of the girl as an African tigress gives place to that of the judo expert Dalila has vowed to become:

Les filles n'apprenaient pas le judo, les leurs, du moins. Certaines d'entre elles avaient demandé à leur père de les inscrire au gymnase. Les pères avaient toujours dit non, avec l'accord de la mère. (65)

[Girls didn't learn judo, not theirs at least. Some of the girls had asked their fathers to enroll them [in judo classes] at the gym. The fathers had always said no, with the mothers' consent.]

Dalila's response to the story is not determined, however, by the older women's expression of disapproval or by the subsequent stories of maternal violence toward daughters who engage in rough play. For in listening to these other stories, Dalila remembers not only "the slap her mother had given her" for making explicit their identity as *bicots*, but also her mother's tears, "the kisses of maternal repentance" (67) that delegitimate the women's violent repression of their daughters and give Dalila the moral strength, some years later, to extricate herself from the cycle of paternal violence in which Fatima is complicit.

Just as Fatima relates her daughter's exploits "as if" they were worthy of note, Sebbar's text relates various versions of the Maghrebian girl's confinement "as if" it deserved serious consideration as a social problem—one that impugns not just the preservation of Islamic traditions in immigrant communities, but postcolonial politics in France, as well. The story of Dalila is mirrored by that of her Moroccan friend, whose forced marriage to a man who beats her prompts her to flee the conjugal abode. The figure that recurs in each of these stories is that of seclusion in the space of a single room—Dalila "in the bedroom with the little ones" (9), the Moroccan girl in the "nuptial chamber" where she is seized by nausea (186). But although the girls' entrapment and beating by the father or husband is presented as the gravest and most immediate danger, the "outside" is construed as a threatening place, as well. The Moroccan girl temporarily takes shelter in yet another single room, the studio apartment she shares with two friends (204); like Dalila, she finds that her "escape" has placed her at the door of homelessness, unemployment, prostitution, and drug trafficking.

These two stories are echoed in turn by the tale of Aïcha, a young wife and mother of five who confines herself to the squalid two-room apartment behind her husband's grocery store, not because she is forbidden to go out, but because she is afraid to do so, not knowing how to get along in Paris. The emblem of Aïcha's misery is a little alcove in her apartment, "the nook that served as both kitchen and bathroom":

> Elle avait du mal à faire les lessives dans le petit évier . . . le linge ne séchait pas, les draps et les culottes s'accumulaient, ça sentait mauvais. (75)

> [She had trouble doing the wash in the little sink. . . . The laundry didn't dry, the sheets and underwear accumulated, it smelled bad.]

Aïcha repeatedly beats one of her five children, Mustapha, a three-and-a-half-year-old bedwetter whose sheets and clothing she cannot keep clean. After being hospitalized twice for bruises and broken bones, the boy is sent to live for some months with a French foster family in Normandy. As in the stories of Dalila and the Moroccan girl, domestic violence is linked to women's confinement, although here, the young woman is the perpetrator rather than the victim of physical abuse.

The nook piled with urine-soaked laundry stands for more, however, than Aïcha's frustration and Mustapha's victimization, for it signals the widespread effects, in immigrant communities, of the housing crisis in Paris. Aïcha, her husband Ali, the well-meaning but ineffectual social worker, the politically committed and sympathetic physician who treats Mustapha—every actor in the story knows that space is the fundamental problem, yet no one is able to obtain a suitable apartment for Aïcha's family; the social worker's advice is that they return to Algeria:

> Vous n'aurez pas de F4 avant deux ans. . . . Vous n'allez pas vivre là-dedans avec cinq enfants. . . . C'est insalubre. Il fait froid.

C'est mal chauffé. Dites à votre mari que vous voulez revenir au pays. . . . Au moins là-bas, il fait beau. (78)

[You won't get the larger place for two more years. . . . You can't live in there with five children. . . . It's unhealthy. It's cold. It's badly heated. Tell your husband you want to go back home. . . . At least the weather's nice back there.]

In this story, domestic violence and the removal of the victim from the family stem less from the encounter between Islamic tradition and modern French life than from the absence of effective political action to provide adequate housing to poor Parisians, particularly immigrants. In the space of Aïcha's laundry nook, the "positive" effects of Algeria's postcolonial relation to France (such as Mustapha's access to medical care) take on a grim aspect as they collide with the economic dependency generated by international capitalism and with the French bureaucracy, which, to paraphrase Laclau and Mouffe, depoliticizes the new antagonisms emerging in civil society, imposing new forms of subordination rather than fostering true democratization.[43]

The story of Aïcha and Mustapha and the fragmentary way in which it is related do more, however, than mark the isolation of Maghrebian women in France, the painful scattering of their families, and the "illiterate deportation" of immigrant groups who are, in Sebbar's words, "divided and weak to the point of being incapable of protecting their own children." For this story, produced during the encounters of Algerian women at the square, also participates in and enables processes of gathering that hold the promise, at least, of transforming the Maghrebians' illiterate deportation into an acceptable form of integration into modern France. Little Dalila, who listens to the fragments of this story while resting her head on her mother's lap, is always anxious to learn the outcome, and has to prompt the women to return to the subject that preoccupies her by interjecting, at every meeting, "What about Mustapha?"

Elle avait remarqué que lorsqu'elles bavardaient, les amies de sa mère, sa mère aussi d'ailleurs, sautaient souvent d'un sujet à un autre, sans aucune suite et c'était elle qui devait refaire l'histoire dans sa tête en rassemblant comme elle pouvait les morceaux qu'elle n'avait pas oubliés. (111)

[She had noticed that when they chatted, her mother's friends—
her mother too, for that matter—kept jumping from one topic to
another at random, and that it was up to her to remake the story
in her head, reassembling as best she could the pieces she hadn't
forgotten.]

Eventually we learn that Mustapha's story ends much the way Dalila's will, that is, he is neither expelled (taken) from his family nor
returned to the fold: against all odds, he finds happiness at the Le-
terrier farm in Normandy and ends up spending vacations there
for years afterward, moving back and forth between the Norman
countryside and the Parisian suburbs. In characterizing Mustapha's relation to the Leterriers, Sebbar sustains the humor, the
gentle irony, and also the sense of unease or even revulsion that
infuse her figurations of encounters with racial others. Far from
purging them of their contradictions and ambiguities and containing them within a static, idealized notion of family, region, or
country, she at once gives full play to their shifting, uncertain character *and* grounds them in the history of colonialism and its aftermath.

Parodying the oriental tales of the eighteenth century by making
France appear strange to foreigners who are neither mouthpieces
for liberal French thinkers nor oriental despots, Sebbar confronts
Ali and Aïcha, who have just come to Normandy to retrieve their
son, with "an old man who looked at them, squinting his eyes.
Maybe he had never seen Arabs before? Or only on colonial postcards [with captions reading] Moorish women . . . beautiful Fatima; Aïcha and Zorah" (225). Sebbar uses the free indirect style
both to ironize the cultural codes that will enable the Norman peasants to "recognize" Aïcha, and to convey Ali's unease with the
manners of Frenchmen who keep pictures of nude Moorish
women in boxes, taking them out to show to guests "when the
children are sleeping." As for Aïcha, she is "reassured to see that
Mustapha didn't seem as unhappy as she might have thought he
would be living with strangers, Norman peasants who spoke only
French, who went to mass on Sundays, ate pork . . . and knew
nothing about Algerian customs" (228). The Algerian couple's
mixed response to the Norman peasants is matched by the peasants' ambivalence toward Mustapha: "Everyone liked him right

away, though in these parts people didn't like Arabs much, and liked Negroes even less" (227).

The pastoral setting that momentarily brings happiness to Ali, Aïcha, and their children, who "were throwing stones into the hedges and trees as though they had always lived in the country" (224), is soon replaced by the suburban one they had fled. This shift not only underlines the obstacles the immigrants encounter in trying to leave the "sad and dusty squares," but also establishes a connection between the unlikely pleasure they experienced among the French peasants and the festival of the Aïd, held in the cement high-rises. The celebration involves slaughtering sheep bought from "farmers on the Normandy coast" (230), and if the flow of blood in the bathtubs of the Arab apartments provokes racist comments from the French women looking on ("Savages, Arabs, Barbarians"), Sebbar's construction of the scene suggests that this results less from the *differences* between the two ethnic groups than from the *similarities* between them: both inhabit the same housing complexes and have "barbaric" peasant ancestors who learned to tolerate "the starts and muted bleating of the sheep . . . the knife that groped for the best spot under the neck, and the bleeding slit throat, the final quivering of its body" (231-32).

Here too Sebbar's text echoes Sibony's when he writes:

> *Racism* is exasperated by *seeing difference come down to the same [thing]*, come back to infiltrate the same and reveal it to be different from itself, threaten to interrogate it on the supports of its identity, reveal them to be too fragile in their tenseness, too rigid in their play, threaten to divulge their secrets or rend their semblances. As for the difference of others, it can irritate when the reign of the Same imposes itself; one can demand and grant the "rights to difference," which are but the banal acknowledgment that everyone has the right to be *oneself*. But there's the rub: the human being doesn't know which "oneself" to become, and when he does know it, he experiences differences as threats to his identity only when he sees them come too close to him, sees them want to assimilate themselves to him, assimilate him to them. (10)

Unlike Sibony, though, Sebbar points to the importance, for Maghrebians, of simultaneously acknowledging the unfounded, the unjustifiable, the irreconcilable in their own and in others' being *and* affirming their origins, even if every articulation of their ethnic identity is necessarily divided and contradictory. For instance, she notes with sympathy—though not without irony, given the context I have just described—how Dalila's father "insisted on slaughtering the sheep of the Aïd himself, on initiating his sons, and reminding his French-born children that they were not from here, that they had a country and a religion, that in spite of laws and decrees that might make of them little French children, they were Algerian and Muslim before anything else" (232-33). The juxtaposition of this scene with Dalila's departure suggests that in part, it is the pleasure and horror inspired by the festival and its function of affirming Algeria as a point of origin that propels Dalila's search for new forms of cultural existence in France, rather than trapping her in a nostalgic, sterile, or dangerous form of nationalism.

The story of Aïcha thus gathers scattered elements of French and Maghrebian communities and histories as well as dispersed moments of Dalila's subjectivity and sociality in such a way as to affirm the girl's departure without severing her ties to her culture or to her family, particularly her mother, Fatima. To a certain extent, this story also ties together the broken and divergent strands of Sebbar's text, which is itself figured by the Algerian women's storytelling at the square. By means of the recurrent textile motif, the illiterate women's storytelling is not only interwoven with a key metaphor of the literary text as *tissue*, but is also meshed with the women's everyday tasks of housekeeping, child care, and mediation between the family and the French bureaucracy. The endless washing and drying of sheets, the unknitting of old sweaters and the knitting of new ones from the used yarn, the arrangement of children's clothing in the armoire, Fatima's use of an old sheet to wrap all the family documents so that her illiteracy doesn't prevent her from conducting bureaucratic business—these figurations of making, maintaining, and remaking the social fabric do more than serve as points of departure for and metaphors of storytelling. They signal the need to investigate the relation between "weaving" as a metaphor for text production (a "feminine" process by which subjectivity and sociality are raveled and unraveled) and the material reality of women: women who read and women who have not been taught to read; women who write and women who work in the textile mills of the first and third world; intellectuals and activists like Sebbar and the Algerian immigrants she writes about.[44]

Sebbar's refashioning of the privileged figure of textuality calls upon readers to invent new interpretive strategies and new practices of writing that articulate women's needs and desires rather than pretending to go beyond the category of gender. And here, as in the *Lettres parisiennes* and *Shérazade*, her refashioning of the trope of exile shows that minority groups can be represented without reinscribing totalizing identities: rather than speaking for minorities, Sebbar's texts suggest ways to open new spaces within which minority discourses might unfold in France today.

Chapter 4

Out of France

> Each time a subject "falls" in love, he revives a fragment of the archaic time when men were supposed to carry off women (in order to ensure exogamy): every lover who falls in love at first sight has something of a Sabine Woman (or of some other celebrated victim of ravishment).
>
> —Roland Barthes, *A Lover's Discourse*

In the margin of the entry "ravishment" from which my epigraph is taken, Barthes cites the Algerian scholar Tahar Labib Djedidi, noting that "in Arabic, for instance, *fitna* refers to both material (or ideological) warfare and the enterprise of sexual seduction."[1] This marginal note in Barthes's text stands as an emblem of the interconnection, still potent in the French imagination, between the experience of ravishment and that of conquest by the orient, particularly the Maghrebian territories conquered by France in the colonial period. As ravishment is an experience that, according to Barthes, is always feminized and fraught with ambivalence, it is not surprising that in French literary representations the Maghreb assumes numerous guises that reflect France's multiple and contradictory responses to the Maghreb's perceived power of seduction: it is by turns hated as a usurper of French power, feared as a threat to the nation's purity, and loved as the object of France's enthrallment. The Maghreb is loved, too, as the agent who induces France to take pleasure in her feelings of powerlessness, her loss of clear boundaries—a loss circumscribed, reassuringly, by France's retention of economic and military power over her imaginary abductor.

Given France's ambivalence about being carried away in her

guise as a Sabine, her ravishment by the Maghreb is often rele-
gated to the margins of discourse in a gesture of disavowal—one to
which Barthes's text pointedly and ironically calls attention. Yet the
opposite also occurs with great frequency. I showed in the last
chapter, for instance, how in Sebbar's *Shérazade* France's ravishment, played out in Julien's relation to Shérazade and in Théophile
Gautier's relation to Algiers, is prominently displayed as the indis-
putable sign of the European nation's conquest *by* (not *of*) the
Maghreb. Sebbar's ironic presentation of this dynamic discloses
how the trope of ravishment inverts the hierarchized relation between France and the Maghreb as a way of denying French colonial
and neocolonial domination and the structuring of both by patriarchy.

   In the present chapter, on the other hand, I will be looking at the
critical staging of ravishment in French novels of the 1980s that attempt to confront colonial and postcolonial violence and establish
solidarity between France and the Maghreb. Evelyne Sullerot's
L'Aman, Marie Cardinal's *Au pays de mes racines*, J. M. G. Le Clézio's
Désert, Michel Tournier's *La Goutte d'or*, and Guy Hocquenghem's
L'Amour en relief all enact liberatory transformations in the dynamics of postcolonial encounters between France and its former colonies in the Maghreb, most often on Maghrebian or French terrain,
but in the case of Hocquenghem, in other parts of Europe and in
the United States as well.[2] All mobilize sexuality—notably heterosexual female and gay male sexuality—in effecting this transformation and, although they are far from being uniformly feminist in
their orientation, they rely centrally on female or "feminized" figures in representing the economic, social, psychic, and erotic
struggles that could potentially reshape postcolonial politics in
France. Finally, all are authored by well-known intellectuals and
writers whom I want to identify as French, despite the ambiguities
in Cardinal's identity as a Pied-Noir, for example, or in Le Clézio's
identity as a native of Mauritius who was educated in England.[3]
However eccentric their relation to metropolitan France may be in
terms of their geographical origins, culture, and politics, these
writers are nonetheless questioning Frenchness from the inside, as
it were.

   To varying degrees, the French texts that concern me here participate in what Françoise Lionnet, echoing the Martinican writer
and theorist Edouard Glissant, calls a "cultural politics of *métis-*

sage," or braiding of heterogeneous cultural forms, which challenges essentialist notions of racial, sexual, and national identity — notions that inform France's complacent self-understanding as well as reductive French conceptions of the Maghreb. In the same way, these novels engage in the process of reclaiming buried histories and constructing countermemories that give voice to marginalized, often feminized, values of both third-world and first-world cultures. In doing so, they work in solidarity with the texts of Francophone writers like Glissant by opening a space where, in Lionnet's words, "multiplicity and diversity are affirmed. This space is not a territory staked out by exclusionary practices. Rather, it functions as a sheltering site, one that can nurture our differences without enclosing us within facile oppositional practices or sterile denunciations and disavowals. For it is only by imagining nonhierarchical modes of relation among cultures that we can address the crucial issues of indeterminacy [that is, the nonessential character of identity] and solidarity."[4]

At the same time, however, I want to suggest that these French texts on the Maghreb reinscribe regressive notions of female identity, race, and national culture. At certain moments, for instance, the affirmation of the Maghrebian nations' right to self-determination is barely distinguishable from the abandonment of poor countries to the economic fate imposed on them by multinational capitalism. In the same way, the expression of respect for the national and cultural autonomy of Maghrebian societies sometimes does less to foster that autonomy than to provide the French writers with a pretext for focusing on their own cultural situation and above all their own subjectivity. The counterpart of this exclusionary dynamic is an appropriative one in which the interweaving of archaic and modern features of individual and collective experience in French and Maghrebian histories sometimes has the effect of leveling important differences between sexes, races, and cultures, and thus of effacing inequalities rather than encouraging us to redress them. In certain respects, the indeterminacy of identities in French-authored fiction undermines solidarity by putting the old wine of assimilation in new postmodern bottles ("we are the world"). Although I do not believe this confirms the thesis that a politically conservative leveling tendency has so far characterized all postmodern cultural production, as Fredric Jameson has suggested, I think it does signal the need to assess carefully the way the art form of late capitalism is used in particular cases, and to take account of who is using it in determining its social and political significance.[5]

Before turning to a consideration of 1980s fiction on the Maghreb and the issues it raises for postcolonial politics and for feminism, let me briefly situate this fiction in the literary and political contexts from which it emerged. In the last twenty years or so, French literature dealing with the Maghreb has become an object of critical interest in its own right: bibliographies, anthologies, and collections of critical essays are now routinely devoted to this body of work, which, as Jean-Robert Henry shows in his introduction to *Le Maghreb dans l'imaginaire français*, comprises many different kinds of texts: the orientalist writings of travelers like Fromentin, Daudet, Loti, and Gide in the nineteenth and early twentieth centuries; the early twentieth-century writings of *colons*, both colonialist and anticolonial, which affirm a distinctly Algerian identity; the Saharan adventure novels of the interwar period and the 1950s, of which the most famous is Saint-Exupéry's *Le Petit Prince*, still the most widely read novel of French literature; and the texts of the Ecole d'Alger (a contested grouping) by writers like Albert Camus, Jules Roy, and Emmanuel Roblès, who are esteemed for their supposed achievement of "converting the material base of colonial malaise into universalist discourse" and for "fostering the emergence of a good Maghrebian literature."[6]

While a number of the Ecole d'Alger writers straddle the colonial-postcolonial divide, other French writers who deal critically with France's relation to the Maghreb do so mainly from a postindependence standpoint. To be counted among the latter are the novelist Claude Ollier, who lived in the Maghreb as a government attaché in the years after independence; the Pied-Noir writer Marie Cardinal, who left Algeria during the revolution and who addresses the divisions and conflicts within national and cultural identities; and J. M. G. Le Clézio, who writes of colonial conquest from the victims' point of view and, like Michel Tournier and Leïla Sebbar, portrays Maghrebian immigrants in such a way as to unsettle unitary notions of Frenchness. Recent French literature on the Maghreb also includes texts reflecting on the Jewish community there, written by Jews still residing in North Africa and by those now living in exile. In addition, there is much popular cultural production in the form of neoexotic films, children's books, comic books, video games, and detective novels, which are often more openly racist or paternalistic than their high-cultural counterparts, and which figure in the "quality" novels of writers like Tournier and Sebbar, both as symptoms of neocolonialism and as potential forces for positive social change. Finally, there has been a resurgence of uncritical nostalgic writing on the Maghreb, often memoirs or autobiographies by Pieds-Noirs published at the authors' expense.

It is probably no coincidence that an outpouring of French literature on the Maghreb comes in the 1970s and 1980s, a time when France finds itself in a political and cultural void. For in this literature, the Maghreb often functions symbolically as a source of salvation or, more productively, of cultural renewal that does not seek to suppress social divisions. In its nostalgic incarnations, it variously enables France phantasmally to project itself back to a point in time preceding the brutality and ugliness of colonial conquest and its aftermath; it resurrects colonial domination as an "ideal" state from which the memory of the fall is expunged, or merely offers an exotic imaginary alternative to the French workaday world. In its more critical, forward-looking guises, on the other hand, it attempts to revive an innovative leftist cultural politics in response to the void left by Giscard's technocratic legacy and Mitterrand's rather lackluster approach to culture.

Despite their profession of support for vanguard art that shakes up established notions of Frenchness, Mitterrand and his Socialist ministers tend, in the 1980s, either to foster art of mediocre, often folkloric, quality and limited interest (for instance in the projects funded through provincial *maisons de la culture*) or, on the other hand, to perpetuate the centuries-old tradition of state-sponsored high art, a conservative tradition that relies on economic, political, and ideological centralization as a means of quality control (exercised for example in the literary academies, the Comédie Française, and the cultural programming on state-controlled television). This conservative tradition neutralizes, or at best blunts, art's critical function. In short, although the Socialists claim to favor artistic iconoclasm, their policies in fact encourage the endless reproduction of traditional art forms and at the same time betray their suspicion of modern art, particularly insofar as it engages with and often celebrates uneven historical development, sociocultural heterogeneity, and technology.

As Guy Hocquenghem points out, "It's easy to see that the Socialists have a problem with modern art in general. They don't understand it and they don't like it. They consider it to be directly tied
to the capitalist market, which is true to some extent. Another
problem for them is that modern art is, more than any other art
form, cosmopolitan. The Socialists don't like art without roots."[7]
This may explain why Mitterrand, himself a writer—although one
who has been described as a "lyrical notary"—makes the flamboy-
ant Jack Lang his minister of culture: the former revolutionary ex-
cels as a "postmodern politician" who gives the lie to the Socialists'
deep distrust of the rootlessness, or cosmopolitanism, of modern
art.[8] Against these developments, critical fiction on the Maghreb
tries to uproot the metropole, making it the point of departure for
writers who, like Hocquenghem, want to become cultural voyagers
and "decline our nationality as one declines an invitation"; alternatively, it makes France the site of cultural mixing for those who,
like Tournier, basically welcome and try to carry forward the dislo-
cations of national identity wrought by immigrants.[9]

Of course, the Socialists' undertakings in the realm of culture
are not uniformly nationalist and antimodern in this period; in fact,
some of them are very compatible with the work of writers like
Tournier and Hocquenghem. For example, the Ministry of Culture
sponsors initiatives that explore France's relation to dominant and
marginal societies in the new transnational networks of culture,
communication, and information. One such project is the investigation, led by Armand Mattelart in 1982-83, into the possibility of
creating a "Latin cinema space" that would facilitate exchange and
collaboration among France, Italy, Spain, Portugal, Mexico, Brazil,
and other Latin nations in the production, distribution, and recep-
tion of audiovisual art. The "technical" obstacles confronted by
Mattelart's research group were these:

> the rigidity of the home market, giving rise to little variety in
> productions; ignorance of well-known authors and actors from the
> Third World; a tendency to consume the latest novelty, thus
> favoring those countries able to produce on a large scale; long
> delays from distributors, who demand firm commitments from
> television channels before buying up the rights to a film; the rules
> governing how long films are allowed to run at commercial
> cinemas (for example, the number of admissions on the first
> day)—disastrous for alternative films, which need time to

establish themselves; the exponential increase in promotion costs . . . ; the almost total incapacity of Third World countries to launch films internationally, because of their weak production capacity and limited local outlets; and the extraordinary barriers built up by sluggish, disinterested bureaucracies.[10]

Mattelart emphasizes the fact that although these technical obstacles are real, they cannot be overcome by purely technical means and should not be conceived in purely technical terms: producers and distributors of film and video must reckon with the historical and social conditions of production within particular nations and negotiate the North-South economic networks in which they are entangled.

To be sure, the process of negotiating international economic and information networks has stimulated a certain amount of productive change with respect to access, fair representation, and so forth. For example, in response to the domination of world news by a few information agencies owned by the industrialized countries, many third-world countries have formed alliances to ensure that they have some control over what is "covered" and how it is covered. However, local responses to the functioning of international networks have also served reactionary ends in both the first and third worlds. Mattelart notes, for instance, that authoritarian regimes in Latin America often shore up the oppressive status quo by welcoming a cultural and informational "internationalism" whose main function is to stifle local cultural initiatives linked to leftist opposition movements.[11] And in France, resistance to U.S. cultural imperialism—which includes everything from ITT and "Dallas" to rock music and cinema—has sometimes involved an abandonment of transnational mixing and cooperation in favor of a chauvinism embodied in groups like the "committee for national identity" formed in the wake of the patriotic fervor sparked by Jack Lang's principled refusal to preside at the American Film Festival in Deauville in 1981.[12]

Thus, if the Socialist government can be credited with sponsoring "cosmopolitan" research projects like Mattelart's, it is simultaneously complicit with a backward-looking nationalism, one that implicitly places France's victimization by the U.S. culture industry on the same plane as Brazil's or Mexico's. A related point is that government-sponsored investigations into the possibility of developing new mechanically reproducible art forms and technology-based distribution networks peaceably stand side by side with, rather than challenging prevailing views of, auratic art forms whose value derives largely from their nontechnological character. In culture, the watchword is reconciliation or, at the very least, peaceful coexistence of conflictual norms and forms.

What is true in the realm of culture is equally true in politics. As Hocquenghem complains in his *Open Letter to Those Who Left the Maoist Collective for the Rotary Club,* the massive betrayal of the left by both the Socialist party and the ex-revolutionaries of May '68 who have come to rule France has resulted in their "reconciliation" with each other and with the right, their unabashed espousal of yuppie values, and their call for military and theological rearmament through spokesmen like Bernard-Henri Lévy, for whom God is a policeman, "the crusher of infidels and Arabs."[13] This betrayal has resulted, too, in a veritable anti-third-world panic of which Pascal Bruckner's *Le Sanglot de l'homme blanc* (1984) is but the most depraved instance: "When will the U.N. list anti-Westernism and antiwhite racism among the crimes against humanity?"[14] Even Régis Debray, a noted defender of third-world nations, goes over to the other side in *Les Empires contre l'Europe,* where he presents Europe as a fortress against the evil empires, particularly, according to Hocquenghem, "the empire of third-world Muslim nationalisms" (174).[15] But then the Socialists have a history of betraying the third world: "After being elected to end the Algerian War, for example, they immediately doubled the number of troops in Algeria" and were equally unscrupulous in invading Chad some twenty years later.[16]

Of course, the Socialist government does inspire enthusiasm on the left in some of its efforts, particularly in its first months in power after a surprise electoral victory, for example in creating a new Ministry on National Solidarity to deal with the problems of foreigners, the handicapped, and homosexuals—heterogeneous groups united by the consciousness of, and the struggle against, their common experience of discrimination in housing, employment, and education.[17] Generally speaking, though, the Socialists' policies are politically wishy-washy or downright conservative, and their rhetoric celebrating the new national "consensus" serves mainly to mask, on the one hand, the racial, ethnic, and class conflicts I discussed in the previous chapter, and on the other, the post-'68 political and cultural void from which many people in France are suffering. In what follows, I hope to show what is at stake in the ways French fiction of the eighties takes up the rhetoric of consensus or reconciliation in addressing the problem of the cultural void, and why it is significant that it should do so under the sign of ravishment by the Maghreb.

Postfeminism as Postcolonial Politics in Evelyne Sullerot

> Dictionnaire français:
> Aman, n.m.: en pays musulman, octroi de la vie sauve à un ennemi vaincu.
> Demander l'aman: Faire sa soumission.
>
> Dictionnaire arabe-français:
> Aman: Paix, trêve, sécurité, sauvegarde, salut; confiance; fidélité à la parole donnée.
> Aahad el Aman: promesse solonnelle de la paix des coeurs et des esprits.
>
> French dictionary:
> Aman, masculine noun: in Muslim countries, the act of sparing the life of a defeated enemy.
> To request aman: to surrender.
>
> Arabic-French dictionary:
> Aman: peace, truce, security, safekeeping, safety; confidence; the keeping of promises.
> Aahad el Aman: the solemn promise of peace in hearts and minds.

Beginning her novel as she does by contrasting the terse, ungiving, monolingual dictionary definition of *aman* with its ample and generous bilingual counterpart, Evelyne Sullerot suggests an answer to the question that will organize her quasi-autobiographical narrative centered on the life of an accomplished French woman named Edith Chaligny: "What counted for her?" (15). What is said to count for Edith is a certain type of relation between individuals and collectivities, a supple relation bodied forth in the interplay of two languages in the Arabic-French dictionary definition of *aman*. Edith embraces *aman* not as mere abstention from lethal violence, but as an ethical principle prescribing the safekeeping of those she loves, including herself, and the keeping of promises that ensure confidence and peace.

At first glance, Sullerot's novel seems to invite the reader to find an embodiment of the positive, prescriptive sense of *aman* in Edith's love affair with Sedik, an Algerian revolutionary whom she meets in France during the Algerian War. Appalled that her country is hunting down Algerians and torturing them in the name of "national security" (49), Edith offers refuge to Sedik and subsequently helps him in his effort to garner financial and political support for Algeria's struggle. Their relationship is characterized as "a real alliance" based on mutual trust, a pleasurable mingling of the lovers' identities, and a joint effort to end French aggression toward Algeria (236). Insofar as it embodies *aman*, the love affair is also clearly meant to figure equitable relations between France and Algeria and, more generally, between first-world and third-world countries. The mixed couple formed by Edith and Sedik between 1957 and 1961 seems to hold the promise of a just resolution to the Algerian War ("We are the opposite of war," proclaim the lovers [226]), as well as peace and justice in future relations between France and Algeria.

Ultimately, however, it is not the five-year love affair itself, but rather the renewal of friendship between Edith and Sedik when they meet in Paris in 1978 that is presented as an allegory of productive relations between France and Algeria. Retrospectively, the love affair is deemed a "failure" by Edith (238), for despite the aging Sedik's insistence that in their youth they were "love itself" (238), Edith remembers all too clearly that their love was increasingly fraught with conflicts in which her interests and desires were systematically subordinated to his. In particular, she recalls his refusal to use contraception, which resulted in pregnancy and a nearly fatal illegal abortion for Edith; Sedik's repeated infidelities, which filled her with jealousy, humiliation, and self-contempt; his brutal insistence that she pose as his submissive wife in their clandestine meetings with Maghrebian freedom fighters ("You're Swiss and you keep your trap shut as much as possible" [210]); and finally, his abandonment of her, in the middle of the peace negotiations, for a "typist or salesgirl who . . . didn't know what the National Liberation Front was" (232)—a cruel and ignoble act that plunged her into debilitating depression. In short, the pleasures and triumphs of the relationship are overshadowed, in Edith's mind, by the pain and injustice of it.

As Sullerot's text makes clear, a key factor in the love affair's failure is that the possibilities it offers Edith for reconstructing her own identity are eclipsed by her experience of coming dangerously close to losing her sense of self when her lover deserts her. On the one hand, Edith's relationship with Sedik enables her to move beyond the constraints of her family situation—her sexually and emotionally unsatisfying marriage and the consuming task of raising five young children—to enjoy what, for a time at least, was a more satisfying love relationship made possible by, and contributing to, both her struggle to end French colonial rule in Algeria and Sedik's struggle to liberate his country. The clearest emblem of the interrelation of these efforts is the composite name "Sedithek" (Sedik and Edith) used by Aimé Césaire, at Sedik's request, to address Edith in dedicating one of his books to her: the poet and theoretician of black identity and resistance to colonialism recognizes Edith as one "who knows what the struggle for identity is" (203-4). Yet on the other hand, it is precisely her relationship to Sedik that, in its abusive aspects, nearly obliterates Edith's sense of identity. For this reason, Edith cautions Sedik not to "rewrite history" (231) by construing their love affair as a success.

The text authorizes Edith's view that it is the renewal of friendship between Edith and Sedik, rather than the love affair itself, that must ultimately be seen as the figure for *aman*. For instance, as Sedik lies in his hospital bed toward the end of his stay in France, the third-person narrator says that Edith, looking on, "is in Sedik's place. She becomes Sedik again, as in the past" (279), with the difference that she now retains, at the same time, a clearer sense of her own interests and desires and thus remains "intact" (239). The empathic mingling of the friends' personal and cultural identities is presented again, although less directly, in a passage linking the figures of Sedik's mother, Edith's mother, and Edith herself, whom Sedik identifies as "his mother in love," since she had "brought him into the world" through her love for him, giving him "what he would never find anywhere else again" (236). Thinking about the nurturing women awaiting the stricken Sedik's return to Algeria, Edith imagines his toothless mother thus:

> [Elle] buvait, lèvres rentrées, son café dans la tasse de Sèvres
> qu'elle lui avait donnée il y a vingt ans, la tasse qu'elle tenait de
> sa propre mère. (281)

[[She] was drinking her coffee, with sunken lips, from the Sèvres porcelain cup [Edith] had given her twenty years ago, the cup that had belonged to her own mother.]

Particularly in these lines emphasizing the maternal, life-giving aspect of their friendship, it is evident that Edith and Sedik are meant to embody the possibility of generous, fruitful, equitable relations between France and Algeria.

Against the claims of Sullerot's protagonist and narrator, however, I want to argue that the 1978 friendship is no more equitable than the love affair had been, and that the appearance of equity in the former depends on a simple reversal of the sexual hierarchy that had organized the latter: with the woman on top, justice appears to have been done. At the time of her 1978 encounter with Sedik, Edith's femininity (I use the term advisedly) is but a thin disguise for her superior intelligence, wealth, and political power, a disguise that does double service. On the one hand, it fools Sedik into accepting his subordination, insofar as it prevents him from recognizing that subordination for what it is. Sedik's Maghrebian machismo supposedly blinds him to *everything but* Edith's femininity—blinds him, that is, to other aspects of her identity that ensure her superior strength: her accomplishments as a researcher at the Institut national de la statistique et des études économiques, her international reputation as a specialist on women's economic issues, and her visibility in France as a potential candidate for a government ministry. On the other hand, Edith's femininity is clearly intended to underwrite a key notion advanced by the novel, namely that Edith's superior strength is never used against Sedik. Noting the reversal of positions that has made her a well-known public figure while consigning the once-notorious Sedik to anonymity, Edith muses about her reluctance to alert her old friend to the change despite his condescension toward her:

Est-ce seulement indulgence? Puissante et douce revanche que la force dont on n'use pas . . . Mais n'est-ce pas de la tendresse, tout aussi bien? (23)

[Is it simply indulgence? Force one doesn't use is also powerful and sweet revenge. But isn't it affection as well?]

Now it is important to note here that because the lovers figure their respective nations, Edith's femininity serves not only to disavow France's continuing domination of Algeria in the postcolonial period, but at the same time, implicitly, to justify that domination: the woman who endured sexual oppression in the past seems to deserve to dominate her former oppressor, particularly since she represents an "enlightened" Western society that supposedly ensures women's equality with men and thus has the moral authority to impose its will on a country whose official policies often favor men. In the analysis that follows, I hope to show that Sullerot enlists certain axioms of postfeminism in France to present an unusually self-serving picture of postcolonial relations between France and its former colonies. The two main axioms are that women have an instinctive aversion to power, and that femininity—that is, traditional constructions of female identity in France, particularly maternity—is an antidote to power.[18] My reading of *L'Aman* will show that, contrary to the text's explicit claims, France *does* use its superior force against Algeria and other Maghrebian societies, and that the main function of femininity in the novel is to disavow this aspect of postcolonial relations. At the same time, I will argue that femininity provides the basis for what Hocquenghem mockingly calls the "reconciliation" of left- and right-wing forces in France, with the result that a leftist critique of France's relations to the Maghreb is made to appear historically obsolete and even harmful to the Maghreb's interests.

Edith's 1978 encounter with Sedik occurs long after the lovers' passion has subsided, and at a point in history when France is presumably disposed to improve relations with its former colony since, according to Edith, the "passion" inspired by the Algerian War is now but a "peaceful memory" (36). Moreover, because the president of Algeria, Boumedienne, is dying, it is suggested that his successor may introduce reforms in domestic and foreign policy that would lay the foundation for better relations with France. In particular, Algeria's "xenophobia," its oppression of women, and its neglect of rural populations are cited as problems ignored not only by Boumedienne but by liberal French supporters such as reporters for *Le Monde* (171).

Already, Boumedienne himself is gesturing toward stronger bonds with France by urging President Giscard "further to improve Algerian-French relations while simultaneously expanding and consolidating cooperative ties" (119). But since the Algerian president's official discourse remains formulaic, it is unclear whether it will produce concrete results. Boumedienne's hackneyed pronouncements are corrected, as it were, by the warmth and vitality of Edith's exchanges with Sedik, which, at first glance, seem more likely to bear fruit. The most telling example is the friends' discussion of the Western Sahara crisis and the fate of the nomadic Saharawi tribes. The Saharawis reject the Moroccan king Hassan's claims that the Western Sahara forms part of Greater Morocco and that its inhabitants are therefore his subjects. Against the king's view, the Saharawis assert both their people's right to self-determination *and* the sovereignty of their Saharawi Arab Democratic Republic (SADR) in the Western Sahara, which has been established in accordance with democratic processes of decolonization. The Saharawis' political arm, the Polisario, is backed by the World Court, the Organization of African Unity, and many Arab countries, including Algeria, where thousands of Saharawis are living in refugee camps.[19] Taking issue with her nephew's and daughter's expression of support for the Saharawis, which consisted in signing a public manifesto, Edith passionately opposes any form of French intervention in the dispute, insisting that the matter be settled by the Maghrebian peoples involved. Edith's rebuke of her nephew and daughter implies a judgment that French intellectuals' and activists' efforts to shape public opinion on this matter constitute undue interference in Maghrebian affairs. Addressing Sedik, Edith says that France's role should be simply to provide a meeting place for the Maghrebian parties to the conflict so that they can work out their differences on their own:

> L'intérêt profond du Maghreb est de ne pas se laisser déchirer de guerres intestines. . . . Il vous faudra bien parler, et parler maghrébin. J'espère pour vous, pour les Sahraouis, pour le Maroc, pour la Mauritanie, que ce sera le plus vite possible. (209)

> [The Maghreb's fundamental interest is not to allow itself to be torn apart by internal strife. . . . You [Maghrebians] will have to talk, and do your talking in Maghrebian. For your [Algeria's] sake and for the sake of the Saharawis, Morocco, and Mauritania, I hope it will happen as soon as possible.]

To which Sedik replies exuberantly, "Edith for president!"

I take it that exchanges such as these are intended to body forth a truly transnational relation between France and Maghrebian countries, one that acknowledges and preserves the nations' historical bonds and intercultural mixing without compromising the former colonies' autonomy. Yet the terms in which Sullerot casts the debate about the Western Sahara bear closer inspection because they distort the international picture in a number of ways and, in fact, finally underwrite French domination of the Maghreb. Sullerot's presentation of the Western Sahara dispute suggests that the principal external threat to the sovereignty of Maghrebian countries comes from the French left, specifically, supporters of the Saharawis such as Edith's daughter, Nadine, and her nephew, Francis. Edith goes so far as to attribute imperialist tendencies to Francis, whom she pictures as "president" of the Saharawis, a figure who would inevitably become a regional bully:

> Je te vois très bien président de la nation Sahraouie et imposant tes vues indépendantes à ta puissante voisine qui vient juste d'accoucher de ton pays par la guerre et à grands frais! (208)

> [I can just see you as president of the Saharawi nation imposing your independent views on your powerful neighbor [Algeria] who just gave birth to your country, and did so at great expense.]

What Sullerot suppresses entirely from the discussion of the Western Sahara dispute, however, is the threat posed to the Saharawi people by the French center and right—the government and the arms dealers who are backing Morocco. Although there is mention of France's "crypto-diplomats itching to meddle in the affair and . . . businessmen eager to carve out a place for themselves," their intervention is cast as no more than an unfortunate possibility (208). In fact, however, France is already supplying most of the arms to Morocco at this time, and although France's official position is neutral, President Giscard, King Hassan's personal friend, is openly hostile to the self-determination of the Saharawis. Despite the Giscard administration's active and lethal involvement in the Western Sahara dispute in 1978, then, only the supposedly intrusive role of the French left is cited as a problem in Sullerot's account.

In supporting the right-wing regime of King Hassan against the SADR and the socialist government of Algeria, which affirm democracy at least in principle, the French president is aligned with Presidents Ford and Carter of the United States. Like Giscard, Ford and Carter maintain an official stance of neutrality on the Western Sahara issue while arming King Hassan, only they do so with weapons paid for by a conservative Saudi regime eagerly helping its American allies in the Oval Office and in Congress to circumvent the law prohibiting the sale of arms abroad for offensive use.[20] Considering Morocco's backing by a number of powerful conservative governments in its repression of the Saharawis, it is clear that Sullerot had to go to some lengths to construe the French left as the primary imperialist force in the region.

A related issue is that Sullerot occults Morocco's *actual* aggression against a relatively weak SADR in order to focus the reader's attention instead on the *potential* aggression of the SADR toward its present supporter, Algeria, on whom it would supposedly "impose" its views. Seen from this angle, the Western Sahara dispute seems to arise from instabilities that are purely internal to the Maghreb, so that French intervention—from the right or the left—is no longer an issue. The only way to account for this new focus on the unlikely prospect of SADR violence toward Algeria is to say that the problem has now become not a particular instance of the abuse of power, but rather the dangers of power in general, particularly when power represses the interests it represents and the material relations that produced it. Sullerot's depiction of the nascent SADR's will to power calls to mind Marguerite Duras's contention that "power of whatever kind, the power of the people or of a faction, is always a nauseating episode in the history of man and the world," and that the abuse of power stems principally from men's fear of sorrow and pain: "Man cannot bear sorrow, he palms it off, he has to get away from it, he projects it outside himself in hallowed, ancestral demonstrations which are his recognized transfers—battle, outcries, the show of discourse, cruelty."[21]

It is worth noting here that Sullerot writes of the SADR's potential violence toward Algeria in terms of an ungrateful male child's rejection of the loving mother who has "just given birth" to him, as if masculine violence and feminine nurture were antithetical essences; the evocation of "maternal" processes, both corporeal and semiotic, in Edith's plea for nonintervention is apparently intended to forestall an abuse of power in the Maghreb. However, as a response to the Western Sahara crisis, Sullerot's inscription of the maternal merely diverts attention from the main issue—Morocco's power over the SADR—and functions instead as a sentimental show of discourse providing an alibi for power. In the Western Sahara dispute, the significant mother figure is not Algeria but Morocco, a bad mother waging deadly war on a people whose minority status she is intent on enforcing with French-supplied radar sensors and U.S.-supplied cluster bombs developed during the Vietnam War, "mother bombs" and baby "bomblets" like those that would be used more than a decade later in the U.S. assault on Iraq in what Saddam Hussein would call "the mother of all battles."[22]

Equally disturbing in this context is Sullerot's presentation of France as a helpmate blessed with feminine tact, a mother country who provides her warring sons, the "enemy brothers" Morocco and Algeria, with a "discreet villa" where they can settle their differences "discreetly" (209). The repeated references to discretion in fact betray the immodesty of Mother France, who seems intent on ravishing her Maghrebian sons, just as Edith ravishes Sedik with her display of respect for Maghrebian autonomy: Edith's show of discourse makes Sedik desire her power over him. If readers are seduced by this maternal vision, it is perhaps because France's power over Morocco, Algeria, and the Western Sahara is embodied in the character of Edith, a researcher concerned with the lives and well-being of women throughout the world, a woman who claims to be "allergic" to power (29). Without bitterness, Edith renews her bond with Sedik even though he had betrayed her many years earlier, just before the negotiations that would formalize Algeria's independence from France. Thus, when Sedik cries out triumphantly, in English, "Edith for president," we are encouraged to see Edith not as the French counterpart to Jimmy Carter in the Maghreb, but rather as a capable and level-headed woman who instinctively protects her Maghrebian offspring just as she nurtures her native French children in her work as a researcher and government planner:

> Des vies, des vies, des âges, des emplois, des cuisines, des chambres avec des lits secrets, des vies échelonnées. . . . Prévoir pour eux. Les ramasser du regard en grands chiffres en grandes courbes, avec cette excitation étrangement maternelle de la responsabilité, comme si elle les avait tous mis au monde et en était comptable et redevable envers l'avenir. (29)

> [Lives, lives, ages, jobs, kitchens, bedrooms with hidden beds, lives spread out. . . . To provide for them. To gather them with a look into large figures, large curves, with this strangely maternal excitement of responsibility, as if she had brought them all into

the world and, from the standpoint of the future, was accountable
for them, owed something to them.]

In short, Edith's maternal vocation is both an allegory of and the
alibi for France's aggressive actions in the Maghreb.

By deploying the figures of the feminine helpmate and the essentially maternal woman in her presentation of Franco-Algerian
relations, Sullerot resurrects the twin myths of women's instinctive
aversion to power and true womanhood as the antidote to power,
putting them in the service of an antiegalitarian postcolonial politics. France assumes the guise of a woman who, like Edith, has
proved capable of accepting great "responsibility" yet remains "allergic" to power, a woman who uses her wealth and position the
way Edith uses her furs and her fame—not to embarrass her less
fortunate Algerian friend, but to seduce the internal forces of repression, such as the agent from the DST (the equivalent of the
FBI), in order to persuade them that people like Sedik are lovable
human beings rather than "terrorists" (113). France nurtures her
children and mediates relations among them in such a way as to
foster their growth and autonomy; the gun she will use if the children get out of hand remains concealed in her purse. Like Edith,
France is a mature woman who tactfully spares the unfaithful lover
of her youth, Algeria, the pain of knowing that she is now the
stronger partner: "he's got enough to deal with in resigning himself to anonymity, without her going and inflicting her own little
notoriety on him" (24). With equal delicacy, France deftly refrains
from pointing out to her former lover (Algeria) that his successor
(the United States?) was a better partner, one who "did not disap-
point" her (232). In short, France's hold on Algeria is acknowledged on condition that it be understood in terms of maternal so-
licitude: we must view her youthful passion as a force that has
been transmuted into tenderness—a tenderness haunted, to be
sure, by the desire for revenge, but untainted by *acts* of revenge:
"force one doesn't use is . . . powerful and sweet revenge." We
must interpret France's superior strength as a benevolent force
("isn't it affection as well?"), a woman's just reward for the effort of
overcoming despair in the face of abandonment.

Of course, it should be noted that the idealization of France as a
tactful companion and bountiful mother is undercut, to a limited
extent, by the functioning of the text, which embraces postmod-

ernism by self-consciously interweaving contradictory narratives of national identity reflecting social, political, and cultural divisions in France at various historical moments. For example, Edith's view of France as an innocent bystander or a potential helpmate to Algeria in the Western Sahara crisis is contradicted by developments in the frame narrative, where the DST agent reveals to Edith that Sedik has been followed throughout his stay in Paris either because he has a role in the negotiation of the Western Sahara conflict or because he is likely to occupy an influential position in the government of Boumedienne's successor. It is clear that the DST regards Sedik as a "terrorist" on account of his activity during the Algerian Revolution and, more generally, on account of his Arab identity (113). Moreover, the DST agent's disapproval of Edith for harboring Sedik during the Algerian Revolution mirrors that of her father, who could not reconcile her support for Algeria's struggle with his notion of patriotism despite the fact that, during World War II, he had harbored Jewish children in the same country house where Edith hid Sedik.

Monolithic and idealized notions of French identity are undercut by other means as well, including the narrator's use of oxymoron in characterizing the French as a "hypercivilized tribe" and the reference to caricatures of "l'esprit français" found in "German, Russian, and English novels of the nineteenth century whose heroes, brave and true, come up against the caustic capriciousness they think they encounter in Paris" (69). To the extent that the novel's protagonist is associated with these "heroes," Edith herself offers a counterimage of French identity, although one that is no more reliable than those generated by romantics who "think" they know what Frenchness really is. Named for a character in an Alexandre Dumas play—a "horrible melodrama" inspired by a painting with the "hyper-romantic" title *Edith with the Long Hair Searching for the Body of Harold at the Battle of Hastings* (76)—Edith is aware of casting herself in two contradictory roles in recalling her love affair with Sedik. In the first, she is a brave and true French freedom fighter who has risked her life carrying money across international borders and into embassies in support of Algeria's cause, a faithful woman carelessly impregnated and ignobly betrayed by her Algerian lover. In the second, on the other hand, she is a prima donna determined to play the most flattering part in the drama, that of innocent victim (234). In short, Sullerot's postmodern figuration of

French identity calls attention not just to the sheer instability and multiplicity of images of Frenchness, but to the ways in which conflicting yet overlapping interests, be they national, aesthetic, feminist, or unreconstructed "feminine" ones, come into play in the generation and interpretation of those images.

However, Sullerot's novel does not allow the incongruities of French identity to stand, but rather attempts to resolve them in the last pages, mainly by eliminating the conflicts between Edith and the DST agent on the one hand, and between Edith's recollections and the frame narrative on the other. Although it is still uncertain whether Sedik came to France "discreetly to meet with Moroccans" on the Western Sahara issue, to "make contacts for the post-Boumedienne era," or to fulfill his promise to return to the country house, La Clairière, before dying (280), it is evident that, thanks to Edith's powers of seduction, the DST agent has been purged of his hostility toward Sedik. His gentle behavior makes clear that he now shares Edith's benevolent desire to know why the Algerian traveled to France: "The commissioner touches [Edith's] shoulder and leans toward her. He speaks very softly. . . . He has a kind smile" (280).

In attenuating the disjuncture between the frame narrative and Edith's recollections, the postfeminism of Sullerot's text not only reconciles the right and the left in Giscard's France but also makes of this reconciliation the rose-colored lens through which the colonial past and the postcolonial present are to be read. Together, Edith and the DST agent read the letter Sedik has left for Edith before disappearing, a letter in which he addresses Edith as "Sedithek," the composite name Aimé Césaire had used in acknowledging the importance of Edith's "struggle for identity." As Edith explains the meaning of the name in hushed tones, the figure of the couple she forms with the agent merges with that of Edith and Sedik, with the result that the Franco-Algerian pair engaged in revolutionary struggle in the 1950s is *equated* with the French pair embodying the political "consensus" in France in the late 1970s, as if these very different alliances were alike in fostering egalitarian relations between France and Algeria.

At this point in the narrative, the agent's reading of the Algerian War is no longer at odds with Edith's; his "kind smile" tells us that for him, as for Edith, that conflict is now but a "great, peaceful memory." As for the present, it bears the mark of Algeria's demise—Sedik has heart trouble and is undoubtedly near death—but this mark is repressed, expelled from the frame of Edith's, and France's, love story: "Neither his old age, nor his illness, nor, least of all, his death could be part of our story," says Edith (282). The bond between France and Algeria thus survives in Sullerot's text only as an untroubling memory and does so, as it were, with Algeria's blessing: Sedik's letter closes with the Arabic expression, "Allah-i-Khalek," which Edith translates as "God's blessing, so that He will protect me" (282). In *L'Aman*, the bond between the French left and the French right finally prevails over both the transnational experience of ravishment and the friendship that grows out of it, a friendship that serves, in the last analysis, mainly to strengthen France's grip on Algeria.

Marie Cardinal's Roots and the Flowering of Neocolonialism

With the publication of *Au pays de mes racines* in 1980, the Pied-Noir writer Marie Cardinal returns to the feminist critique of colonialism that figured centrally in the 1975 autobiographical novel that made her famous, *The Words to Say It*. At issue in the later text, presented as a diary and travel narrative, is the fifty-year-old narrator's return to her motherland, Algeria, after a twenty-four-year absence in an attempt to recover the life-sustaining "archaic" pleasures she had enjoyed there as a child (88). In Cardinal's text "Algeria" is a figure for these pleasures, which find their theoretical articulation in Julia Kristeva's notion of the semiotic—signifying processes associated with presymbolic "maternal" relations and with the experience of jouissance.[23] I want to argue that in *Au pays de mes racines* the trope "Algeria" and the semiotic processes it figures have two contradictory functions that are at odds with each other politically: one is historical and politicized, while the other is ahistorical and essentializing. On the one hand, in accordance with Kristeva's early formulations of the semiotic/symbolic relation, "Algeria" appears as a potentially revolutionary force operating at various levels in the life of the independent nation, not only within and between subjectivities but also in concrete democratic struggles for social change. Distinct from the forms of power and subjection that constitute Algeria as a nation state—material and symbolic forms that, for Cardinal as for Kristeva in the early 1970s, are themselves inherently unstable and subject to change—Cardinal's "Algeria" seems capable of unsettling the hierarchies organizing social relations in that country, hierarchies that have survived from the colonial period or have been instituted and legitimated by nationalist ideologies since independence.

On the other hand, however, "Algeria" also appears as a non-manipulable force operating in a space that is absolutely divorced from democratic struggles and the institutions they seek to change. Simultaneously subjective and cosmic, this space is always coded feminine and always situated outside of power, outside of history. In this version, Cardinal's presentation of the "Algeria"/Algeria relation corresponds to Kristeva's later articulations of the semiotic/symbolic relation, notably in her studies of the abject, where the semiotic no longer plays a role in political struggles but is seen instead mainly as a place of retreat for the beleaguered individual, especially the avant-garde writer or artist whose freedom is increasingly threatened in modern bureaucratic societies, particularly authoritarian societies.[24] In its feminine guise as a refuge from power and politics, Cardinal's "Algeria" bears a striking resemblance to Sullerot's France in L'Aman. Whereas Sullerot casts France as a benevolent woman who is "allergic" to power, mobilizing the feminine flatly to deny French aggression against North Africa in the Giscard era, Cardinal uses it more subtly, suggesting that what she calls the "essential" Algeria (193)—the feminine Algeria that eternally eludes power—can never be an object of aggression for any power.

In terms of the narrator's subjective experience, "Algeria" also has a double, contradictory meaning that has important implications for her and other French people's relations with Algerians. It figures, on the one hand, what Kathleen Woodward calls "mature narcissism, a benevolent narcissism" facilitated by aging—one that is progressive rather than retrogressive insofar as it has let go its aggressive component and "coexists with mature relations with others"; indeed, it might be seen as "a condition for benevolent relations with others."[25] On the other hand, however, "Algeria" also figures the reversion to a primary narcissism characterized by Freud, in his essay "On Narcissism," as a childlike "self-contentment *and inaccessibility*"[26] that, in the adult, according to J.-B. Pontalis, constitutes a nostalgic retreat from social relations in the effort to "preserve an undivided totality," an idyllic primary state.[27]

Thus, if the mature, benevolent narcissism of Cardinal's narrator fosters relations with Algerians that can help to bring about the subjective and social transformations called for in Cardinal's text, her retrogressive narcissism ignores these transformations or even hinders them by encouraging blissful acceptance of the nonegalitarian postcolonial status quo.

For the narrator of *Au pays de mes racines,* the prospect of returning to the motherland is cause for joy but also for considerable anxiety. Roughly the first half of the narrative interweaves the narrator's childhood memories of Algeria with reflections on her ambivalence about the return in the weeks preceding her departure from Paris. As we will see, the narrator's experience of family conflict and colonial war and her attendant "bad conscience" (73) make her fear the return to Algeria as much as she desires it. In the latter part of the book, childhood memories are interwoven with accounts of the narrator's impassioned responses to the independent nation that had once been her home. Declaring that the present "fills [her] with enthusiasm" (142), she says she is particularly eager to see how the Algerian people are negotiating three major questions facing them nearly twenty years after independence: the means and ends of modernizing the nation, the role of Islam in contemporary life, and the social and political situation of women.

The hinge between the two parts of the book—between colonial Algeria and the independent nation, between past and present, childhood and adulthood, the loss of life-sustaining pleasures and their recovery—is made explicit only in the last pages. These pages disclose the sources of the narrator's ambivalence about her return to Algeria and the force that allows her to overcome them—what she calls her "will to jouissance" (192). Toward the end of the narrative, we learn of the narrator's panic upon arriving in Algiers and her reflex to fight it in order to have access to the pleasures Algeria promises the Pied-Noir woman of fifty. What triggers her panic is the sight of the main post office in Algiers, which was the site of two related traumas of her youth. First, it was the place where, in the narrator's early adolescence, her mother had inflicted upon her a "horrible, incurable wound" (179) with the revelation that many years before, because she was pregnant on the eve of her divorce, she had done everything possible to abort the pregnancy that finally resulted, in spite of everything, in her daughter's birth. A victim of patriarchy and colonial ideology but also their willing accomplice, the narrator's mother had taught her daughter a lesson she would never forget: she must fear her sexual desires and suppress them as much as possible, in keeping with Catholic beliefs that subordinated women's desires to men's, just as they legitimated French Catholics' domination of Algerian Muslims who supposedly worshiped a false god. At the same time that her mother had taught her a cruel and lasting lesson, however, she had brutally rejected her daughter, the fruit of her own hated sexual desire, "mutilating" the girl's body and mind (179) and causing her to turn to what was immediately available—Algeria itself—as a surrogate mother:

> Je me suis accrochée à ce que j'ai pu, à la ville, au ciel, à la mer, au Djurdjura. Je me suis agrippée à eux, ils sont devenus ma mère et je les ai aimés comme j'aurais voulu l'aimer, elle. (181)

> [I hung onto whatever I could—the city, the sky, the sea, the Djurdjura Mountains. I clung to them; they became my mother and I loved them as I would have liked to love her.]

A second trauma associated with the main post office is a bloody massacre the narrator witnessed there during the Algerian War, years after her abandonment by her mother. For the narrator, the post office recalls the violence and injustice of a colonial war that was murdering Algeria, the adoptive mother she loved.

Once she confronts the anxiety-inducing personal memories of family conflict and war, however, she is able to "evacuate" (192) them into a realm of memory that lies beyond her self. Having overcome the trauma of seeing the main post office, she is able to gain access to the Algeria she had loved as a child: she finds it "intact, as beautiful as in my fondest memories, and sometimes even more beautiful" (160). She writes:

> Et puis, très rapidement, cette base immuable et magnifique s'est transformée en présent. Un présent qui ressemble aux champs fleuris de mon enfance. (160)

> [And then, very quickly, this magnificent and immutable base was transformed into the present—a present resembling the flowering fields of my childhood.]

The narrator's contact with this "immutable base" at once dispels her ambivalence about returning to her motherland and enables her to yield completely to her will to jouissance, the force linking the sensuous childhood pleasures related in the first part of the book to the adult pleasures related in the second part, that is, the recovery of sensuous delight in the earliest signifying processes, but also the discovery of transformative processes at work in the independent nation at the time of the writing.

Yet the will to jouissance is not simply an irresistible force that triumphs over ambivalence, for it is itself a source of ambivalence associated with the return to Algeria, the place where the narrator first experienced jouissance:

> Je voulais jouir d'Alger et de l'Algérie. Cette volonté de jouissance était énorme, je m'en rends compte maintenant. C'est probablement elle qui me faisait peur avant de partir, elle qui m'a tenue si longtemps de ma terre. . . . Ainsi, dès la première heure, j'ai été libérée du passé. Il était là, partout, il aurait fallu que je sois aveugle pour ne pas le voir, mais il ne me pesait pas. J'étais certaine de ne pas être venue pour lui. Ce que je désirais retrouver était au-delà de lui, c'était à la fois plus ancien et vivant, je désirais retrouver l'essentiel de ce pays, son souffle, son feu, son dedans. Ils étaient là, intacts eux aussi, et je m'y suis livrée dans la joie et la sérénité. (192-93)

> [I wanted to enjoy Algiers and Algeria. I now realize that this will to jouissance was immense. Thus, from the first hour of my stay, I was freed from the past. It was there all around—I would have had to be blind not to see it—but it didn't weigh me down. I was sure I hadn't come for its sake. What I wanted to retrieve was beyond the past—it was older and it was alive. I wanted to recover what was essential about this country, its breath, its fire, its inside. They were there, intact as well, and I yielded to them joyfully and serenely.]

Because fear of the will to jouissance ultimately takes priority over personal trauma, guilt, and colonial war as an obstacle to recovering what is "essential" about Algeria, and because of the emphasis on experiences of jouissance *in* Algeria throughout the text, it seems clear that, for Cardinal's narrator, the "essential" Algeria is first and foremost the site of jouissance.

In *Au pays de mes racines*, jouissance is presented mainly as a motility associated with early childhood experiences that are seen as "archaic, primary, primordial" (88). Frequently, it is cast in terms of an infant's relation to her mother, as when the narrator speaks of the soothing sound of the waves lapping the shore at Tipasa:

> [Les vagues] entrent dans mon berceau comme des nourrices pleines de lait. . . . Bercez-moi encore, j'ai besoin de vos seins lourds. (161)
>
> [(The waves) come into my cradle like wet-nurses full of milk. . . . Rock me some more, I need your heavy breasts.]

As in the passage just cited, the figure for the mother is often a feature of the Algerian landscape (here, the waves at Tipasa). However, the mother (or adoptive mother) may also assume the aspect of the entire cosmos, holding the child in an oceanic embrace. For instance, floating in the Mediterranean Sea, the narrator exclaims euphorically:

> Le monde est ma nourrice, il me tient en sécurité dans ses bras, il m'enchante. (186)
>
> [The world is my nurse; it holds me safely in its arms, it delights me.]

The cosmic, rhythmic sensation of contentment and plenitude, evoked in the above passages not only through the images but through the lilting rhythms of Cardinal's prose, is given a name by the narrator: "love." And this is what she claims to be seeking in Algeria:

> Je sais que le rythme invariable qui fait se balancer la mer et mon corps est celui de l'amour. . . . Et c'est peut-être parce que je suis incapable de nommer l'amour qu'il est si grand, si important, si grave. Rythme régulier, alternatif: l'autre-moi, moi-l'ailleurs, le différent-moi, moi-le-dehors. L'univers et moi, moi dedans lui, lui dedans moi. Parfaits. (94)
>
> [I know that the invariable rhythm that rocks the sea and my body is that of love. . . . And it is perhaps because I'm incapable of naming love that it is so great, so important, so grave. Regular, alternating rhythm: the other-me, me-elsewhere, the different-me, me-the-outside. The universe and me, me in it, it in me. Perfect.]

Now, as I indicated earlier, "Algeria" as a trope for semiotic processes and the site of jouissance sometimes works to unsettle symbolic formations; it has revolutionary political effects that are most clearly figured in, but are not restricted to, the realm of poetic language. For example, the semiotic "Algeria" is integral to struggles that will productively change the meanings and social functions of modernization, Islam, and female identity in the psychic, libidinal, ideological, economic, and political formations of the independent nation. Most often it takes the form of an irrepressible motility, as in the image of the Algerian people who, unlike their rulers, still regard the revolution as a reality: they are "still mobilized, ready to brandish their pitchforks and raise their fists" (167). The transformative power of "Algeria" is evident, too, in the "agility" of the Algerian university women with whom the narrator converses, women whose "slender, lively gestures" now inform their teaching, their arguments, their efforts to convince others: "they're professors, they're no longer *fatmas*" (158). It can be discerned as well in rhythms and figures of the Algerian language that convey the mobility and inexhaustibility of the Algerians' desire. Says a bartender to the narrator:

> En arabe on dit: "Quand le ciel est rouge, selle ton cheval, mets ta gandoura et prépare-toi à galoper." (166)
>
> [In Arabic there is a saying, "When the sky is red, saddle your horse, put on your gandoura, and get ready to gallop."]

As for the transformative power of Islam, it is apparent in the narrator's recollection of figures from popular culture that peopled the stories told to her as a child by the Arab women who worked for her family, for instance, "Mohammed and his winged horse" (18).

The narrator is not content merely to observe these forces at work in Algeria, but wants to imbue her own writing with them in order to foster "permanent revolution" in the world and in her own being (184). Yet she is reluctant to use the words "permanent revolution" because "they have already been recuperated . . . by the usual blindness and the usual avidity of the powers that be" (184); accordingly, she tries to find other words, "floating words, images on the move" (166) capable of eluding the powers that "put uniforms on bodies and minds" (168). As is evident from the above examples and from repeated references to the narrator's "desire to talk about the revolution, desire to talk about women" (160), "Algeria"—at once the site of jouissance and the figure for politically productive semiotic processes—signifies both the transformations observed by the narrator and her attempts to inscribe them in her own writing.

Without presuming to speak for Algerians, the narrator situates herself on the side of those who are "still mobilized" for revolution and against those who "are no longer making revolution but rather are organizing it"—the "scribes . . . who are defining once and for all the institutions of the Algerian people" (167). Similarly, she is with the Algerian women, whose "lively gestures" inform their efforts to change their lives, and against those who serve as mouthpieces for the phallocratic state, for example the bacteriologist writing for the national newspaper *El Moudjahid*, who denies the existence of women's subordination in modern Algeria and places all the blame for women's oppression in the past on the colonizers. The woman's article asserts that "since 1970 women have been participating unselfconsciously in the construction of the nation, and I am part of this new generation of women" (118-19), but her claims are contradicted by the narrator's observations about the women she sees:

> [A la plage] on en voit quelquefois qui arrivent surchargées de couffins, le haïk en bataille, le hadjar de travers. Elles restent tout habillées sous le soleil de plomb à s'occuper des enfants, à préparer les repas. Elles ne bougent pas de leur place. (172)

> [(At the beach) one sometimes sees [women] arriving, loaded down with baskets, their *haik* flapping wildly, their *hadjar* askew. They remain completely dressed in the blazing heat, taking care of the children, preparing the meal. They don't budge from their places.]

Where economic development is concerned, the narrator criticizes the proponents of a modernization that would force Algerians to adopt both Western work rhythms and the ideologies that justify them. In particular, she points to the neocolonial paternalism and hypocrisy of the European advisers who "see Algeria as a dependent country" (168), saying:

> Je pense à ce qui se passe dans les pays respectifs de ces hommes et je me demande comment ils peuvent avoir autant d'assurance. Le goulag, l'apartheid, les ingérences de la CIA, la planification de toutes les formes de racisme, la pollution, est-ce que c'est ça qui leur donne leurs certitudes? (169)

[I think of what is happening in the respective countries of these men and I wonder how they can be so self-assured. The Gulag, apartheid, CIA meddling, the institutionalization of every form of racism, pollution—is that what makes them so sure of themselves?]

Yet she recognizes the economic necessity of modernizing in accordance with democratic principles, citing with approval the poet Malek Haddad who wrote, "Without Islam we are nothing. Without socialism we can do nothing" (163). Acknowledging the importance of Islam for the identity of the Algerian people, she candidly promotes its progressive force (figured as Mohammed's "winged horse") while registering disapproval of its oppressive effects in the political field. Says an old friend of the narrator's who has resettled in Algeria, for example, "The regime is hardening; it demands more discipline and is becoming more bureaucratized. Islamism is gaining ground and fueling intolerance of foreigners" (134). In sum, by various means Cardinal casts "Algeria" both as an experience of presymbolic pleasures *and* a force capable of disrupting oppressive power formations and fueling struggles to reconfigure the modern nation.[28] At the same time, she presents "Algeria" as a set of processes that enable her narrator to identify with the *differences* that distinguish her from Algerians, rather than with the similarities between them; she can move between the two cultures that have formed her without "cutting off one of her two heads" (17). Like the storks who migrate continually between Alsace and the ancient city of Timgad, she is a "hybrid" (108) who embodies not only war and the long history of European conquest in the Maghreb, but also birth and renewal in Euro-Maghrebian relations. In short, "Algeria" enables the narrator to engage with Algerians in the effort to change the world both subjectively and socially.

On the other hand, however, "Algeria" functions in Cardinal's text as a retreat from engagement in democratic cultural-political struggles. In fact, her text discredits those struggles by situating them alongside other power formations that are no longer seen as inherently heterogeneous, unstable, and changeable but rather as monolithic and all but immutable. Power becomes a uniformly oppressive, masculine force located in a sphere from which an "immutable," idealized, feminine "Algeria" is said to be excluded entirely. Insofar as "Algeria" is the site of semiotic processes that produce jouissance, its pleasurable, inexhaustible, nonmanipulable force now operates in a realm apart, where the individual's relation with the cosmos is at issue, but not social relations themselves:

> Oui, je l'avoue, c'est ce qu'il y en a en moi d'archaïque que je recherche et j'ai l'impression que c'est par la terre elle-même que je l'aborderai, pas par les gens. Les gens portent une culture qui embrouille l'archaïsme; je le voudrais brut. (42-43)

> [Yes, I admit that I'm after what is most archaic in me, and it seems to me that it's through the land itself that I'll gain access to it, not through the people. People carry in them a culture that obscures archaism, whereas I want it raw.]

The retreat from culture into an unproblematic natural world is especially apparent in the figure of the garden paradise in which the narrator no longer feels the need for social connection. For example, upon rediscovering the gardens that had delighted her as a child, she says:

> Maintenant, je sais que ces jardins sont à la fois le paradis et Dieu et que ma jouissance à y être ne doit pas se laisser troubler par la recherche d'autre chose. (129-30)

> [Now I know that these gardens are at once paradise and God and that my enjoyment of them must not let itself be troubled by the search for something else.]

At certain moments, then, what is important about the gardens and other features of the Algerian landscape is that "the rhythms of the universe common to all human beings entered me there" (88); they now have little to do with Algeria per se. Unlike the "flowering fields" that had connected the narrator's past and present experience with that of the Algerians, the "gardens" serve mainly to revitalize the narrator emotionally and professionally. We are told, for instance, that in the weeks preceding her journey to Algeria, the narrator is unable to write because of her feeling of "emptiness" (84), which recalls the "emptiness" (127) she had felt as a young girl mutilated and abandoned by her mother. We can infer from this that a key function of the trip to Algeria is to restore the narrator's desire to live and to write. The uprooted Pied-Noir writer returns, then, not only to the open "fields" where she min-

gles with the Algerian people, but also to the bounded territory of
the gardens—"gardens enclosed by high yellow walls and rusted
grilles"—in order that her "desires again sprout wings" (19).

Under the guise of freeing her narrator from the "moorings of
humanity" (87) so that she may find her roots in jouissance, Cardinal makes two highly problematic moves. First, she implicitly opposes a "natural," feminine subject of jouissance to an artificial,
masculine subject of national, colonial, and postcolonial culture,
casting archaic subjective processes less as the product of social in-
teractions and cultural inscription than as a precultural paradise,
one that is the same for all human beings and is utterly immune to
the "spectacle" of power (54). In Lacanian terms, she relies on a
notion of the Imaginary as an autonomous primary gestalt, presenting it as a blissful state of assumed plenitude untroubled by the
hostility, rivalry, and aggressivity associated with that moment in
Lacan's early formulations.[29] In other words, precisely at the moment where her text claims to be attending to radical alterity, it
banishes a host of differences, construing femininity as a site unmarked not only by aggressivity but by history, nationality, class,
and race. In short, it discounts the play of difference and desire—
the big Other of discourse—in "the distance taken up by the subject in its relation to the other, which is opposed to it as the small
other, as belonging to the imaginary dyad."[30] So, for example, contrasting women's experience with the workings of power, Cardinal's narrator says:

> Comme le pouvoir est bête et manque d'humilité! Il devrait de
> temps en temps faire du couscous, ou du pot-au-feu s'il préfère.
> . . . Il apprendrait le respect, la patience, la confiance, il serait à
> l'écoute de l'ailleurs, de l'autre, du différent, de ce qui a une vie
> propre et ne peut, en aucune manière, être manipulé n'importe
> comment. (53-54)

> [How stupid power is, and how lacking in humility! He should
> make couscous once in a while, or pot roast if he prefers. . . . He
> would learn respect, patience, confidence; he would listen for the
> elsewhere, the other, the different, that which has a life of its own
> and cannot in any way be manipulated at will.]

Clearly, the narrator would have us believe that on both sides of
the Mediterranean, true women constitute a homogeneous class

that attends to the differences that power, by its very nature, denies.

Second, in making "Algeria" the figure for an ahistorical, acultural paradise, Cardinal draws on and inadvertently underwrites the very colonialist stereotypes that she is at pains to criticize in other parts of the narrative, namely the notions that Algeria is uncivilized, underdeveloped, and feminine, that is, vulnerable to penetration. It makes little difference, ultimately, that in Cardinal's version these attributes are "good" rather than "bad" because, like many of her French literary predecessors (notably André Gide in *L'Immoraliste*), she leaves the structure of colonial domination in place, provisionally inverting its terms in service of the European traveler's pleasure.

Cardinal's strategy of casting "Algeria" as an autonomous, idyllic primary state has unfortunate repercussions in parts of the text where contemporary postcolonial politics is thematized. The most obvious one is that Algeria, as modern nation-state, is conflated with the idealized "Algeria" insofar as it is presented as a completely autonomous entity whose conflicts, far from being bound up with the international division of labor as they had been in the opening pages, are now seen as purely internal. Still fraught with ambivalence about her return to Algeria on the eve of her departure from Paris, the narrator muses ironically:

> Les éboueurs sont en train de ramasser les ordures. . . . Ils sont tous africains. Je me demande si demain ce seront des Français qui ramasseront les ordures à Alger. (106)

> [The sanitation workers are collecting the trash. . . . They're all African. I wonder if the French will be the ones collecting the trash in Algiers tomorrow.]

Once she is in Algeria, however, the international networks that impose Algeria's dependence on wealthy nations fade from view. For although the narrator acknowledges and comments critically on the function of Algeria's "advisers," suggesting, as we have seen, that their assurance derives from disavowal of racial conflicts, environmental disaster, and imperialism in their own countries, she nonetheless states categorically in the last pages that while the socialist revolution brought "miraculous" changes at the time of independence, offering land and houses to dispossessed Algerians, the socialism of today is an economic failure for which the inefficient and corrupt Algerian government alone is responsible:

> Il n'y a plus à attendre que les colons s'en aillent pour que la
> misère soit moins lourde. (195)

> [It's no longer a matter of waiting for the *colons* to go away so that
> the poverty may be alleviated.]

Similarly, where Algerian women's oppression is concerned, she disavows any possible connection between it and the functioning of international capitalism, declaring flatly, "The [colonial] oppressors are gone" (119).

The bad faith in attributing absolute autonomy to Algeria is especially apparent in the narrator's paternalistic view of the Algerian masses. Fervent partisans of the social transformations begun at the time of independence, the Algerian people are said to believe that the revolution is still in progress (and thus to be dupes of the government), whereas the narrator sees that the revolution is over and is now being "organized" as an oppressive instance of power: "[The Algerian people] aren't really aware that the scribes have already moved in" (167). At this juncture, the observations of Cardinal's narrator imply that Algeria is autonomous only in the sense that it produces its own problems; it must still rely on first-world observers like herself to theorize them.

To a certain extent, then, the narrator colludes with neocolonial ideologies that underwrite economic policies of enforced dependence. Yet she remains unaware of her collusion, in part because she regards her past—that is, her unequivocal opposition to French colonialism long before the Algerian War—as the guarantee of her solidarity with Algeria in the present:

> Je n'ai rien à me faire pardonner. . . . J'ai été contre ce que
> représentait ma famille: la France et ses conquêtes, son empire
> colonial, sa morgue, son mépris, son racisme, son humanitarisme
> hypocrite. . . . Il n'a jamais été question pour moi de faire le
> moindre compromis à ce sujet. (153-54)

> [There's nothing to forgive me for. I was against everything my
> family stood for: France and its conquests, its colonial empire, its
> arrogance, its disdain, its racism, its hypocritical humanitarianism.
> . . . I never made the slightest compromise in that regard.][31]

Rather than coming to terms with the ways her narrator is implicated in postcolonial structures of domination, Cardinal construes "Algeria" as an autonomous, acultural, ahistorical realm of jouissance, thereby displacing her more differentiated articulations in which "Algeria" involves a continual interplay of culturally diverse and often conflicting elements. The latter include, for example, not only the pleasures of bilingual glossolalia—"*laroulila, ladiguedondaine*" (19)—but, at the same time, the assignment of the adult singers of nonsense rhymes and lullabies to positions in the colonial and class hierarchies, as in this evocation of the bedtime rituals performed by a Spanish servant, an Algerian servant, and the narrator's French mother:

> Quand c'est Carmen, [la berceuse] est plus proche de moi. Quand c'est Daïba, elle me plaît tout à fait, pourtant je me sens déjà coupable de me laisser endormir par elle. Je sais déjà que c'est le rythme de ma mère qui est le "meilleur." (27)

> [When it's Carmen, [the lullaby] is closer to me. When it's Daïba, it pleases me no end, yet I already feel guilty for letting myself be put to sleep by her. I already know that my mother's rhythm is the "best."]

It is the imbrication of social conflict in pleasure—and the play of pleasure in the social transformations wrought by conflict—that is most compelling about *Au pays de mes racines*, yet this feature of the text is continually muted by the disavowal of conflict in the narrator's nostalgia for an imagined childhood paradise.

Unfortunately, Cardinal's effort to disavow the conflicts of the postcolonial situation leads her to deny, simultaneously, the possibility or even the desirability of productive postcolonial political engagement between the French and the Algerians and, more generally, between peoples in the first and the third worlds. In *Au pays de mes racines*, as in Sullerot's *L'Aman*, such political engagement can only reproduce imperialist relations; it can never productively alter identities shaped by race, gender, sexuality, class, and nationality, or change the relations between them so that difference is acknowledged and accepted rather than reified as an other/opposite. This is made clear, in particular, in Cardinal's presentation of relations between Iranian women at the time of the 1979 revolution and the women from Europe and North America who went to Tehran to protest the revolutionary government's abrogation of women's rights. Of the first-world protesters the narrator writes:

Elles y sont allées avec les meilleures intentions du monde chrétien, sans savoir que les meilleures intentions du monde musulman n'ont rien de chrétien. Elles ont parlé au nom de leurs soeurs opprimées et elles se sont plantées comme on dit vulgairement. (52)

[They went there with the best intentions in the Christian world, not knowing that the best intentions of the Muslim world are not the least bit Christian. They spoke in the name of their oppressed sisters and took their stand, as the saying goes.]

The alternative posed by the narrator is a strategy of nonintervention except in the form of listening:

L'image de la Mauresque qui chemine, chargée de ballots, au côté de l'homme somnolant sur son âne est une image odieuse. . . . Mais cette femme-là, l'Occident ne la connaît pas, ni cet homme, ni cet âne, ni même ces ballots. Si bien que l'image a un autre sens que celui qui lui est donné et vouloir la détruire avec les armes occidentales—même celles des femmes—est une grande maladresse, un abus de pouvoir. Il faut laisser les femmes arabes déposer leurs ballots et dire: "Je ne marche plus." Les raisons qu'elles donneront de leur révolte étonneront, de même qu'étonnent les agissements du peuple iranien et de ses chefs. (52)

[The image of the Moorish Woman, loaded down with bundles, walking beside the man dozing on his donkey is an odious image. . . . But the West knows neither that woman, nor that man, nor that mule, nor even those bundles. So the image has a different meaning than the one assigned to it, and to want to destroy it with Western weapons—even women's weapons—is a terrible blunder, an abuse of power. It is necessary to let Arab women put down their bundles and say, "I'm not walking another step." The reasons they'll give for their revolt will be surprising, just as the maneuvers of the Iranian people and their leaders are surprising.]

Now, it appears that the narrator's encounter with Algerian university women is to be taken as a model for proper postcolonial behavior on the part of the first-world woman, insofar as the narrator enters into a receptive relation to the Algerians; she "listens to them attentively" (158) without speaking for them or assimilating their struggles to hers:

Elles commencent à parler de leurs existences qui sont pleines à

craquer. Elles ont un pays à construire, des étudiants à instruire et
leurs vies de femmes à faire admettre. (158)

[They start talking about their lives, which are filled to the brim.
They have a country to build and students to teach, and they are
demanding acknowledgment of their lives as women.]

The result: "For me, knowledge. I'm learning what the specific demands of Algerian women are" (158). The problem is that under
the guise of respecting the autonomy of the women with whom
she is conversing, the narrator encloses the "specific demands of
Algerian women"—demands that remain unspecified in her
account—in a bounded space entirely separate from the one she
occupies and from the international networks that partially determine, for example, Algeria's rising rate of unemployment and economic dependency, factors that inevitably shape the demands of
Algerian women.

Equally important, for Cardinal's narrator, the demands of Algerian women become an object of "knowledge" that in no way re-
flects on her own subjectivity or on her understanding of, or action
upon, French women's demands. What is significant about the encounter for the narrator is not that it suggests ways to erode the
inequalities between France and Algeria, either at the level of her
personal contacts or at the level of organized, politicized networks.
Rather, it is meaningful because the Algerian women "recognize"
her; their "smiling faces" tell her she must have succeeded in her
goal of writing authentically while avoiding "indecency" (157). Her
relation to them—especially her desire to "thank" them for
something—has mainly to do, she says, with her "life as a writer"
(154), because for her, Algerian women represent an important
sector of her readership:

En Algérie, qu'est-ce qu'elles pensaient? Leur jugement me
manquait et leur silence était une torture. (157)

[In Algeria, what did they think? I wanted to know their opinion
and their silence tortured me.]

What the encounter with the Algerian women points up, finally, is
not that the narrator avoids the cultural imperialism of which she
accuses the first-world feminist protesters in Tehran, but rather
that her own "life as a writer" comes perilously close, at times, to
occupying "Algeria" as its exclusive domain, the place where *her*

freedom and jouissance can flourish, far from the struggles of "official feminism" and the conflicts of postcolonial politics.[32] Unfortunately, the alternative to the French writer's occupation of "Algeria" in this episode is the establishment of discrete homelands for her on the one hand and the Algerian women on the other, homelands that the reader is invited to regard as separate but equal.

Clearly, a real change takes place in Cardinal's writing between *Les Mots pour le dire* and *Au pays de mes racines*, one that is symptomatic of political shifts in France in the late seventies. Whereas *Les Mots pour le dire* ends with a reference to May '68, suggesting the need to politicize the psychic and sexual struggles Cardinal's narrator has waged, *Au pays de mes racines* ends with a critique of socialism—not just its corrupt, inefficient form in present-day Algeria, but socialism in general as a set of political principles and practices alien to Algerians' (especially Algerian men's) supposedly intractable individualism. Significantly, the references to May in the later text deal with the colonial past rather than the postcolonial present, in keeping with the general pattern of politicizing the past while naturalizing and idealizing the here and now in presenting the aspect of "Algeria" I have just been discussing.

In *Au pays de mes racines*, "May" refers, on the one hand, to the rituals surrounding the narrator's first communion, the differences between Catholic boys' and girls' rites of passage, and the differences between Christian and Muslim ideologies shaping female identity. On the other hand, it recalls the army officers' revolt of May 13, 1958 (a revolt against orders from Paris to cease operations in Algeria), which sparked the furious passions of Pieds-Noirs intent upon preserving the purity and integrity of an idealized and inaccessible Mother France: in their eyes, "no woman is more beautiful, no sacrifice is too great for her" (67). Their "passionate love" for France—"a passion that was blind, brutal, stupid, yet authentic and archaically pure" (67)—was matched only by their "mad love" for Algeria, the accessible woman with whom they lived, and who provided them with treasures they eagerly offered to a disdainful France: "boughs of jasmine, garlands of orange blossoms, wine at fourteen degrees centigrade, wheat flour, fruits swollen with juice, fish of gold and silver" (68). While acknowledging the role played in the war by Pied-Noir economic interests, the narrator's account underscores the deadly power of archaic passions once "mad love" is threatened and its twin, mad aggression, is unleashed. In these pages, love cohabits with aggression rather than occupying a separate sphere, and both passions figure, negatively, in the violence of colonial war.

When the postcolonial period is at issue, however, the bonds are dissolved between love and aggression, and often, between passion and politics as well. As socialism dies in the closing lines, possessive individualism is reborn:

> L'espoir est dans le socialisme, c'est-à-dire dans l'enrichissement collectif. Je ne suis pas certaine que ces mots aient un sens pour le fellah. Je crois qu'il pense encore individuellement la richesse et que la propriété, pour lui, n'a rien perdu de son éclat. Les Algériens sont accueillants, hospitaliers, mais ils ne partagent pas leurs femmes, ils les cachent. (195)

> [People still place their hope in socialism, that is, in collective enrichment. I am not certain that these words have any meaning for the *fellah* [the Algerian peasant]. I think that he still conceives of wealth in individual terms and that property, for him, has lost none of its appeal. Algerians are welcoming, hospitable, but they don't share their women, they hide them.]

The parallels with Kristeva's work are clear, for there, too, the value of the individual, epitomized by the dissident aesthete, eventually takes precedence over that of collective engagement in oppositional politics. A similar shift can be observed in the writing of Jean-François Lyotard, Jean-Luc Nancy, and others intent on bearing witness to intractable difference, having abandoned politics as a lost cause. Thus, despite the productive cultural-political aspects of Cardinal's writing that I have tried to analyze here, her search for *l'état sauvage*[33] is complicit with the self-serving neoliberal politics that has become a Paris fashion.

J. M. G. Le Clézio's Sahara: Roots of Ethnic Purity

If in Cardinal's *Au pays de mes racines* and Sullerot's *L'Aman* the Maghreb functions, at times, merely as a space where French neoliberal values are reinscribed and where the social and psychic conflicts of the postcolonial world dissolve as the French subject phantasmatically returns to a state of plenitude and sensuous delight, the case seems at first glance to be quite different in J. M. G.

Le Clézio's *Désert*. For whereas Sullerot's and Cardinal's autobiographical texts place French women at the center of the narratives, positing their protagonists' struggles as the only ones French women can write about authentically, thus relegating Maghrebians' struggles to a separate, subordinate realm, Le Clézio's text adopts the conventions of the historical novel, making Maghrebians the subjects of the narrative and focusing throughout on their struggles against colonial and postcolonial domination by France. Unlike Cardinal's Algeria, Le Clézio's Morocco is always the site of a sensuous experience associated with Moroccans' history: on the one hand, the suffering of nomadic Saharawi tribes who, having fled their lands in southern Morocco in the face of French invasion in the winter of 1909-10, undertake a seemingly interminable and ultimately futile march through the desert to the promised land in the North; and on the other hand, the pleasures of the nomads' descendants whose enjoyment of the light, sounds, smells, and tactile sensations of the desert signals the possibility of freedom from both French and Moroccan domination in 1980, a freedom fundamentally dependent on the recovery of both precolonial cultural traditions and the history of collective anticolonial struggle.

Yet despite Le Clézio's focus on Moroccans' struggles and his unequivocal denunciation not only of colonialism but also of the postcolonial violence that Cardinal and Sullerot virtually ignore, we must ask whether his text in fact avoids the phantasmatic dissolution of contemporary conflicts and the reaffirmation of neoliberal values. For its response to the squalid, solitary life of ordinary Maghrebians in urban centers such as Marseilles and Tangiers is to encourage an impossible retreat into the idealized space of an oasis at the edge of the desert where, supposedly, capitalist exploitation is unknown, an unadulterated precolonial culture survives intact, and racism and xenophobia do not exist because there is "not a single foreigner in this land" (113). To resolve the problems posed by multinational capitalism and immigration in this way is to sidestep the crucial questions of the day: how to negotiate France's ethnic and racial diversity, a process that will vary according to the particular identities of the individuals and groups involved (that is, their gender, sexuality, class, and so forth); how to negotiate social conflicts arising within Morocco's borders; and how equitably to restructure political, economic, and cultural relations between first-

and third-world nations, particularly France's relations with its former protectorate.

It can be said that Le Clézio's phantasmatic dissolution of the conflicts and contradictions within and among individuals and national groups reaffirms liberal values insofar as it relies on the humanist notion of an originary, unitary state—figured by a garden, an oasis—from which the human race has been expelled and to which it must return if it is to live in harmony. Le Clézio's novel has the classic structure of a search for the lost origin, a series of trials in the desert that will culminate in the return to the garden or oasis—here, the fig tree in the shade of which his protagonist Lalla gives birth to a child after returning to Morocco from a brief, alienating stay in Marseilles. In the highly naturalized and dehistoricized presentation of the act of childbirth (and thus of female experience), the Saharawi culture of Lalla's ancestors is reborn, innocent of foreign influence.

Ultimately, nothing is changed by the fact that in *Désert* the space of refuge is figured alternately as the desert itself, a boundless country that "has no name" (331), or by the fact that Lalla's ancestors are said to search endlessly for an origin that cannot be fully recovered, an origin imaged by the tomb of the ancestor Al Azraq, "spirit of my father, spirit of my grandfather" (26). Far from being free-floating signifiers, the Saharawis are a bounded community defined by their relation to the ancestor, and the infinite deferral of the ancestor's presence is itself the groundless ground of his authority: although it is said of the nomads that "there was no end to freedom, it was vast like the expanse of the earth, beautiful and cruel like the light" (411), this freedom is nonetheless constrained by the authority to whom their "wordless prayer" (411) is addressed. The constraint of the ancestor's authority is equally operative in the nomads' recollection of "the oasis where the water is green, where the palm trees are immense and give fruit as sweet as honey," a recollection expressed in "a language that was strange and sweet like that of prayers" (220).

Lalla's act of giving birth under the fig tree functions in Le Clézio's text not only as a figuration of the return to the garden/oasis as point of origin—the fulfillment of the nomads' desires, expressed in prayer—but also as the embodiment of the *memory* of the lost origin, which secures its authority from generation to generation. However many gaps there may be between evocations of that

memory, however variable its articulations, it nonetheless defines
and lends stability to the identity of Lalla's people, an identity that
is clearly marked off from that of Moroccans in the North, Moroccan immigrants in France, and Europeans. Although they may
wander endlesslessly through a boundless, unnamed territory, Le
Clézio's Saharawi tribes form a closed community that engages in
no reciprocal exchange with the other communities with which
they are inextricably entwined historically. In *Désert*, the necessarily exclusionary gesture that founds Saharawi identity is recalled in
the cataclysmic scenes that function to reaffirm that identity by annihilating the "cities of beggars and prostitutes" (334) on both sides
of the Mediterranean, or by incorporating them into the idealized
Saharawi group. In these scenes, the Saharawi community is embodied not in Lalla but in the all-seeing, godlike figure of Al Azraq,
or Es Ser (the Secret), as Lalla calls him, a figure who stands for the
imposition of a unitary, fixed identity on the peoples of Morocco.

It is striking that Morocco's recovery of an imaginary oneness
through Al Azraq and Lalla in Le Clézio's *Désert* is structurally parallel to French Algeria's recovery of its supposed unitary origin in
Albert Camus's "The Adulterous Woman."[34] In Camus's story, the
nomads of the Algerian desert—particularly the "tall Arab" who
closely resembles Al Azraq, "thin, vigorous, wearing a sky-blue
burnoose . . . and bearing his bronze aquiline face loftily" (19)—
are "signs" (23) that the French protagonist Janine must decipher,
instruments in the middle-class European woman's transcendence
of her culture's values. Janine's transcendence consists in opening
herself to the supposedly universal experience of human freedom,
thereby entering a realm where the differences between her and
the Algerians are erased, and where no rules are given except that
which obliges human beings to exercise their freedom, preferably
in a conscious and deliberate fashion. As she sheds the distinguishing marks of her age, class, and nationality and merges pleasurably with the cosmos in a moment of jouissance, both Janine
and the Algerian nomads whose meaning she has grasped become
generic human nomads, "men . . . ceaselessly trudging, possessing nothing but serving no one, poverty-stricken but free lords of a
strange kingdom" (24).

The structural homology between these texts suggests that
Désert, no less than "The Adulterous Woman," relies on essentialist notions of human identity and a logic of assimilation of all hu-

man groups to a single identity. The structural parallel suggests, too, that the power of both texts to legitimate their essentializing, assimilationist solutions to cultural conflicts stems, at least in part, from their common strategy of naturalizing those solutions by embodying them in women's supposedly transcultural, transhistorical experiences of childbirth and jouissance. Just as Janine merges with the land at the moment of jouissance, assuming the aspect of a tree—"she seemed to recover her roots and the sap again rose in her body" (32)—Lalla communes with nature while she is in labor, taking shelter in the shadow of the fig tree that will function as midwife: "The powerful odor of the tree penetrates her, surrounds her, and this soothes her ravaged body, mixes with the odor of the sea and the algae" (393).

This is not to say that there is no difference between Le Clézio's configuration of Saharawi identity as an ethicopolitical norm and Camus's thinly disguised reassertion of hegemonic French identity as a norm. Camus is responding to Algeria's anticolonial struggle by granting the Algerians' refusal to conform to French norms, only to assimilate colonized Maghrebians to a supposedly higher, supranational human order that is still quite obviously defined in European terms. Le Clézio, on the other hand, is clearly responding critically to the Saharawis' oppression by French colonizers and subsequently by the French- and U.S.-armed Moroccan government, which refuses to recognize the sovereignty of the Saharawi Arab Democratic Republic. His text deftly combines the nomadic aspect of Saharawi society—which suggests that its freedom, like that of all other sociopolitical entities, depends on the recognition that it can never be fully constituted—with its necessary strategic fixation as a stable identity, that is, as a people who can legitimately affirm their right to self-determination and the sovereignty of their government. The problem is that the "fixed" aspect ends up dominating not only Saharawi identity but Moroccan and Mediterranean identity in such a way that the Saharawi norm disturbingly resembles the colonialist norm it was intended to challenge. I want to stress that in the context of France in the eighties—presented in *Désert* as a "void" (270), a social desert plagued by economic and emotional poverty and various kinds of real and symbolic prostitution—we must ask whether the imagined plenitude of an idealized, naturalized Saharawi community does as much to encourage affinity and affiliation with Saharawi tribes and other oppressed Moroccans as to undermine affiliation by displacing onto the Western Sahara the fantasy of *France* as a land without foreigners, without internal divisions and conflicts—a country that all dissatisfied immigrants might flee, as Lalla did, in order to preserve their dignity. We must ask, in other words, whether *Désert*, like "La Femme adultère" and, for that matter, texts such as Albert Memmi's *Le Désert* and Driss Chraïbi's *Naissance à l'aube*, fuels the nostalgic fantasy of a return to oneness underlying the disavowal and violent repression of differences of race, sex, sexuality, class, and culture both in France and in North Africa.[35]

Le Clézio's novel comprises two narratives that are intercut with each other and ask to be read through each other: one is set in the colonial past and is replete with historical detail, while the other is a fiction set in the postcolonial present. The former centers on a boy's experience of the Saharawis' legendary march through the desert to the cities on the northern Moroccan coast in search of freedom from Christian invaders, the latter on a girl's solitary voyage north from a Moroccan coastal city to Marseilles in search of freedom from economic exploitation in the labor market and sexual exploitation in marriage. Just as the boy finds not the promised land he was seeking but "the new order" (225) of colonialism, which forces him and his fellow survivors to retrace their steps through the desert, the girl finds in the industrialized cities of France not a better life, but an existence so empty and degrading that she returns to her native Morocco.

The boy, Nour, and the other Saharawis following the scholar, holy man, and political leader Sheikh Ma al-'Aynayn hope to reach the place "where there would be water and grazing ground for the animals, and land for all men" (234). The poignancy of Le Clézio's account of the fatal desert march derives, in part, from the fact that neither young Nour nor the majority of his fellow travelers understand that they are recruits in a *jihad* against the Christian invaders; rather, they are counting on their leader to guide them to a place where they may again live in peace. The crushing defeat of these unarmed people in rags at the hands of General Moinier in June 1910 is thus shown to be particularly abhorrent and tragic.[36] The same is true of the massacre of the Saharawis at Agadir in April 1912:

Ils se sont réunis sur le lit du fleuve, si nombreux qu'ils

recouvraient toute la vallée. Mais ce n'étaient pas des guerriers pour la plupart. C'étaient des femmes et des enfants, des hommes blessés, des vieillards, tous ceux qui avaient fui sans cesse sur les routes de poussière, chassés par l'arrivée des soldats étrangers, et qui ne savaient plus où aller. La mer les avait arrêtés ici, devant la grande ville d'Agadir. Pour la plupart, ils ne savaient pas pourquoi ils étaient venus ici. (398)

[They gathered on the riverbed in such great numbers that they covered the entire valley. But they were not warriors for the most part. They were women and children, wounded men, old people—all those who had fled unceasingly on the roads of dust, driven away by the arrival of foreign soldiers, and who no longer knew where to go. The sea had stopped them here, before the great city of Agadir. For the most part, they did not know why they had come here.]

The point here is not that Le Clézio confirms the colonialist view of Ma al-'Aynayn as "a savage, a fanatic who tells his warriors . . . that he will make them invincible and immortal, who has them brave rifles and machine guns, armed only with spears and sabers" (357). On the contrary, he ironizes this view, presenting the sheikh instead as a political and religious leader concerned to preserve a form of collective existence now threatened with extinction, a man whose power to move his people extended well beyond the frame of the armed resistance movement he was leading against the French in the early twentieth century.[37] In fact, in *Désert*, it is precisely the sheikh's loyalty to his people and their way of life that explains his alleged failure to comprehend that it was money, not arms, that defeated him in the end:

Savait-il ce qu'était la Banque de Paris et des Pays-Bas, savait-il ce qu'était un emprunt pour la construction des chemins de fer, savait-il ce qu'était une Société pour l'exploitation des nitrates du Gourara-Touat? Savait-il seulement que, pendant qu'il priait et donnait sa bénédiction aux hommes du désert, les gouvernements de la France et de la Grande Bretagne signaient un accord qui donnait à l'un un pays nommé Maroc, à l'autre un pays nommé Egypte? . . . Le vieux cheikh ne savait pas cela, parce que ses guerriers ne combattaient pas pour de l'or, mais seulement pour une bénédiction, et que la terre qu'ils défendaient ne leur appartenait pas, ni à personne, parce qu'elle était seulement l'espace libre de leur regard, un don de Dieu. (356-57)

[Did he know what the Bank of Paris and the Netherlands was?
Did he know what a loan for the construction of railroads was?
Did he know what a company for mining the nitrates of the
Gourara-Touat was? Did he even know that while he was blessing
the men of the desert, the governments of France and Great
Britain were signing an agreement that granted to one party a
country named Morocco, and to the other a country named
Egypt? . . . He didn't know these things, because his warriors
were not fighting for gold, but only for a blessing, and because
the land they were defending did not belong to them or to
anyone, for [to them] it was only the free space of their look, a
gift of God.]

The Nour narrative thus ends in defeat insofar as the blue men, or
warriors, of Ma al-'Aynayn fail to prevent the French from taking
power in Morocco. We read in the last lines of the novel that the
Saharawi tribes are fading from view now that the French have occupied center stage in the historical drama: "They were going
away, as in a dream, they were disappearing" (411). Still, because
the survivors' wandering never ceases, because there is "no end to
[their] freedom" (411), we are invited to read the other narrative,
centered on their descendant, Lalla, as the sequel to their story, the
resurgence of their people and the fulfillment of their dream.

Lalla's links to her ancestors are provided by her father's sister,
Aamma, who raises her, and by the Shluh shepherd Hartani.
Aamma tells Lalla stories of her mother, Hawa, who was born in
the South and who like Nour is a descendant of the blue man of the
desert Al Azraq, the sage who instructed Ma al-'Aynayn to build
the holy city of Smara, which was to become a legendary site of
Saharawi resistance to colonization. Transmitting to her niece Hawa's various and often conflicting stories of Lalla's birth in the
shade of a fig tree in the mountains of the South, Aamma also tells
how Hawa sang songs in Shluh, songs that, we know from the
Nour narrative, were familiar to Nour. Aamma's stories, then, give
Lalla access to an oral tradition that accounts for her personal origins and binds her and other members of the Saharawi tribes
across generations.

Hartani, a foundling born in the South and left by the edge of a
well by a blue man, has cultural ties to Lalla's mother and her
people, although his name—"the nickname he was given because
he had black skin like the slaves of the South" (104)—differentiates

him from them as well. Conversely, he is a "stranger" (105) to all the city dwellers on the coast except Lalla. Hartani never goes into the city but rather occupies the uncertain zone between the suburban shantytown and the desert, keeping company only with animals and plants unless Lalla crosses his path. Shunning the language of humans, Hartani communicates exclusively by gesture and by example, hovering on the border between the human and the natural world and initiating Lalla into the mysteries of the desert.

Like the shepherd, Lalla "is not afraid to come often to the rocky plateau, in spite of the silence and the emptiness of the wind" (89-90), for she is looking for something other than the life that lies before her in the coastal city. In fact, both Lalla and Hartani are waiting for something, but the shepherd "is perhaps the only one who knows what he is waiting for":

> C'est comme si une partie de lui-même était restée au lieu de sa naissance, au-delà des collines de pierres et des montagnes enneigées, dans l'immensité du désert, et qu'il devait un jour retrouver cette partie de lui-même, pour être tout à fait un. (175)

> [It is as if a part of himself had remained at the place of his birth, beyond the hills of rock and the snowy mountains, in the boundlessness of the desert, as if he was to find this part of himself one day, to be completely one.]

Thanks to Hartani's teachings, Lalla discovers that she, too, is waiting for this sense of oneness with a people and with the land. Having learned Hartani's natural language—"his language of very beautiful things, which stirs the inside of her body and makes her tremble" (90)—Lalla begins to "search in her memory for the tracks of the words her mother used to say" (143) and is eventually able to hear her mother's singing "vibrating inside her" (192).

It is "on the border of the desert" (110) where she has been following the tracks of her mother's words that Lalla begins to sense the presence—that is, the look—of the being she calls Es Ser, the Secret, whom she later recognizes as her ancestor Al Azraq: "what Lalla sees above all is a white tomb. . . . That is where the light of the look seems to come from, and Lalla understands that it is the resting place of the Blue Man" (192). Just as Hartani's voice and her mother's singing stir her, penetrating her inner being, Es Ser's look caresses her body and rends it: "Lalla feels the heat of his look moving over her face and her body" (89); "it is as if something deep inside her was tearing and breaking, letting death and the unknown enter. The burning of the desert radiates in her" (192). Es Ser's penetrating look, which at once fractures Lalla's being and "illuminates" (147) it, seems to be quintessentially masculine and yet is associated in Lalla's imagination with the look of the sea, the look of a woman:

> Peut-être que c'est la mer qui regarde comme cela sans cesse, regard profond des vagues de l'eau, regard éblouissant des vagues des dunes de sable et de sel? Naman le pêcheur dit que la mer est comme une femme, mais il n'explique jamais cela. Le regard vient de tous les côtés à la fois. (147)

> [Maybe it is the sea that is looking like that incessantly, the deep look of the sea waves, the dazzling look of the waves of the dunes of sand and salt? Naman the fisherman says that the sea is like a woman, but he never explains that. The look comes from all sides at once.]

This shifting array of sexually ambiguous looks and voices that "come from all sides at once" will enable Lalla to recover the memory of her personal and cultural origins in the country that "has no name." Paradoxically, these unsettling looks and voices will also enable her to find the oneness she has been waiting for, but we will see that in the process, their multiplicity and ambiguity will be reduced as Lalla comes to incorporate the annihilating, unifying, theological gaze of Es Ser.

As she internalizes the look associated with Es Ser and the feminized sea, Lalla begins to commune with her ancestral past:

> Alors, pendant longtemps, elle cesse d'être elle-même; elle devient quelqu'un d'autre, de lointain, d'oublié. Elle voit d'autres formes. . . . Elle voit cela, car ce n'est pas un rêve, mais le souvenir d'une autre mémoire dans laquelle elle est entrée sans le savoir. Elle entend le bruit des hommes, les chants des femmes, la musique, et peut-être qu'elle danse elle-même, en tournant sur elle-même . . . en faisant résonner les bracelets de cuivre et les lourds colliers. (91-92)

> [Then, for a long time, she is no longer herself; she becomes someone else, someone far away and forgotten. She sees other forms. . . . She sees this, for it is not a dream, but the recollection of another memory that she has entered without knowing it. She

hears the noise of men, the songs of women, the music, and
perhaps she is dancing herself, turning in circles . . . making the
copper bracelets and heavy necklaces resonate.]

Although her transformation here is only momentary, it has the effect of prompting her to leave the city where she lives with her
aunt, for she realizes that what she is waiting for will come to her
neither through work nor through marriage on the Moroccan
coast. First, Lalla leaves the carpet factory where her aunt has
found employment for her because the manager, Zora, beats the
young girls who work for her, girls who have no money and are for
all practical purposes enslaved to their boss. And shortly afterward, she refuses to marry the rich man from the city who brings
gifts to her aunt's family in exchange for a wife who will serve and
obey him. Moved by the tales told to her by the Jewish fisherman
Naman who has traveled to many European ports, Lalla sets out
for Marseilles after being impregnated by Hartani.

If she suffers from nausea upon arriving in the busy French port,
it is less because of morning sickness than because of "the emptiness of the streets" (281) and the barred windows that make "prisoners" (283) of the city's inhabitants. In the Marseilles slums, she
does menial labor and lives in solitude relieved only by her friendship with Hartani's European counterpart, the young gypsy
Radicz, who in the end is run over by a bus as he flees the police
trying to arrest him for stealing goods from parked cars. When Lalla is "discovered" by a photographer and becomes a media star almost overnight, the illiterate model marks her difference from the
postmodern culture that adopts her by autographing her photos
with the sign of her tribe, a small heart. Now identifying herself as
Hawa—that is, as an adult and a mother—Lalla-Hawa troubles the
heart and mind of the photographer (with whom she cohabits for a
short time) and resists assimilation to the glitzy society he represents:

> Le visage de Hawa est partout, partout. . . . [Mais] les yeux
> regardent ailleurs . . . de l'autre côté du monde. . . . Elle donne
> [au photographe] sa forme, son image, rien d'autre. (327)

> [Hawa's face is everywhere, everywhere. (But) her eyes are
> looking elsewhere . . . at the other side of the world. . . . She
> gives [the photographer] her form, her image, but nothing else.]

Relying on a simple opposition between image and substance, Le Clézio's text asks us to dissociate the "real" Hawa (the inassimilable immigrant? the working-class Moroccan girl? the wanderer on the dunes beyond the shantytown? Es Ser's communicant?) from the photographic images of her circulating in the postmodern metropolitan center, while simultaneously maintaining her intimate association with her Saharan ancestors.

Ultimately, the text interrupts the endless proliferation of images of Hawa, containing it in the young woman's all-seeing look as she dances in a Marseilles disco and draws the other dancers into her trancelike state. Envisioning "an endless expanse of dust and white stones, a living expanse of sand and salt, and the waves of the dunes," Hawa is phantasmatically transported to the space of the desert where a totalizing incorporation of all identities and differences is enacted:

> C'est comme autrefois, au bout du sentier des chèvres, là où tout semblait s'arrêter, comme si on était au bout de la terre, au pied du ciel, au seuil du vent. C'est comme quand elle a senti pour la première fois le regard d'Es Ser, celui qu'elle appelait le Secret. (334)

> [It is like before, at the end of the goat path, the place where everything seemed to stop, as if one were at the edge of the earth, at the foot of the sky, on the threshhold of the wind. It is like the moment when she felt for the first time the look of Es Ser, the one she called the Secret.]

According to the logic of *Désert,* once the all-encompassing look of Es Ser imposes itself through the entranced woman, it is no longer necessary or even possible to ask, "But who is Hawa?" (325). For Hawa is now indistinguishable from the look of Es Ser itself, and her fractured, shifting, overlapping identities — constructions whose groundlessness is figured in her relation to the ancestor's tomb — give place to a reified substance or plenitude. This plenitude is embodied first in the pregnant dancer who inspires euphoria in the disco crowd, and subsequently in the woman in labor on the dunes of northern Morocco, a full body sheltered by a fig tree whose "high, powerful branches [are] like the arms of a giant" (393).

As Hawa dances in the Marseilles disco, the look of Es Ser is no longer "strange" (89) and troubling as well as protective, as it had been when she first encountered it. Whereas initially Lalla is "afraid" of Es Ser's seering look and "does not understand why the storm of the man of the desert wants to destroy [the] cities" (110) on both sides of the Mediterranean, she now experiences a pleasurable "intoxication" induced by the look's reassuring function of providing an incontestable frame within which to interpret the signs of the world, whether it be the world of Marseilles, the world of Tangiers, or the desert world. Lalla's intoxication is contagious and spreads to the other dancers, so that the removal of "all the obstacles" (334) to totalizing identification appears as oceanic bliss—the other side of the mass destruction effected by the "empty, imperious look" (110) of Es Ser in the forboding scene on the dunes.

The phantasmatic return to plenitude figured in "Hawa, daughter of Hawa" (395), entails the annihilation of all the hybrid, fractured cultural forms and self-constructions evoked so far in the narrative. If Hawa has functioned as a kind of *femme sauvage* up to this point, she now assumes the familiar aspect of the noble savage who promises salvation for her people and for the French. The child born of the noble Lalla Hawa's full body at once restores authentic Saharawi culture and cancels the artificial French culture figured in the "void" emerging from the wombs of the Marseilles prostitutes, "old women . . . lying under the weight of the men who crush them and dirty their yellow flesh" (296). Although the birth of the child takes place on the dunes near Tangiers, it is attended by no Moroccan city dwellers, for they are excluded by virtue of their alienation from nature and their entanglement in the capitalist, sexist, and racist networks of the urban center. Lalla knows that "only [the fig tree] can help her, like the tree that helped her mother in the past, on the day of her birth" (393).

Absent from the idealized space of the oasis, imaged by the fig tree, are not just the urban masses of the Mediterranean, however, but also Aamma, the woman of the North who raised Lalla; Hartani, who recalls the black slaves from the South; and Naman the Jewish fisherman—the storytellers of various ethnic backgrounds whose voices and gestures implicitly enjoined Lalla earlier in the novel both to recover a cultural memory in danger of being effaced (that of the Saharawis) *and* to preserve other Moroccan cultural memories registering the nation's long history of conflict and commerce with Europe (those conveyed by Naman). Absent too is the refrain of the French song Lalla had heard on the radio and loved as a child although she did not understand its meaning, a refrain she recalls briefly as she disembarks in Tangiers, "Mediterrane-e-e-an" (72). The silencing of this refrain is telling since it suppresses a name disclosing the Saharawis' ties not only to the peoples of northern Morocco but to those in "the countries on the other side of the sea" (110), peoples whose histories are inextricably entwined with their own.

It is true that after her communion with nature and with the nomadic people who embody an ideal human identity, Lalla, like Camus's Janine, returns to everyday life and thus implicitly faces the task of generalizing her quasi-mystical individual experience. Following the birth, Lalla awaits the arrival of "someone from the city of boards and tar paper, a young crab fisherman, an old woman in search of wood, or a little girl who simply likes to walk on the dunes to look at the birds of the sea. . . . For someone always comes along eventually" (396-97). However, since all the people who mediated Lalla's relations with her compatriots are now gone and with them, their languages, it is hard to see how she could possibly communicate to non-Saharawis in the North by means of the "ancestral gestures" she performed "instinctively" (393) in giving birth to her child. How could Lalla communicate the song of Hawa, a song that "goes straight to her heart," to people who have no affective ties to the Saharawis, when she herself "no longer understands the words," which are "in the language of the Shluh" (192)? And even if we assume that Lalla can now speak the languages of Aamma, Hartani, and Naman, is there any guarantee that they will be meaningful or politically useful to the city dwellers of Morocco, or that Lalla will be able to interpret the languages of the city dwellers other than as signs of their speakers' corruption and degradation?

What is needed is not the ecstatic merging of all Moroccans (or all human beings) with the idealized Saharawi community figured in *Désert*. Rather, we must acknowledge the shifting, provisional character of all elaborations of Saharawi identity and the need to form them, whenever possible, through reciprocal exchange with other groups. We must also acknowledge that the territory within which Saharawi and other identities are deployed is never simply "the free space of [a] look" (357) but a space marked off by means of inevitable exclusions of which we must remain critically aware.

In order to avoid colluding with the imperialist look of the French colonizers or with its double, the "imperious look" of Al Azraq, we must relinquish the fantasy of apocalypse and allow instead for the permanent multiplicity, partiality, and ambiguity of the looks and voices that both constitute and unsettle identities—looks and voices that "come from all sides at once."

The Limits of Cultural Mixing in Michel Tournier and Guy Hocquenghem

If Le Clézio's *Désert* seeks to resolve the conflicts and contradictions in the Maghreb's relations with France by falling back on the notion of a substantive Saharawi identity firmly rooted in the precolonial traditions of the Sahara, Michel Tournier's *The Golden Droplet* takes the opposite tack, insisting on the power of Maghrebian traditions—in this case, calligraphy—not only to survive outside their native context but to mix with the elements of French modernity in such a way as to productively unsettle and reconfigure relations between sexes, genders, classes, and cultures in France. Although it displays an awareness of the ways existing social relations limit possibilities for change, Tournier's text is as bouyant and iconoclastic as Le Clézio's is grave and reverent. Rather than relocating the alienated, deracinated Maghrebian in a "pure" native context that provides a protected site from which to critique—or symbolically destroy—French modernity, Tournier affirms both the immigrants' presence in France and the transformative potency of cultural mixing.

Tournier's protagonist, a Berber shepherd from the Algerian oasis of Tabelbala, is moved to leave his native land upon losing a part of himself to a French tourist—a blond woman in a Landrover—who takes his picture but fails to keep her promise to send him a copy of it. In a futile attempt to recover the loss imposed by the foreigner who produces a fundamentally alienating and alienated image of him, the shepherd, Idris, makes his way through the desert to Oran, then to Marseilles, and finally to Paris in a series of adventures that make of *The Golden Droplet* a parodic *Bildungsroman*. In fact, Tournier's novel challenges the very concept of *Bildung*, drawing on the prohibition on imaging the human body in Islamic cultures. In the French capital, Idris's apprenticeship in the traditional art of calligraphy frees him from enslavement to the image, that is, to the economy of loss and imaginary plenitude that organizes the society of the spectacle in the first world and imposes itself on third-world peoples in various forms. Where France's relation to the Maghreb is concerned, some of the most significant forms are the varieties of Saharan lore generated by Father Foucauld, the Foreign Legion, and Saint-Exupéry, all of which are parodied in Idris's adventures: his alienating encounter with the elements of his own culture, transformed into artifacts in the Saharan Museum; his encounter, in the town of Bechar, with the Algerian photographer who makes his living indulging French tourists' orientalist fantasies, providing tawdry decors for would-be sultans dreaming of "reigning over a flock of naked women" (71); and his dealings with the French advertising mogul Monsieur Mage who casts him in a neo-orientalist commercial (complete with camel) for a soft drink called Palm Grove. In his guise as homosexual aesthete, Mage, who is enamored of Idris and wants to reduce him to a culturally manageable object of desire, reads aloud from *The Little Prince,* attributing to the Berber shepherd the "strange little voice" of Saint-Exupéry's legendary protagonist (129). Idris's ties to Mage and the world of matter are loosened as he masters a system of abstract signs and acquires the spiritual qualities attributed to calligraphy: he relinquishes altogether the fantasy of a fully constituted, substantive identity, that is, the "authentic" one he purportedly possessed without knowing it in Tabelbala before the arrival of the blond woman in the Landrover and tries to recover in order to counter the alienating fixed identities imposed on him by foreigners like Mage. "Calligraphy is liberation. . . . The sign is spirit, the image is matter. Calligraphy is the algebra of the soul traced by the most spiritualized organ of the body, its right hand" (184-85).

However, it is not until he takes his spirituality to the streets, as it were, that Idris's personal liberation suggests the possibility of broad-based social change. In the elegant Place Vendôme, "with its emperor [Napoleon] on his column," Idris works as a day laborer breaking up the pavement of Empire with a pneumatic drill. By virtue of the fact that the drill is cast as his "pneumatic dancing partner" (203), Idris's alienated labor becomes a dance, a form of play in which he himself becomes a free-floating signifier. As presented by Tournier, the Algerian laborer's dance exposes the social mechanisms that simultaneously constitute and threaten to disrupt prevailing relations between rich and poor, natives and immigrants, men and women, and masculine and feminine identifications in France. Disputing the idea, put forth by one of the construction workers, that the powerful pneumatic drill is nothing but an instrument of repression, one of "the filthiest things they ever invented to kill Arabs with," Idris's cousin Achour insists upon the instability and alterability of the drill's social function and meaning, declaring:

> C'est ton zob, tu comprends? Un zob de géant. Avec ça, tu crèves Paris, tu niques la France! (255)

> It's your prick, don't you see? A giant prick. With that thing you can stuff Paris, you can screw France! (201)

Yet it is not simply a matter of reversing colonial relations of domination, as Achour's remark suggests. Although many reviewers in the mainstream press read *The Golden Droplet* in terms of such a reversal,[38] the point is not only that at the end of the novel the Berber youth *has* the phallus—the "giant prick" formerly possessed by conquerers like Napoleon and his descendants. The point is also that Idris *is* the phallus, that is, he is engaged in a feminine mascarade insofar as he is now indissociable from his dancing partner who, we are told, is none other than Zett Zobeida, the black woman who danced at wedding ceremonies in Tabelbala, a creature of flesh and blood "metamorphosed into a rapid robot" (203). As Idris dances in the Place Vendôme in the novel's final scene, the stability of the binary structure organizing masculine and feminine identifications is challenged and with it, interlocking structures such as the relation between the French descendants of conquerers like Napoleon and the Algerian descendants of resistance leaders like Abd el-Kader. Moreover, Tournier playfully expands the range of possible identifications by moving beyond the ambiguities of the masculine-feminine relation to include relations with machines: Idris's dance with Zett "metamorphosed into a rapid robot" makes him a cyborg and thus subverts the interpretive grids defining his identity in terms of the oppositions between masculinity and femininity, culture and nature, modernity and archaism, civilization and barbarism.

The final scene of *The Golden Droplet* is clearly meant to enact the deconstruction of these oppositions not only in Idris's dance with the drill but also in its effects: Idris's "delirious frenzy" (203) shatters the shop window separating him and his co-workers from the golden droplet that had once belonged to Zett Zobeida. A "pure sign, absolute form" (22), the droplet is not the full embodiment of the Algerian homeland or even of Idris's native Berber culture, a minority culture in Algeria whose integrity has in any case been challenged in various ways from within the nation's borders. Rather, it is the emblem of the processes by which cultural and other identities are figured and transfigured, as is clear from the many overlapping and conflicting meanings assigned the golden droplet in the text, which Tournier explicitly signals in his postscript. *La goutte d'or* is the geometrically shaped Berber jewel Idris found by chance after Zett's dance at a wedding ceremony in Tabelbala—a jewel he lost to a Marseilles prostitute, only to rediscover it in the window of the jewlery shop in the Place Vendôme. It is also the Etruscan (later the Roman) *bulla aurea* that free youths wore as their emblem, exchanging it for a toga upon reaching adulthood. *La rue de la Goutte-d'Or* in Paris is the street where proletarians drank themselves to ruin in the tavern of Emile Zola's *L'Assommoir*. Today this street is "the center of the district where African immigrant workers congregate, and it was the scene of violent clashes during the Algerian War" (204).

Idris's dance with the pneumatic drill in the Place Vendôme shatters the shop window that defines the droplet as a luxury commodity, apparently shaking the foundations of multinational capitalism and the class structure it requires and supports in France: Idris and the other immigrant workers have the chance, momentarily at least, to make of the droplet something other than the symbol of their economic and social subordination and the attendant inaccessibility of the commodities sold on the international market, "jewels and gems from Africa and the Middle East" (202). The shattering of the window also signals a challenge to the race relations that consign immigrants like Idris to the lowest rungs of the class ladder in France. The young Berber's liberation and the droplet's reconfiguration as "absolute form" are only momentary, to be sure, for as soon as the shop window shatters, "the alarm bell is triggered off by the vibration sensors" and "helmeted policemen in bullet-proof vests" pour out of the vans that have rushed to the scene (203). However, even as it acknowledges the forces aligned against the transformations sparked by Idris, Tournier's text affirms their potency in its presentation of the youth's dance. Their potency is evident, too, in the "phantasmagoria" that fills the boy's head as he dances: "dragonflies, crickets, and jewels all jumping up and down in delirous frenzy" (203), jumbled fragments of Zett Zobeida's dance and enigmatic song:

La libellule libelle la ruse de la mort
Le criquet écrit le secret de la vie. (35)

The dragonfly phrases the tricks of death
The cricket writes the secret of life. (21)

This is not to say, however, that the colonial relation or its reincarnation in imperialism is adequately challenged by *The Golden Droplet*. As the "phantasmagoria" suggests, Idris's liberatory dance is made possible by his appropriation of Zett's dance. Accordingly, contrary to the injunctions of Tournier's narrator, the droplet should be read, among other things, as the emblem of the third-world populations figured by Zett, populations whose activity forms the material base of Idris's liberation as well as the liberation of the sign. Even as it spiritualizes the individual male immigrant, integrating him into the mobile, hybrid culture taking shape under the banner of the "pure sign"—an amalgam of Islamic prohibitions against imaging the human form, the art of calligraphy, and French poststructuralism in today's ethnically diverse France—Tournier's text consigns the populations figured by Zett to the realm of pure matter, the realm of the body robbed of its signifying potency and reduced to a presymbolic surface on which meanings are inscribed by those who reserve for themselves the power to signify. In short, Idris's appropriation of Zett's dance represses and exploits the "autonomous and intensely expressive life" of the African (woman's) body:

[Ce ventre] était la bouche sans lèvres de tout ce corps, la partie parlante, souriante, grimaçante et chantante de tout ce corps. (35)

This belly was the lipless mouth of her entire body, the speaking, smiling, grimacing, singing part of the entire body. (21)

The feminized African body—the material base of the male immigrant's liberation—is never successfully contained within the African homeland, however, for it also finds expression in the figure of the Egyptian singer Oum Kalsoum, "'the Star of the Orient,'

. . . quite simply known as 'the Lady' (as Sett)" (177), whose name recalls that of the black dancer Zett. Broadcast on the radio, the voice of Oum Kalsoum, "the soul of Egypt and of the entire Arab world" (178), brings into being in France an "almost exclusively masculine" (177) Arab community that enables Idris to fashion a "defense against the maleficent power of the image" (176). And naturally, Idris's liberation has a material base in the metropole itself, figured in the bleached-blond Marseilles prostitute, the peepshow dancer, and the blond model and prostitute with whom Idris must contend on the road to absolute form. As is always the case in Tournier's texts, the liberatory blurring of boundaries between sexes, genders, classes, and cultures takes place in and for male subjects.[39]

Thus, it would be a mistake to accept at face value the text's association of Zett and Oum Kalsoum with the sphere of the sign — Zett because "[she] and her golden droplet were the emanation of a world without images, the antithesis of, and perhaps the antidote to, the platinized woman with the camera" (22); Oum Kalsoum because of her status as "vestal" of the Arab people (177), that is, as disembodied voice. The African and metropolitan female figures do not belong to the separate spheres of sign (spirit) and image (matter). In fact, the absolute break between image and sign asserted by Tournier's narrator is contradicted by the text's disclosure of historical developments linking the two regimes, specifically the emergence of mass culture in which the sheer proliferation of mechanically reproducible images undermines the neat distinction between the object and its image, enabling the theorization of the sign as "absolute form." In this view, the sign has no substantive basis in a preexisting reality yet partakes of reality and produces it performatively. It is in terms of the "dissolving power" (167) of mass-produced images that we should read the episodes in *The Golden Droplet* dealing with photography, television, and other contemporary forms of image making in which Idris gets caught up before freeing himself from them. One such episode involves the passport photo that in no way resembles the young Berber yet has more reality in the eyes of French officials than Idris himself. Another involves the flickering televised images of the French seen by Idris and his fellow travelers on the boat to Marseilles, images that unsettle the Algerians' preconceptions of their wealthy neighbors across the Mediterranean — for example, a demonstration in the

Latin Quarter in which students are confronted by a "riot squad using tear gas" and are beaten and bloodied by the police (92). But the most telling episode deals with the fetishist Etienne Milan's fascination by the empty forms of boy mannequins, images of the human form that have completely replaced the "natural" love object in Milan's perverse libidinal economy. The virtue of these images, according to Milan, lies in their power to dissolve reality, to "undermine [it] at its very foundations" (167). It is the dissolving power of mass-produced images that links image and sign, and the passage from the first regime to the second is inextricably tied to dynamics of first-world industrialization, a process whose material base is class exploitation within first-world societies, attenuated by the colonial and imperialist exploitation of third-world societies. Thus, if the golden droplet, like the spiritualized male immigrant, is a "pure sign" in Tournier's text, it is also the mark of the exclusions that enable its emergence as such: the exclusion of feminized third-world populations (particularly in North Africa), of female immigrants, of French workers, and of sex workers, cast as heterosexual women and homosexual men.

If many readers are disappointed by *The Golden Droplet*, it is not, apparently, because they object to these exclusions. As I noted earlier, many readers see in Tournier's novel a reversal of the colonial relation, which improperly gives third-world peoples license to determine the shape and meaning of national identity in France. Moreover, because reviews and critical essays praise Tournier's treatment of the hotly debated question of immigration in terms of supposedly timeless myths (for instance, the calligrapher's legend of the Blond Queen and its counterpart, the tale of the Levantine pirate Barbarossa) rather than from a realistic *misérabiliste* standpoint, we can infer that the exclusions in *The Golden Droplet* are welcome: they relieve the highly educated French reading public of its guilty conscience and simultaneously discourage critical reflection on immigration questions by dismissing their relevance to literature.[40]

It is also hard to explain readers' disappointment with *The Golden Droplet* in terms of charges that the novel is mediocre, the work of an "official writer" of the state who is now resting on his laurels as a member of the Goncourt Academy and capitalizing on his high visibility as President Mitterrand's dining companion.[41] The charges have a false ring since no criticism of the state is ever offered, nor even any convincing criticism of Tournier's text: at most, it is feebly asserted that the novel lacks emotion; relies on dry ethnographic, geographical, and historical documentation; and above all is demogogic in its blunt criticism of France ("The Maghrebian is always good, the Frenchman is always bad, when he is not grotesque").[42]

It seems to me that *The Golden Droplet* disappoints many French readers not because of its demagogy or its mediocrity, much less its affirmation of the male immigrant's integration into French life at the expense of third-world populations and women. Rather, it disappoints them because in casting a Berber immigrant and the culturally mixed community he emblematizes as signs lacking any fixed substance, Tournier frustrates his compatriots' desire for a specifically ethnic or national incarnation of plenitude.[43] As we saw in the case of Cardinal's *Au pays de mes racines* and Le Clézio's *Désert*, that desire need not be satisfied by a direct affirmation of France's full presence: the Saharawi nation embodying precolonial ethnic purity or the Pied-Noir's Algeria as the site of both pre- and postcolonial plenitude can satisfy it as well. The effect of these satisfactions, as I argued earlier, is to divert attention from the problems of cultural mixing that Tournier takes as his central concern.

Yet, as I have tried to show in my discussion of *The Golden Droplet*, Tournier's affirmation of the potency of cultural mixing depends entirely on the stability and inequality of existing relations between first- and third-world nations. Although his text signals the limits of any politics of identity based on nationality, ethnicity, race, gender, or sex, it fails to acknowledge that the conditions under which cultural mixing takes place in France are not general conditions. Nor is *The Golden Droplet* the only text in which this problem arises: there is abundant evidence of Tournier's tendency to make faulty generalizations about the world based on a wealthy white man's view of developments in France, for instance his claim that "the world is rapidly evolving toward a situation in which all but one threat [nuclear destruction] will have disappeared. Science and technology will have eliminated disease and hunger. Eroticism will have finally become a way a life and will have given birth to a sexuality completely detached from procreation and no longer leading, as it does today, to overpopulation or abortion."[44] And even where he confronts the abject material conditions in which, say, certain African populations live, he tends to view them not as an effect of Africa's subordinate relation to Europe, but rather as the *equivalent* of European forms of abjection. This is the case, for instance, when he writes of his visit to a garbage dump outside Cairo where poor people have constructed houses out of foul-smelling refuse. Quoting with approval the nuns who are administering medical services to the residents of the dump, he corrects his original impression of it, suggesting that the place is "purgatory" rather than "hell," a purgatory that has analogues in the first world. Says Sister Anne: "You see, I just worked for seventeen years in a clinic in Geneva. [I came here because] I needed to detox."[45]

A similar disregard for the ways global inequalities affect first-world cultural politics is apparent in Guy Hocquenghem's *Love in Relief,* which, like *The Golden Droplet,* exposes the limits of the politics of identity through the figures of the cyborg and the foreigner, and through a critique of the image as the ground of identity. Hocquenghem's protagonist is a Tunisian boy, Amar, who encounters an unlikely group of French tourists consisting of several gay men and a single madwoman who are vacationing in an equally unlikely spot—the cold, windy, rocky island of Kerkenna off the coast of Tunisia, a place devoid of exotic appeal. The drunkenness, sexual depravity, and distraction of the French men and woman lead to Amar's being blinded in a motorcycle accident, which becomes the pretext for his departure from Kerkenna, his motherland. His search for a medical cure to his blindness takes him to Old Europe, where he meets an aged American woman of great wealth, Mrs. Halloween. In her company, Amar learns to negotiate the world not as a blind person—for his companion never fixes his identity in that way—but as a youth integrated into a high-tech society through various sophisticated devices *and,* at the same time, physically attached to the ghoulish maternal body of Mrs. Halloween, which unfailingly guides his steps.

Mrs. Halloween's death more or less coincides with Amar's exit from the Old World and entrance into the New World of the United States, the site of his definitive liberation from the maternal body and its promise of plenitude. There, the figure of the French madwoman, Andrea, reappears as the shadowy replacement of Mrs. Halloween: rather than guiding the boy as Mrs. Halloween had done, Andrea follows him, partly because she is in love with him and hopes one day to find fulfillment in possessing him, partly because she is fascinated by his elusiveness and wants to acquire that quality herself. Amar's life of bisexual cruising in West Hollywood puts him in contact with Larry, a mad scientist from "Neurone Valley," California, who insists on making Amar see again. After installing in Amar's brain a television camera that forces the boy to "see" images constantly, Larry subjects him to brutal experiments that result in the cyborg's dysfunction and death.

What is interesting about Hocquenghem's novel is the way the Amar figure crystallizes myriad forms of social marginality—gay and bisexuality, blindness, foreignness, third world-ness, cyborg tendencies. The figure of Amar indicts and explodes categories and institutions like heterosexuality, sightedness, national belonging, and even human being. Amar's travels are explicitly cast as a post-'68 cultural politics that moves beyond both party politics and identity politics, especially feminism, gay liberation, and racial, ethnic, and national minorities' struggles. Like Tournier's Idris, Amar figures a pleasurably disorienting mix of traditional and modern oriental and occidental cultures, for instance in his researches in the New York Public Library, where he listens to tape recordings of the work of the ancient Tunisian historian Ibn Khaldoun in English translation (as well as the only other text listed under "Arabia": *The Seven Pillars of Wisdom*, by Colonel Lawrence). Amar's aural relation to ancient oriental and modern orientalist texts in the New York Public Library, far from merely substituting for a supposedly "normal" or "dominant" mode of "reading," brings into play his childhood training at the Koranic school in Tunisia, which consisted in recitation of verses spoken, rather than "read," by his teacher.

In the New York Public Library Amar also listens to recordings of French histories of philanthropy directed toward the blind, which enable him to construct a critical counterhistory of the specification of blindness as a disability. In addition, he reads Arabic poetry using a machine that makes the characters on the printed page "appear much enlarged, and in relief" (162). Like Idris, he gets in touch with his ancestral past by reading "real literature, works in calligraphy [that] . . . distilled poetry down to the letter" (162). Yet he emphasizes that what becomes available to him through technology is not just Arab culture but "the entire cultural universe" (162). The concrete transformative power of this contact with the "cultural universe" is figured in Amar's use of a newer model of the reading machine mentioned above, the Optacon, whose "stimulators . . . translate the images and signs [in books] into pressure upon my back . . . [which] meant that I could read several lines of a text at once . . . [and] acquire a sense of simultaneity" (164): "rapid brushing by a multitude of points ends up forming a near image" (164) without ever confining the reader to any one fixed or complete image defined by ethnic or national belonging.

However, although Hocquenghem is committed to problematizing his own national identity by "speaking through the mouth of the foreigner" and by projecting his Maghrebian protagonist out of France into the high-tech world of the United States, he ultimately refuses, in *Love in Relief*, to admit of any difference between what it means for a European male intellectual to "decline his national identity as one declines an invitation" and what it means for a member of a national minority or a third-world national group to do so.[46] Like Tournier, he implicitly views the two situations as equivalent. Moreover, to a certain extent, despite his refusal of exoticism in *Love in Relief*, Hocquenghem reproduces the Gidean appropriation of the Arab boy as an instrument and figure for a very specific type of liberation, that of the European gay or bisexual male. And it is worth noting that the freedom of the ambiguously gendered but stereotypically promiscuous male is thrown into relief by the European woman's failed liberation. Andrea, whose voice echoes and alternates with Amar's throughout the text, tries in vain to become a protean figure like Amar. Far from exploding the identities that contain her, as her male counterpart is able to do up to a point, she merely tries unsuccessfully to escape from them by fleeing her psychoanalysts and the clinics where she is treated. Andrea ends by reconciling herself with constraining identities inside the walls of a mental institution: she marries her analyst, making sure that the baby she has conceived with Amar is born in Paris ("so the child will be born French" [216]). Although Andrea is in some ways barely distinguishable from Amar insofar as both are *folles* (a term meaning both "madwomen" and "gay men"), her main function in the novel is to be the male figure's foil, much as Zett Zobeida is Idris's foil in *The Golden Droplet*.

The disturbing conclusion of *Love in Relief* is that Amar, who appears only as the effect of a long succession of desiring machines, is killed off in the end. His death is presented neither as the divine punishment of immorality nor as the natural result of unnatural sexual practices (which amounts to the same thing). Rather, Amar is destroyed by scientific and geopolitical systems policing the territorial borders from which they profit, borders whose necessity, and whose very existence, Amar puts into question. As I have tried to suggest, however, the figure of Amar's radical alterity comes into view only against the ground of Andrea's restricted sociosexual economy, which is but a modified version of the essentially reproductive, maternal sociosexual economy assigned to Amar's Tunisian mother. The writing of a self-proclaimed "Francophobe" like Hocquenghem is therefore very similar to that of a quasi-official writer like Tournier, at least in terms of its uncritical globalization of a first-world masculine cultural politics. And although *Love in Relief* and *The Golden Droplet* go further than *L'Aman, Désert,* and *Au pays de mes racines* in unsettling the categories of sexual, ethnic, and national identity, they share with these other texts an impulse to preserve Europe's privileges under the guise of being ravished by the Maghreb.

Conclusion

Maghrebian writing since the mid-1950s, as well as French writing on the Maghreb and on today's ethnically diverse French nation, suggests a need to alter the terms of recent debates about cultural politics in which poststructuralist theory is pitted against a return to history and to identitarian politics. On the one hand, poststructuralism is too often dismissed by proponents of historicization as a simple evasion of politics. And on the other, defenders of poststructuralism stubbornly interpret the demand for historicization in reductive terms, claiming that it can only mean a return to the Hegelian understanding of history as a rational process that is driven by, and that ends with the full realization of, human freedom and autonomy.

In recent years, poststructuralism's critique of representational politics and the politics of representation has frequently been ignored, rather than taken seriously into account. Theorists such as Jean-François Lyotard have shown that the politics of representation tends to translate all social possibilities into the language of capitalism and bureaucracy, rather than attending to their resistant singularity. Because the politics of representation continually converts intractable difference into manageable oppositions, he argues, it is necessary to invent another politics, one that refuses the homogenization of all demands and desires. Similarly, for Abdelkebir Khatibi, a politics that resists capitalism and bureaucracy while attending to intractable difference is crucial to decolonization.

The alternative politics proposed by Lyotard and, in somewhat different terms, by Khatibi, does not necessarily entail a defection from effective political struggle. The same is true of Michel Foucault's and Gilles Deleuze's alternative politics, which mobilizes "wild" modes of social and cultural analysis in order to elude the politics of representation. The problem is not that the work of these theorists engages a variety of "other" politics but rather that it peremptorily condemns as uniformly oppressive, or dismisses as useless, every engagement in representational politics. It suggests that differences in geopolitical contexts, and of subject positions within those contexts, are of little consequence, and that oppressed groups can opt to avoid representational politics altogether. Moreover, because it is interested primarily in promoting its own understanding of a general dynamic that has been unfolding since the Enlightenment, it remains at a level of abstraction that blinds it to the *gains* of certain oppositional struggles in the contemporary world, and focuses exclusively instead on the ways in which these struggles reinforce the oppressive power of the state. It operates according to a logic that encourages us to see only futility in such activities as the Algerian feminist demonstrations against a 1981 draft of the family law that would have required Algerian married women to obtain their husband's permission to work outside the home: the primary significance of their success in eliminating this provision from the new law, in this view, lies in its reinforcement of state power. The same is true of U.S. feminist struggles to prevent erosion of abortion rights. The women whose bodies and everyday lives are profoundly affected by such legal decisions are not necessarily in a position to assume the Olympian view that their struggles merely strengthen the repressive state, or do no more than to mitigate its repressive force in "insignificant" ways.

Just as poststructuralist critiques of the politics of representation have been mobilized in the wholesale dismissal of representational politics, so too have poststructuralist critiques of History been marshaled against the proponents of historicization. Many defenders of "theory" claim that the force of poststructuralism lies in its deconstruction of the notion of History itself—its dream of rationality, its belief in a redemptive politics that will resolve all social conflicts and contradictions and bring History to an end, and its celebration of an autonomous, universal human subject that is neither indebted to, nor in any way fettered by, its past. But this defense of poststructuralism misses the point of the most interesting recent work in feminist studies, cultural studies, and postcolonial studies—work that is inspired not by Hegel but by Foucault. Far from reviving the dream of an autonomous subject, this work analyzes historically contingent modes of subjection while simultaneously acknowledging that all social orders are founded by exclusions. Rather than supposing that all peoples and cultures are progressing toward Enlightenment (some more rapidly than others), it deconstructs the categories that subtend Enlightenment thought, notably the categories of "tradition" and "modernity," which have been used to explain and justify imperialism. Rather than returning to ethnographic readings of literature and culture, the work of theorists as diverse as Gayatri Spivak, Edward Said, and Martin Bernal shows that the study of a given literature or culture must consider the processes by which it is constituted as an object of knowledge, as well as the political stakes of those processes.

Similar methods of analysis are evident in the work of Judith Butler, who argues for a critical genealogy of the processes by which the category of sex is at once produced as an object of knowledge and naturalized. Her critique is directed not only at the essentialism of white middle-class feminism but also at the essentialist dimensions of poststructuralist psychoanalytic discourses. She shows that the supposedly prediscursive, "true" body—a feminine or homosexual or radically bisexual body—produced by the discourses of Jacques Lacan, Julia Kristeva, and others, discourages the radical interrogation of a symbolic order that renders femininity and homosexuality culturally unintelligible. As I suggested in the opening pages of this study, Butler's work has important implications for the theories of Lyotard and Khatibi, which celebrate femininity's intractable difference while simultaneously assuming the immutability of the symbolic order that attempts to silence it.

The compelling critiques of poststructuralism that have emerged in recent years do not assume that total liberation is possible. They take for granted that every symbolic order founds itself by means of exclusions, but refuse to view any given set of exclusions (including the exclusion of femininity or radical bisexuality) as inevitable. They do not return to identitarian politics, but rather attend to what Homi Bhabha calls the "gatherings" of peoples in shifting, provisional, divided, and conflictual political configurations, such as those of the Beurs in France, who are not enclosed in any identity determined by language, nationality, race, or cultural "tradition," yet affirm their effectiveness as actors in a particular social scene. Like recent literary texts by and about Maghrebians, recent work in feminist studies, postcolonial studies, and cultural studies challenges many of the assumptions that have shaped French studies for the past twenty-five years—in particular, the assumption that poetic language is a special sexual/political discourse that radically subverts discourses of domination. If the notion of a subversive poetics is itself an effect of a repressive law that pretends to be immutable, then subversion is possible, as Judith Butler says, only within the terms of the law itself, and poetic language must be read in relation to other discourses and social practices ordered by that law. A radically "other" politics must not be conceived only in terms of a philosophy or a poetics that can bear witness to intractable difference. It is crucial to acknowledge that intractable difference is at work in other activities as well—notably in social movements—and that intellectuals have a role to play in giving voice to it, without presuming to speak for those whose activities manifest it.

Notes

Introduction

1. Abdelkebir Khatibi, *Maghreb pluriel* (Paris: Denoël, 1983). All translations of this text are mine. Future references will appear in parentheses in the text.

2. Khatibi's notion of the *bi-langue* is elaborated in "Bilinguisme et littérature" in *Maghreb pluriel*, pp. 177-207; reprinted under the title "Incipits" in *Du bilinguisme*, ed. Abdelkebir Khatibi (Paris: Denoël, 1986), pp. 172-95. Translation is mine.

3. For a critique of these concepts, see Carl E. Pletsch, "The Three Worlds, or the Division of Social Scientific Labor, circa 1950-1975," *Comparative Study of Society and History* 4 (Oct. 1981): 565-90.

4. Samir Amin, *The Maghreb in the Modern World* (London: Penguin, 1970); quoted by Samia Mehrez, "The Subversive Poetics of Radical Bilingualism: Postcolonial Francophone North African Literature," in *The Bounds of Race: Perspectives on Hegemony and Resistance*, ed. Dominick La Capra (Ithaca, N.Y.: Cornell University Press, 1991), p. 255.

5. Abdelkebir Khatibi, *Figures de l'étranger dans la littérature française* (Paris: Denoël, 1987), pp. 204, 206-7. Translations are mine. Future references will appear in parentheses in the text.

6. Abdelkebir Khatibi, *Love in Two Languages*, trans. Richard Howard (Minneapolis: University of Minnesota Press, 1990), p. 118; originally *Amour bilingue* (n.p.: Fata Morgana, 1983). Future references will appear in parentheses in the text.

7. *L'intraitable* is the central concern in Jean-François Lyotard's "A l'insu (Unbeknownst)," trans. James Creech and Georges Van Den Abbeele, in *Community at Loose Ends*, ed. the Miami Theory Collective (Minneapolis: University of Minnesota Press, 1991), pp. 42-48; originally "A l'insu," *Le Genre humain: Politiques de l'oubli* (Fall 1988): 37-43. There he writes, for instance, that "May '68 was faithful to the thing that would suffer from its being represented and directed toward the civil sector" (45). Future references to "A l'insu" will appear in parentheses in the text.

8. Jean-François Lyotard, *The Differend: Phrases in Dispute*, trans. Georges Van Den Abbeele (Minneapolis: University of Minnesota Press, 1988), p. xiii; originally *Le Différend* (Paris: Editions de Minuit, 1983). Future references will appear in parentheses in the text. I am indebted to Georges Van Den Abbeele's "*Algérie l'intraitable*: Lyotard's National Front," *L'Esprit créateur* 1 (Spring 1991): 144-57, although I disagree with his assessment of Lyotard's "other" politics.

9. Jean-François Lyotard, "A Memorial for Marxism," trans. Cecile Lindsay, in *Peregrinations: Law, Form, Event* (New York: Columbia University Press, 1988), pp. 45-75; originally "Pierre Souyri: Le marxisme qui n'a pas fini," *Esprit* 61 (Jan. 1982): 11-31. After a split in the Socialisme ou Barbarie collective, the two friends worked together on the newspaper *Pouvoir Ouvrier* from 1964 to 1966.

10. Maurice Olender, prefatory note in *Le Genre humain: Politiques de l'oubli* (Fall 1988): 7.

11. Jean-François Lyotard, "Le Nom d'Algérie," in *La Guerre des Algériens: Ecrits 1956-1963*, ed. Mohammed Ramdani (Paris: Galilée, 1989), pp. 33-39. Future references will appear in parentheses in the text.

12. See Lyotard's "L'Etat et la politique dans la France de 1960," in *La Guerre des Algériens*, ed. Ramdani, pp. 164-96.

13. See Lyotard's *Heidegger and "the jews,"* trans. Andreas Michel and Mark S. Roberts (Minneapolis: University of Minnesota Press, 1990), p. 3 (originally *Heidegger et les juifs* [Paris: Galilée, 1988]), for an explanation of his use of quotation marks and lower case for "the jews."

14. Maurice Blanchot, *The Unavowable Community*, trans. Pierre Joris (Barrytown, N.Y.: Station Hill Press, 1988); originally *La Communauté inavouable* (Paris: Editions de Minuit, 1983); Jean-Luc Nancy, *The Inoperative Community*, ed. Peter Conner, trans. Peter Conner, Lisa Garbus, Michael Holland, and Simona Sawhney (Minneapolis: University of Minnesota Press, 1991); originally "La Communauté désoeuvrée," *Aléa* 4 (1983): 11-50.

15. In reference to his notion of "poverty" in thought, Khatibi specifies that it "is not an appeal to a philosophy of the poor man and to his exaltation, but rather an appeal to a plural thought that does not reduce others (societies and individuals) to the sphere of one's self-sufficiency" (*Maghreb pluriel*, 18).

16. See, for example, the essays by Philippe Lacoue-Labarthe and Jean-Luc Nancy in *Rejouer le politique* (Paris: Galilée, 1982) and also their collection *Le Retrait du politique* (Paris: Galilée, 1983). For a critique of this work, see Nancy Fraser, "The French Derrideans: Politicizing Deconstruction or Deconstructing the Political?" in her *Unruly Practices: Power, Discourse and Gender in Contemporary Social Theory* (Minneapolis: University of Minnesota Press, 1989), pp. 69-92. See also Fraser's "The Uses and Abuses of French Discourse Theories for Feminist Politics," *boundary 2* 2 (1990): 82-101.

17. Abdelwahab Meddeb, *Talismano* (Paris: Bourgois, 1979).

18. This same impulse is already evident in Khatibi's *La Mémoire tatouée: Autobiographie d'un décolonisé* (Paris: Denoël, 1971), p. 177, where he writes: "Remember Mohammed, the prophet without writing, remember his cave, his meditation. What words, what incantation, what breath? He let himself be carried and spoken by a multitude of palpitations. It was his wives, his friends, or his tribe that transcribed his breath" (my translation). Khatibi's references to the "breath" (*souffle*) of Mohammed recall, of course, the bilingual literary review *Souffles* founded in 1966 by Khatibi and other dissident Moroccan writers. Future references to *La Mémoire tatouée* will appear in parentheses in the text.

19. In *Love in Two Languages* bisexuality, or androgyny, truly involves different experiences of being *between* two sexes, rather than of being *both* male and female, as is the case with Ahmed/Zahra, the Moroccan girl who is raised as a boy in Tahar Ben Jelloun's *The Sand Child*, trans. Alan Sheridan (San Diego: Harcourt, Brace, Jovanovich, 1987), and its sequel, *The Sacred Night*, trans. Alan Sheridan (San Diego: Har-

court, Brace, Jovanovich, 1989); originally *L'Enfant de sable* (Paris: Seuil, 1985) and *La Nuit sacrée* (Paris: Seuil, 1987). In the latter novel, the essentialism in Ben Jelloun's treatment of androgyny is particularly apparent, despite the consul's declaration to Zahra that "you know, because you have experienced it bodily, that clarity is deceptive. What is clear or definable in relations between two beings?" (134). Zahra discovers her true being—her true body, her true femininity—in her lovemaking with the blind consul who, she says, "sculpted me into a statue of flesh, desired and desiring. I was no longer a creature of sand and dust of uncertain identity. . . . I needed forgetfulness, wandering, and the grace distilled by love in order to be reborn and live. Alas, this happiness, this plenitude, this self-discovery in the sublime look of a blind man would not last" (138; my translation). Zahra forgets the paternal law (just as the consul is blind to it) only to "discover" in herself exactly the femininity prescribed by that law—its sexual component, if not its economic, legal, and political trappings.

20. In "Fitna ou la différence intraitable de l'amour," in *Imaginaires de l'autre: Khatibi et la mémoire littéraire* (Paris: L'Harmattan, 1987), pp. 36-37, Christine Buci-Glucksmann notes this feminist moment in *Love in Two Languages* only to subject it immediately to a supposedly timeless law of narrative in which "the fiction of a hermaphroditic narrator exceeds every Law."

21. Fatima Mernissi, *Le Maroc raconté par ses femmes* (Rabat: Société Marocaine des Editeurs Réunis, 1986); in English, *Doing Daily Battle: Interviews with Moroccan Women*, trans. Mary Jo Lakeland (New Brunswick, N.J.: Rutgers University Press, 1988). Khatibi's foreword appears only in the Moroccan edition. Future references to this text will appear in parentheses in the text.

22. On the ambiguity of "woman," or femininity, and its antifeminist implications in contemporary French philosophical texts, see Alice A. Jardine, *Gynesis: Configurations of Women and Modernity* (Ithaca, N.Y.: Cornell University Press, 1985), and Rosi Braidotti, *Patterns of Dissonance: A Study of Women in Contemporary Philosophy*, trans. Elizabeth Guild (New York: Routledge, 1991).

23. In the same spirit, Khatibi writes toward the end of this text that "difference is a woman and wild difference is a masked seduction" (*La Mémoire tatouée*, 143). That is, the difference established by paternal law is the binary opposition between man and woman, whereas a supposedly radically other difference—*la différence sauvage*—is approachable only in the language of what will be referred to in *Love in Two Languages* as "intractable love" (57), whose very existence is predicated on the repression of both the mother's body and the infant's polymorphous perversity by the paternal law.

24. Judith Butler, *Gender Trouble: Feminism and the Subversion of Identity* (New York: Routledge, 1990), p. 77. Future references to Butler concern this text and will appear in parentheses in the text.

25. Michel Foucault, *The History of Sexuality, Volume I: An Introduction*, trans. Robert Hurley (New York: Vintage, 1980), p. 154. Quoted by Butler, *Gender Trouble*, p. 91.

26. Hélène Cixous and Catherine Clément, *The Newly Born Woman*, trans. Betsy Wing (Minneapolis: University of Minnesota Press, 1986). Cixous writes in the section titled "Sorties": "The Voice sings from a time before law, before the Symbolic took one's breath away and reappropriated it into language under its authority of separation. . . . Within each woman the first, nameless love is singing" (93). Orig-

inally *La Jeune née* (Paris: Union Générale d'Editions, 1975). Future references will appear in parentheses in the text.

27. Nawal al-Saadawi, *Woman at Point Zero*, trans. Sherif Hetata (London: Zed Books, 1983). I have quoted from Assia Djebar's foreword to the French translation of that novel, *Ferdaous: Une Voix à l'enfer* (Paris: des femmes, 1981), translated by Miriam Cooke in *Opening the Gates: A Century of Arab Feminist Writing*, ed. Margot Badran and Miriam Cooke (Bloomington and Indianapolis: Indiana University Press, 1990), p. 387.

28. In "Poststructuralism, Marginality, Postcoloniality and Value," in *Literary Theory Today*, ed. Peter Collier and Helga Geyer-Ryan (Ithaca, N.Y.: Cornell University Press, 1990), p. 226, Spivak cautions against the Westerner's desire to "fix and diagnose the identity of the most deserving marginal" or, in Jean-Paul Sartre's terms, to "redo in [oneself] the project of the Chinese, or the Indian, or the African" (*Existentialism and Humanism*, trans. Philip Mairet [New York: Haskell House, 1948], pp. 46-47; quoted by Spivak in "Theory in the Margin," in *Consequences of Theory*, ed. Jonathan Arac and Barbara Johnson [Baltimore, Md.: Johns Hopkins University Press, 1991]), p. 155). Still, it seems crucial to transform the sphere of knowledge in which we work by pointing to a fact that is often ignored, namely that third-world women are subjects, not just objects, of knowledge. For another discussion of these issues, see Spivak's "Feminism in Decolonization," *differences* 3 (Fall 1991): 139-70.

29. Abdelkebir Khatibi, preface to Marc Gontard, *La Violence du texte: Etudes sur la littérature marocaine* (Paris: L'Harmattan, 1981), p. 8.

30. Edward W. Said, "Figures, Configurations, Transfigurations," *Race and Class* 1 (1990): 14. One has to wonder whether fear, rather than critical judgment, motivates Khatibi's claim in *Figures de l'étranger*, pp. 208-9, that "the Indian of the Americas or the black [tellingly, Khatibi uses the masculine singular here] has not found, to my knowledge, his founding myth as imaginary space in this literary internationalism, unless it be massively in the myth of the noble savage, the pretext for the most inhospitable folklore in existence." Although he underscores the fact that he "says it calmly, traveling in the United States" (208), it is clear that such a statement could not be made by one who has read Leslie Marmon Silko or Toni Morrison, to name only two writers in the categories he mentions, unless it be under the threat of ostracism by white French philosophers.

Chapter 1. Recasting the Colonial Gaze

1. An example of the first approach is Christine Buci-Glucksmann's "Fitna ou la différence intraitable de l'amour," in *Imaginaires de l'autre: Khatibi et la mémoire littéraire*, ed. Michèle Fay (Paris: L'Harmattan, 1987), pp. 17-43. An example of the second is Ahlem Mosteghanemi's *Algérie: Femme et écritures* (Paris: L'Harmattan, 1985).

2. Chandra Talpade Mohanty, "Under Western Eyes: Feminist Scholarship and Colonial Discourses," *boundary* 2 12 (1984): 334. Following Mohanty, I use the term "Western scholars" to include "third world women in the West, or third world women in the third world writing on [feminist] issues and publishing in the West" (336). I have also adopted Mohanty's capitalization of "Third World" in connection with the reified figure of the "composite Third World woman." Other important discussions of this and related problematics include Gayatri Chakravorty Spivak, "French Feminism in an International Frame," *Yale French Studies* 62 (1981): 154-84, reprinted in Spivak's *In Other Worlds* (New York: Methuen, 1987), pp. 134-53; Spi-

vak, "Can the Subaltern Speak?" in *Marxism and the Interpretation of Culture,* ed. Cary Nelson and Lawrence Grossberg (Urbana: University of Illinois Press, 1988), pp. 271-313; Spivak, "Three Women's Texts and a Critique of Imperialism," *Critical Inquiry* 12 (Autumn 1985): 243-61; and Trinh T. Minh-ha, *Woman, Native, Other: Writing Postcoloniality and Feminism* (Bloomington and Indianapolis: Indiana University Press, 1989), especially pp. 79-116. For an example of the feminist scholarship criticized by Mohanty, Spivak, and Trinh, see Monique Gadant, "Nationalité et citoyenneté: Les Femmes algériennes et leurs droits," *Peuples Méditerranéens* 44-45 (July-Dec. 1988): 293-337.

3. Marnia Lazreg, "Feminism and Difference: The Perils of Writing as a Woman on Women in Algeria," *Feminist Studies* 1 (Spring 1988): 81-107. Homa Hoodfar, "Return to the Veil: Personal Strategy and Public Participation in Egypt," in *Working Women: International Perspectives on Labour and Gender Ideology,* ed. Nanneke Redclift and M. Thea Sinclair (London: Routledge, 1991), p. 111. Future references will appear in parentheses in the text.

4. Mai Ghoussoub, "Feminism—or the Eternal Masculine—in the Arab World," *New Left Review* 161 (Jan.-Feb. 1987): 17.

5. Reza Hammami and Martina Rieker, "Feminist Orientalism and Orientalist Marxism," *New Left Review* 170 (July-Aug., 1988): 93-106.

6. Examples include *Women and Islam,* ed. Azizah al-Hibri (New York: Pergamon Press, 1982), and *Opening the Gates: A Century of Arab Feminist Writing,* ed. Margot Badran and Miriam Cooke (London: Virago, 1990).

7. See Clara Connolly, "Washing Our Linen: One Year of Women Against Fundamentalism," *Feminist Review* 37 (Spring 1991): 68-77. WAF is an international organization composed of women from Muslim countries and others living in the United Kingdom. It is not an antireligious organization. See also Pragna Patel's review essay "Alert for Action: Women Living under Muslim Laws Dossiers 1-6," *Feminist Review* 37 (Spring 1991): 95-102, which discusses the French-based organization and WAF's links to it.

8. Rabia Abdelkrim-Chikh, "Les Femmes exogames: Entre la loi de dieu et les droits de l'homme," *Annuaire de l'Afrique du Nord* 27 (1988): 237. Future references will appear in parentheses in the text.

9. Germaine Tillion, "Les Femmes et le voile," in *Etudes Maghrébines: Mélange Charles-André Julien,* ed. Pierre Marthelot and André Raymond (Paris: Presses Universitaires de France, 1964), p. 29. Future references will appear in parentheses in the text. In *Republic of Cousins: Women's Oppression in Mediterranean Society* (Atlantic Highlands, N.J.: Humanities Press International, 1983), in which another version of this essay appears, Tillion gives a finely nuanced account of the historical shifts in practices such as veiling and the disinheritance of daughters as an effect of endogamy, in terms of relations between men and women, urban and rural societies, and native and *colon* cultures. It is only the problem of women's relation to the emerging nation that is presented in a dualistic manner.

10. In saying this, I am not overlooking, much less condoning, Tillion's opposition to Algerian independence. See *Algeria: The Realities* (New York: Knopf, 1958) for her defense of the French occupation.

11. David C. Gordon, *Women of Algeria* (Cambridge, Mass.: Harvard University Press, 1968), pp. 61, 64. Future references will appear in parentheses in the text. Similar analyses appear in Attilio Gaudio and Renée Pelletier, *Femmes d'Islam, ou le sexe interdit* (Paris: Denoël, 1980), pp. 89-106, and Juliette Minces, "Women in Alge-

ria," trans. Nikki Keddie, in *Women in the Muslim World*, ed. Lois Beck and Nikki Keddie (Cambridge, Mass.: Harvard University Press, 1978), pp. 159-71.

12. Catherine Delcroix, *Espoirs et réalités de la femme arabe (Algérie-Egypte)* (Paris: L'Harmattan, 1986), p. 139. Future references will appear in parentheses in the text.

13. Interview with a combatant in the National Liberation Front's official organ, *El-Moudjahid* 72 (Nov. 1, 1960), in *La Révolution algérienne par les textes*, ed. André Mandouze (Paris: Maspero, 1961), p. 106. See Djamila Amrane's critique of women's subordination in the liberation struggle in *Les Femmes algériennes dans la guerre* (Paris: Plon, 1991).

14. Fadela M'rabet, *La Femme algérienne, suivi de les Algériennes* (Paris: Maspero, 1969).

15. Peter R. Knauss, *The Persistence of Patriarchy: Class, Gender, and Ideology in Twentieth Century Algeria* (New York: Praeger, 1987), p. xiii. Future references will appear in parentheses in the text. The patriarchal character of Algeria's political culture is unselfconsciously affirmed in films like Mohamed Lakhdar-Hamina's *Chronicle of the Years of Embers* (1976), an epic account of events leading to the revolution, and Ahmed Rachedi's *The Mill* (1985), a critique of bureaucratic inefficiency and corruption. In the same period, however, some very popular feature films deal explicitly either with the anxieties bound up with Algerian machismo (Merzak Allouache's *Omar Gatlato*, 1976) or women's dissatisfaction with current family arrangements and obstacles to their participation in public life (Ali Ghalem's *A Wife for My Son*, 1982).

16. M'rabet, *La Femme algérienne*; Knauss, *Patriarchy*, pp. 97-140; Nadia Aïnad-Tabet, "Participation des Algériennes à la vie du pays," in *Femmes et politique autour de la méditerranée*, ed. Christiane Souriau (Paris: L'Harmattan, 1980), pp. 235-50; Marie-Aimée Helie-Lucas, "Women, Nationalism and Religion in the Algerian Liberation Struggle," in *Opening the Gates: A Century of Arab Feminist Writing*, ed. Margot Badran and Miriam Cooke (Bloomington and Indianapolis: Indiana University Press, 1990), pp. 105-14.

17. See Aïnad-Tabet, "Participation," and Camille Lacoste-Dujardin, *Des Mères contre les femmes* (Paris: La Découverte, 1985). On the subject of educated women's employment in Algeria, Fatiha Talahite-Hakiki notes that despite their growing numbers, their level of paid employment in the formal sector remains low (4.5 percent), and they are called upon increasingly to contribute, through domestic labor, "not only to the biological and physiological reproduction of the labor force, but above all to the reproduction of the (male) wage-earning class" ("Scolarisation et formation des filles en Algérie: Préparation au salariat ou production de ménagères modernes?" *Annuaire de l'Afrique du Nord* 19 [1980], p. 298).

18. "Islam Fundamentalism Sweeps over Algeria Like Desert Wind," *Los Angeles Times*, June 16, 1990, sec. A. This chapter was written before the legislative elections of Dec. 27, 1991, in which the FIS won a majority of seats in the first round, prompting a military coup that ousted President Chadli Bendjedid and canceled the second round of elections. Although it appeared that the FIS would not win the two-thirds majority necessary to change the Algerian constitution, many Algerians feared that an FIS victory would bring with it, sooner or later, the establishment of an Islamic state (which is not to say that all those who harbored these fears condoned the military coup).

19. President Chadli, quoted in Knauss, *Patriarchy*, pp. 134-35. For a history of the feminist group that protested the 1981 draft of the family laws, see Rabia Ab-

delkrim-Chikh, "Les Femmes dans le monde arabe. Une seule question: être auto-nome ou pas," *Sou'al* 4 (Nov. 1983).

20. Chadli, quoted in Knauss, *Patriarchy*, p. 135.

21. Ratiba Hadj-Moussa, *Les Femmes algériennes entre l'honneur et la révolution* (Québec: Laboratoire de recherches sociologiques, 1984). Rabia Abdelkrim-Chikh, "Les Enjeux politiques et symboliques de la lutte des femmes pour l'égalité entre les sexes en Algérie," *Peuples Méditerranéens* 48-49 (July-Dec. 1989): 257-78. Future references will appear in parentheses in the text. Marie-Aimée Hélie-Lucas, "Les Stratégies des femmes à l'égard des fondamentalismes dans le monde musulman," *Nouvelles Questions Féministes* 16-18 (1991): 29-61.

22. See "No Future à Bab-el-Oued," *L'Express*, Oct. 6-12, 1989, pp. 27-29; Jean Daniel, "Le Ciel et la rue," *Le Nouvel Observateur*, Feb. 15-21, 1990, pp. 38-40; and Farid Aïchoune, " 'La Femme est une fabrique de musulmans,' " *Le Nouvel Observateur*, Apr. 5-11, 1990, pp. 13-14.

23. See Fatna A. Sabbah, *Woman in the Muslim Unconscious*, trans. Mary Jo Lakeland (New York: Pergamon Press, 1984).

24. *Le Nouvel Observateur*, Feb. 22-28, 1990, p. 23.

25. Fatima Mernissi, "Muslim Women and Fundamentalism," *Middle East Report* 153 (July-Aug. 1988): 11. Future references will appear in parentheses in the text. This essay is adapted from the introduction to the revised edition of Mernissi's *Beyond the Veil: Male-Female Dynamics in Modern Muslim Society* (Bloomington and Indianapolis: Indiana University Press, 1987).

26. Quoted by Mostefa Lacheraf, *L'Algérie: Nation et Société* (Paris: Maspero, 1969), pp. 255-56.

27. Maurice Viollette, *L'Algérie vivra-t-elle?* (Paris: Alcan, 1931), p. 412. Future references will appear in parentheses in the text.

28. See Charles-Robert Ageron, *Histoire de l'Algérie Contemporaine*, 2 volumes (Paris: Presses Universitaires de France, 1979), vol. 2, pp. 449-66. Future references to this text are to volume 2 and will appear in parentheses.

29. On the administration's exploitation of Muslim personal status in order to deny natives voting rights, see Jean Mélia, *Le Triste sort des indigènes musulmans d'Algérie* (Paris: Mercure de France, 1935), pp. 215-29. On feminist reforms in Turkey and Egypt and debates about reform in Algeria in the 1930s, see Ali Merad, *Le Réformisme musulman en Algérie de 1925 à 1940* (Paris: Mouton, 1967), pp. 315-31. See also the Ulemas' (religious reformers) newspaper *La Défense*, May 25, 1934, Nov. 9, 1934, and Nov. 23, 1934, and Leila Ahmed, "Feminism and Feminist Movements in the Middle East," in *Women and Islam*, ed. al-Hibri, pp. 153-68. On the Communist party's program for Algerian women, see N. D'Orient and M. Loew, *La Question algérienne* (Paris: Bureau d'Editions, 1936), pp. 229-31, and Monique Gadant, "Les Communistes algériens et l'émancipation des femmes," *Peuples Méditerranéens* 48-49 (July-Dec. 1989): 199-228.

30. Jean-Robert Henry and François Balique, *La Doctrine coloniale du droit musulman algérien* (Paris: Centre National de la Recherche Scientifique, 1979), p. 37.

31. For a liberal view close to Viollette's, see René Maunier, *Sociologie coloniale* (Paris: Domat-Montchrestien, 1932).

32. Octave Depont, *L'Algérie du Centenaire* (Bordeaux: Cadoret, 1928), p. 46. Future references will appear in parentheses in the text. For similar views, see E.-F. Gautier, *L'Algérie et la métropole* (Paris: Payot, 1920), pp. 207-54, and Arnold Van Gennep, *En Algérie* (Paris: Mercure de France, 1914), pp. 168-77, 192.

33. On medical assistance as a means of regulation, see also Doctor Calmette, "Les Principes de la politique française coloniale," in *L'Empire colonial français*, ed. Gabriel Hanotaux (Paris: Plon, 1929), pp. 143-58.

34. Maunier, *Sociologie coloniale*, pp. 112-13.

35. Abdallah Laroui, *L'Histoire du Maghreb* (Paris: Maspero, 1970), p. 355.

36. Frantz Fanon, "L'Algérie se dévoile," in *Sociologie d'une révolution* (Paris: Maspero, 1968), p. 23. Future references are to this edition and will appear in parentheses in the text. In English, "Algeria Unveiled," in *A Dying Colonialism*, trans. Haakon Chevalier (New York: Grove Press, 1967), pp. 35-67. Pierre Bourdieu discusses this dynamic in similar terms in "Guerre et mutation sociale en Algérie," *Etudes Maghrébines* 7 (Spring 1960): 25-37.

37. See Hal Lehrman, "Battle of the Veil," *New York Times Magazine*, July 13, 1958, pp. 14, 18. Lehrman notes that Algerian women organized a counterdemonstration, demanding the release of political prisoners. In *L'Aliénation colonialiste et la résistance de la famille algérienne* (Lausanne: La Cité, 1961), Saadia and Lakhdar accuse the French organizers of the May 13 event of forcing their maids, as well as Algerian prostitutes, to participate in this "grotesque effort" (143).

38. On the establishment of women's camps, see Patrick Kessel and Giovanni Pirelli, *Le Peuple algérien et la guerre: Lettres et témoignages d'Algériens* (Paris: Maspero, 1962), p. 537, n. 4. On Algerian women's methods of organizing in the prison camps and their political and ideological differences with Algerian men, see Djamila Amrane, *Les Femmes algériennes dans la guerre* (cited in n. 13).

39. Ageron, *Histoire*, (609; my emphasis).

40. See Mostefa Lacheraf's comments in *Révolution Africaine*, Dec. 7, 1963, pp. 18-19, and Dec. 19, 1963, pp. 22-23.

41. André Adam, "Chronique sociale et culturelle," *Annuaire de l'Afrique du Nord* 1 (1962): 545-62. See, for example, "On National Culture," in *The Wretched of the Earth*, trans. Constance Farrington (New York: Grove Press, 1968), where Fanon points out that "the colonized man who writes for his people ought to use the past with the intention of opening the future, as an invitation to action and a basis for hope" (232). He also notes that "we find today the Arab states organically linked once more with societies which are Mediterranean in their culture. The fact is that these states are submitted to modern pressure and to new channels of trade" (216).

42. See Jean-Paul Charnay, *La Vie musulmane en Algérie d'après la jurisprudence* (Paris: Presses Universitaires de France, 1965). For a U.S. view in favor of French reforms, see "Kif-Kif la Française," *Time*, Feb. 23, 1959, p. 26.

43. Simone de Beauvoir and Gisèle Halimi, *Djamila Boupacha*, trans. Peter Green (New York: Macmillan, 1962).

44. Marnia Lazreg ("Feminism and Difference," 90-91) signals the exploitative nature of studies of Algerian women by early twentieth-century French feminists Mathéa Gaudry and Hubertine Auclert. In *Femmes arabes et soeurs musulmanes* (Paris: Editions Tierce, 1984), Denise Brahimi shows that for Gaudry, Auclert, Henriette Celarié, and other feminists writing in the first half of the twentieth century, expressions of sympathy with and admiration for Algerian women emerge alongside manifestations of frustration with the economic, social, and political circumstances of French women, suggesting that French feminism both projected its ideals onto Algerian women and used them as a site for the deployment of French women's power and authority in compensation for defeats suffered at home. Yet however self-serving their relation to Algerian women may have been, I think it is a mistake

to view their work as purely colonialist. It should be acknowledged, for example, that when Mathéa Gaudry applauded the resourcefulness and independence of Chaouïa women in *La Femme Chaouïa de l'Aurès: Etude de sociologie berbère* (Paris: Geuthner, 1929), she was not merely expressing frustration with her own situation or nostalgia for a legendary pre-Islamic Berber past in which women were supposedly powerful; she was also affirming Algerian women's resistance to oppressive indigenous institutions while simultaneously complicating the colonialist view of Algerian women and Berbers (an ethnic minority) as weak links in the nationalist chain. Yvonne Knibiehler and Régine Gontalier's *Femmes et colonisation: Rapport terminal au Ministère des relations extérieures et de la coopération* (Aix-en-Provence: Université de Provence, Institut d'Histoire des Pays d'Outre Mer, 1986) provides much interesting information about early twentieth-century French feminists' activity in the colonies and in the promotion of colonization, although the authors are quite uncritical of French feminism's reliance on colonialism to promote itself.

45. Feminist literary critics have been calling attention to nationalism's counter-revolutionary effects on Algerian women at least since Evelyne Accad's *Veil of Shame: The Role of Women in the Contemporary Fiction of North Africa and the Arab World* (Sherbrooke, Quebec: Editions Naaman, 1978). (See, for example, her discussion of Assia Djebar's writing, pp. 37-48.) However, I know of no treatment of the dynamic that concerns me here, that is, the mobilization of the figure "woman" to contain and mediate, as well as to assume responsibility for, social divisions within the nation.

46. Ahmed, "Feminism and Feminist Movements in the Middle East," p. 163.

47. Kateb Yacine, *Nedjma* (Paris: Seuil, 1956), pp. 128-29; in English, trans. Richard Howard (New York: George Braziller, 1961), pp. 170-71. Future references will appear in parentheses in the text. Charles Bonn's *Kateb Yacine: Nedjma* (Paris: Presses Universitaires de France, 1990) provides a helpful introduction to the novel. It includes an account of the literary context in which it emerged, a textual analysis, a commentary on its relation to Kateb's other work, and a bibliography.

48. Abdelkebir Khatibi, *Le Roman maghrébin* (Rabat: Société Marocaine des Editeurs Réunis, 1979), p. 104. Future references will appear in parentheses in the text.

49. Accad, *Veil of Shame*, p. 90. See also Jacqueline Arnaud, *La Littérature maghrébine de langue française: Le Cas de Kateb Yacine* (Paris: Publisud, 1986), pp. 35-46, 309-14. Future references will appear in parentheses in the text.

50. Barbara Harlow, *Resistance Literature* (New York: Methuen, 1987), p. 82. Future references will appear in parentheses in the text.

51. On Kahina, see Arnaud, *Littérature maghrébine*, pp. 172-74. On the Etoile Nord-Africaine movement, see Ageron, *Histoire*, pp. 349-59.

52. In addition to Arnaud's study, see, for example, Jean Déjeux, "Les Structures de l'imagination dans l'oeuvre de Kateb Yacine," *Revue de l'Occident Musulman et de la Méditerranée* 13-14 (1973): 263-92; Kristine Aurbakken, *L'Etoile d'araignée: Une Lecture de Nedjma de Kateb Yacine* (Paris: Publisud, 1986), pp. 175-204; and Mildred P. Mortimer, "Kateb Yacine in Search of Algeria," *L'Esprit Créateur* 4 (Winter 1972): 274-88.

53. The point here is to show that *Nedjma* exploits for its own purposes, but also alerts readers to the dangers of, the modern uses to which "woman" and women are put in Algeria. This is a different matter from charging Kateb with sexism (or defending him against such charges, as Arnaud is anxious to do). It is well known that until his death in 1989 Kateb supported Algerian feminism, and particularly the women writers of Algeria. He writes, for example, in his preface to Yam-

ina Méchakra's *La Grotte éclatée* (Algiers: Entreprise National du Livre, 1986), that "at present, in our country, a woman who writes is worth her weight in gunpowder" (8).

54. Aurbakken, *L'Etoile d'araignée*, p. 199. Future references will appear in parentheses in the text.

55. Antoine Raybaud, "Roman algérien et quête d'identité," *Europe* 567-68 (July-Aug. 1976): 54-62.

56. Malek Alloula, *The Colonial Harem*, trans. Myrna Godzich and Wlad Godzich (Minneapolis: University of Minnesota Press, 1986). Future references will appear in parentheses in the text.

57. On the displacement of Algerians as a result of colonial land policies, see Lacheraf, *L'Algérie*, pp. 16-25, 70-71, and Pierre Nora, *Les Français d'Algérie* (Paris: Julliard, 1961), pp. 90-93. On the prostitution that results, see Yvonne Knibiehler and Régine Gontalier, *La Femme au temps des colonies* (Paris: Stock, 1985), p. 248, and Jacques Berque, *Le Maghreb entre deux guerres* (Paris: Seuil, 1962), pp. 357-59.

58. Mathéa Gaudry, *La Société féminine au Djebel Amour et au Ksel* (Algiers: Société Algérienne d'Impressions Diverses, 1961).

59. On the second-class economic and social status of French Algerians by comparison with their metropolitan compatriots, and on Frenchness as the main force mitigating ethnic and class conflicts among them by differentiating them from the Algerian natives, see Nora, *Les Français d'Algérie*, pp. 133-43, 150-51.

60. Maurice Besson, "La Première Exposition Coloniale," *Bulletin du Comité de l'Afrique Française* 2 (Feb. 1931): 123.

61. Quoted by C. M., "Autour de l'Exposition coloniale," *Bulletin du Comité de l'Afrique Française* 11 (Nov. 1931): 734.

62. Text of a speech by Gustave Mercier, general commissioner, "The Results of the Algerian Centenary," *Bulletin du Comité de l'Afrique Française* 6 (1930): 391, 393.

63. Roland Barthes, *Camera Lucida*, trans. Richard Howard (New York: Hill and Wang, 1982), p. 98; quoted by Alloula, *Colonial Harem*, p. 131 n. 28.

64. Proceedings of the Congress on Rural Colonization, *Bulletin du Comité de l'Afrique Française* 9 (Sept. 1930): 521-22.

65. The implantation (and negative reinterpretation) of this ideology is evident from the 1930s through the 1960s. On the Muslim reformers' view of the beaches and dance halls as scenes of "fornication," see Merad, *Réformisme musulman*, pp. 328, 329 n. 2. On the official pronouncements of the Algerian government after independence regarding Western women's eternal and inevitable subordination in "consumer society," see Hadj-Moussa, *Femmes algériennes*, pp. 166-69.

66. Marc Garanger, *Femmes algériennes 1960* (Paris: Contrejour, 1982). In *Révolution en Algérie* (Paris: France Empire, 1956), René Schaefer notes that during the revolution certain Algerian women were required to unveil for photos that appeared on food cards needed to obtain provisions (147). On the "resettlement" of Algerian populations during the revolution, see Lacheraf, *Algérie*, pp. 265-66; Bourdieu, "Guerre et mutation sociale," pp. 32-33; and Patrick Eveno and Jean Planchais, *La Guerre d'Algérie* (Paris: La Découverte, 1989), pp. 221, 223-28.

67. Leïla Sebbar, *Shérazade, brune, frisée, les yeux verts* (Paris: Stock, 1982), p. 220.

68. In "Algeria, Conquered by Postcard" (*New York Times Book Review*, Jan. 11, 1987, p. 24), Carol Schloss remarks in a similar vein that despite Alloula's effort to construct a countermemory by restoring the postcards to their original context, "the cultural dialogue he initiates remains male-centered and concerned with women as

property and as symbolic marks of (dis)honor or status for the men in their families." However, Schloss accepts Alloula's view of the postcards as a "surrogate" for political and military conquest. Another brief critique of Alloula's male-centered interpretation appears in Cynthia Enloe, *Bananas, Beaches, and Bases: Making Feminist Sense of International Politics* (London: Pandora Press, 1989), pp. 42-44.

69. See, for instance, Fatima Mernissi, *Beyond the Veil*, and Assia Djebar, "Forbidden Sight, Interrupted Sound," *Discourse* 8 (Fall-Winter, 1986-87): 39-56.

70. Ghoussoub, "Feminism—or the Eternal Masculine—in the Arab World," p. 17. In the discussion that follows (pp. 17-18), she illustrates changes in the work of Ijlal Khalifa, author of books on the history of the women's movement in Egypt and Palestine; Aziza al-Hibri, a feminist Marxist philosopher; and noted Egyptian feminists Leila Ahmed and Nawal al-Saadawi, all of whom have recently subordinated feminism to class struggle or defended antifeminist Islamic practices in the name of anti-imperialism.

71. Nayereh Tohidi, "Gender and Islamic Fundamentalism: Feminist Politics in Iran," in *Third World Women and the Politics of Feminism*, ed. Chandra Talpade Mohanty, Ann Russo, and Lourdes Torres (Bloomington and Indianapolis: Indiana University Press, 1991), p. 260.

72. Connolly, "Washing Our Linen," p. 69.

73. See Diana Johnstone, "In 'Great Kerchief Quarrel' French Unite against 'Anglo-Saxon Ghettos,' " *In These Times*, Jan. 24-30, 1990, pp. 10-11, and Christian Casteron, "La 'Guerre du foulard' aura-t-elle lieu?" *Jeune Afrique*, Nov. 6, 1989, pp. 40-41.

74. Florence Assouline, *Musulmanes: Une Chance pour l'islam* (Paris: Flammarion, 1992), pp. 127-42.

75. Mernissi, "Muslim Women," p. 9.

Chapter 2. Wild Femininity and Historical Countermemory

1. Mohammed Dib, *Who Remembers the Sea*, trans. Louis Tremaine (Washington, D.C.: Three Continents Press, 1985). Originally *Qui se souvient de la mer* (Paris: Seuil, 1962). On the author's search for new forms capable of giving voice to the cataclysmic events of which he is writing, see Dib's postface to this novel. Future references to these texts will appear in parentheses.

2. All three volumes of Dib's trilogy were published in Paris by Seuil. Mouloud Feraoun, *La Terre et le sang* (Paris: Seuil, 1953); Mouloud Mammeri, *La Colline oubliée* (Paris: Plon, 1952).

3. For instance, Dib declares that the books he wrote prior to *Who Remembers the Sea* continue to be considered as indispensable testimonies. "But," he says, "with the mass of documents and testimonies accumulated on the subject of the Algerian War and on Algeria *tout court*, the Algerian author feels freed from his responsibility in relation to current events: he is no longer obliged to follow the events step by step. And it becomes possible for him to deepen his reflection and even to seek adventure (I mean literary adventure, the adventure of creation), in short, by taking risks." *Les Lettres françaises*, Feb. 7, 1963, p. 5.

4. Ronnie Scharfman, "Starting from Talismano: Abdelwahab Meddeb's Nomadic Writing," *L'Esprit Créateur* 1 (1986): 41.

5. In "Le Desserrage des structures romanesques dans *Le Champ des oliviers* de Nabile Farès et *Talismano* d'Abdelwahab Meddeb," *Itinéraires et Contacts de Cultures*

4-5 (1984): 158, Anne Roche writes, for instance: "This analysis of techniques certainly defers the question of meaning. What can the commentator say about war, horror, loss, etc.? More important, what can one say that cannot be 'diverted'? It is through the violence of his narration, more than through the violence of what is narrated, that Farès proffers an 'unacceptable' discourse." Charles Bonn makes a similar claim in *Le Roman algérien de langue française* (Paris: L'Harmattan, 1985), p. 286, where he maintains that the text of *L'Exil et le désarroi* "escapes" from ideological discourse, and that "its author . . . knows that an ideological discourse can always be used against its intended aims, whereas the *song* can never be diverted or led astray" (emphasis is Bonn's). Already in *Le Roman maghrébin* (Rabat: Société Marocaine des Editeurs Réunis, 1979), Abdelkebir Khatibi was often moving abruptly from the analysis of political content to universalizing claims about Maghrebian writing as pure literariness, especially in the texts of Kateb Yacine. Raybaud is the exception here, for although he, too, places greater emphasis in the eighties on literariness (drawing mainly on Kristeva's work), he consistently grounds his readings historically. See his "Le Travail du poème dans le roman maghrébin (II): L'Exemple du *Champ des oliviers* de Nabile Farès," *Itinéraires et Contacts de Cultures* 4-5 (1984): 105-45.

6. Some attacks on Francophone Maghrebian writers were published in *Les Temps Modernes* 375 bis (Oct. 1977), a special issue titled *Du Maghreb*. For an excellent critical response to these attacks, see Antoine Raybaud and Anne Roche, "La Littérature maghrébine d'expression française en mutation," *Annuaire de l'Afrique du Nord* (1978): 887-97.

7. Martine Gozlan, "Femmes: Ce que nous avons à redouter des islamistes," *L'Evénement du jeudi*, Jan. 9-15, 1992, p. 30.

8. "Assocations de femmes/Droit d'exister," El *Watan*, Jan. 3-4, 1992.

9. Florence Assouline, *Musulmanes, une chance pour l'islam* (Paris: Flammarion, 1992), p. 178. Dalal Bizri examines religious conservatives' discourses on Arab women in "La Femme arabe dans le discours islamiste contemporain," *Peuples Méditerranéens* 48-49 (July-Dec. 1989): 309-27, but unfortunately she tends to treat Islamic fundamentalism as a monolithic movement.

10. Fazia Hacène, "Associations féminines. Objectif: La coordination," *El Moudjahid*, Nov. 20, 1989, p. 20.

11. Aissa Khelladi, "L'homme est-il l'avenir de la femme?" *Ounoutha* 1 (Apr. 1991): 19.

12. Assouline, *Musulmanes*, pp. 178-79. In Assouline's text, the expression "will to servitude" is in quotation marks.

13. Fatima Mernissi, *Doing Daily Battle: Interviews with Moroccan Women*, trans. Mary Jo Lakeland (New Brunswick, N.J.: Rutgers University Press, 1989).

14. Fatima Mernissi, "Women, Saints, and Sanctuaries," in *Women and National Development*, ed. Wellesley Editorial Committee (Chicago: University of Chicago Press, 1977), p. 107. Future references will appear in parentheses in the text. For a study of female singers of *ray* music in Algeria—economically and socially marginalized singers who, like the women in Mernissi's study, at once contest and reinvest practices that consolidate their marginalization—see Marie Virolle-Souibes, "Le Ray, côté femmes: Entre alchimie de la douleur et spleen sans idéal, quelques fragments de discours hédonique," *Peuples Méditerranéens* 44-45 (July-Dec. 1988): 193-220. Unfortunately, as her subtitle suggests, Virolle-Souibes uncritically attributes to Algerian subaltern women a "hedonist" ideal, which, more than anything else,

seems to reflect the author's nostalgia for a certain current in European feminism of the 1970s, filtered through modern French poetry.

15. Fatima Mernissi, *Beyond the Veil: Male-Female Dynamics in a Modern Muslim Society* (Bloomington and Indianapolis: Indiana University Press, 1987). An adapted version of the introduction to this volume, which I am quoting in my discussion, appears under the title "Muslim Women and Fundamentalism" in *Middle East Report* 153 (July-Aug. 1988): 8-11. Future references will appear in parentheses in the text.

16. Fatima Mernissi, *Sultanes oubliées: Femmes chefs d'état en islam* (Paris: Albin Michel, 1990), and *Le Harem politique: Le Prophète et les femmes* (Paris: Albin Michel, 1987); in English, *The Veil and the Male Elite: A Feminist Interpretation of Women's Rights in Islam*, trans. Mary Jo Lakeland (Reading, Mass.: Addison-Wesley, 1991). Assia Djebar, *Loin de Médine* (Paris: Albin Michel, 1991). For an analysis of these texts, see my "Feminism and Islamic Tradition," *Studies in Twentieth Century Literature* 1(Winter 1993): 27-44. For an analysis of the historically changing forms and functions of Islam in Algeria in various urban and rural contexts, see Paul Vieille, "L'Urbain et le mal de modernité," *Peuples Méditerranéens* 37 (Oct.-Dec. 1986): 141-54.

17. See Camille Lacoste-Dujardin, *Le Conte Kabyle: Etude ethnologique* (Paris: Maspero, 1970), p. 101. Unlike Kateb and Farès, Lacoste-Dujardin interprets the ogress's negativity (pp. 95-107) as a social evil that the male hero Mquides must overcome in order to restabilize a community threatened by female insubordination and male rivalry. For Lacoste-Dujardin, "Mquides must refuse to engage with the *teryel* [the ogress] in a system of exchanges, of gifts and countergifts, that could introduce this asocial woman into the society of men, and must denounce her 'savagery' " (97). For a more critical view, see Nabile Farès, "Littérature orale et anthropologie, signification de l'Ogresse" (Thèse de troisième cycle, Faculté des Lettres, Université de Paris X-Nanterre, 1971).

18. Nabile Farès, *Le Champ des oliviers* (Paris: Seuil, 1972), p. 32. Future references will appear in parentheses in the text.

19. Kateb Yacine, *Nedjma*, trans. Richard Howard (New York: George Braziller, 1961), pp. 179, 112.

20. Kateb Yacine, "La Femme sauvage/1," *Les Lettres nouvelles* 67 (Jan. 1959): 1-6; reprinted in *Kateb Yacine: L'Oeuvre en fragments*, ed. Jacqueline Arnaud (Paris: Sindbad, 1986), pp. 165-66. The translation is mine. On Kateb's play *La Femme sauvage*, comprising various texts written at different times and performed in Brussels after the war of liberation, see Taïeb Sbouaï, *La Femme sauvage de Kateb Yacine* (Paris: Arcantère, 1985).

21. In an essay on Mouloud Feraoun's *Le Fils du pauvre* (Paris: Seuil, 1950), Naget Khadda takes a position close to mine when she claims that "the feminine puts pressure on and unsettles established identities at the same time that it is itself pressured and unsettled by the changes made" ("Allégorie de la féminité," *Peuples Méditerranéens* 44-45 [July-Dec. 1988]: 86). Khadda argues in "Mohammed Dib: Esquisse d'un itinéraire," *Itinéraires et Contacts de Cultures* 4-5 (1984): 197-234, that Dib constructs a "defense" (223) against Nafissa's revolutionary force by means of doubling, that is, by splitting the familiar maternal figure from the lover, whose mysterious qualities make her a "stranger" or "foreigner" (221). She maintains that the mysterious Nafissa seems at times to be working for the enemy and that her feminism is thus misogynistically construed as being alien to nationalist ideology. I am trying to show, on the other hand, that while Nafissa's commitment to the revolu-

tionary struggle is uncertain only insofar as it is seen through the eyes of a narrator who at first only dimly perceives the existence and import of that struggle, Dib's text *is* equivocal about the place of feminism in postindependence Algeria: it substitutes the male narrator/writer for Nafissa and does not articulate the (possibly altered) genders of the "neighbors" and "strangers" (108) who will negotiate Algeria's identity in the new historical context figured by an underground city in communication with other worlds—a context that cannot be mapped in terms of nationalist ideology.

Let me add here that critics of Algerian literature—particularly Algerian women's literature—invariably point to "the couple" as a site of critical reflection and social transformation without examining the ways in which the texts problematize the very notion of "the couple" as a discrete unit that can be considered independently of political change in other spheres, such as government. In addition to Dib's *Who Remembers the Sea*, it is interesting to consider, for example, Assia Djebar's *Les Alouettes naïves* (Paris: Julliard, 1967), in which the trope of naiveté semiotically links three aspects of Algerian history that display with particular clarity the imbrication of sexual and political forms of domination: (1) the colonial exploitation of Algerian women as prostitutes, referred to as "naive larks" (*alouettes naïves* rather than *Ouled Naïl*, p. 423) by French soldiers and settlers; (2) the political naiveté of those who believed that after independence slogans such as "bread for all" and "a total awakening" (395) would become a reality; and (3) the "naive force" (420) of Algerian women, particularly Djebar's female protagonist, Nfissa, who avidly embraces life as both a militant and a lover while her husband, Rachid, like the narrator of *Who Remembers the Sea*, draws on and tries to articulate his partner's force in his writing. So although it is stated in the last pages of the novel that "war that ends between peoples is reborn between couples" (423), there is no reason to confine gender relations to "the couple" or to construe the transformation of gender identities as a "women's" issue.

22. This same dynamic is evident in Dib's "Naëma disparue" in *Le Talisman* (Paris: Seuil, 1966), pp. 65–85, where the bewildered male narrator is always confronted with "the same incertitude, the same madness" (80), whereas his wife Naëma and the revolutionaries she fought with "know why they died" (85). In *Habel* (Paris: Seuil, 1977), the male protagonist is torn between two opposing female figures, Sabine and Lily, who embody the extremes of fixity and boundlessness that, in *Qui se souvient de la mer*, are both figured by Nafissa. In *Habel*, too, it is the male alone who negotiates uncertainty (as opposed to repressing it, as Sabine does, or succumbing to it in madness, as Lily does).

23. Nabile Farès, *Un passager de l'occident* (Paris: Seuil, 1971), p. 20.

24. Nabile Farès, *Mémoire de l'absent* (Paris: Seuil, 1974), and *L'Exil et le désarroi* (Paris: Maspero, 1976).

25. Antoine Raybaud, "Le Travail du poème dans le roman maghrébin (II): L'Exemple du *Champ des oliviers* de Nabile Farès," *Itinéraires et Contacts de Cultures* 4-5 (1984): 119.

26. See Antoine Raybaud and Anne Roche, "Pas," *Littérature* 27 (Oct. 1977): 116-128.

27. Not that the Berber kingdom was culturally "pure" before the Arab conquest. Denise Brahimi notes, for instance, in *Femmes arabes et soeurs musulmanes* (Paris: Editions Tierce, 1984), pp. 133-66, that Kahena practiced a mix of Judaism and the traditional Berber religion.

28. Raybaud and Roche, "Pas," p. 120.

29. Nabile Farès, *Yahia, pas de chance* (Paris: Seuil, 1970).

30. Charles Bonn, *Le Roman algérien*, p. 283. Bonn is quoting *L'Exil*, p. 37. Future references to *Le Roman algérien* will appear in parentheses in the text.

31. The recognizably female energy source is naturalized and neutered by Roche, who refers to the "*nourishment* of [Farès's] text by a *compost* of folktales and popular traditions," elements that are "reutilized . . . in a construction of another type, here, a book, a 'literary' book" ("Le Desserrage des structures romanesques," p. 156; my emphasis).

32. Here I have borrowed a phrase from Elizabeth Fox-Genovese, "Placing Women's History in History," *New Left Review* 133 (May-June 1982): 5-29. Fox-Genovese argues that historians should be more attentive to the ways analyses of gender make history ambiguous, rather than merely adding women's history to the existing body of historical work. I have of course been arguing that literary critics, who are no strangers to ambiguity, should be attentive to women's history, which places limits on the usefulness of ambiguity as a critical category.

33. Rachid Boudjedra, *La Répudiation* (Paris: Denoël, 1969) and *L'Insolation* (Paris: Denoël, 1972). Future references will appear in parentheses in the text. Translations are mine. In these novels, there are in fact few attempts to affirm anyone's agency other than the narrator's own. For example, although the oppressed Algerian people are sometimes termed "recalcitrant" (*Répudiation*, p. 247) to authoritarian rule, they are more often depicted as "sleeping in their majestic indifference to everything that emanated from the Clan [the Algerian ruling elites], good or bad, licit or iniquitous, true or false" (*Répudiation*, p. 248). In "La Femme, l'émigré, et l'écriture romanesque maghrébine, ou la triple productivité de l'étrange," *Peuples Méditerranéens* 44-45 (July-Dec. 1988): 221-33, Charles Bonn notes the limited formal purpose served by the main female characters in Boudjedra's first two novels, but is content to discuss them, along with emigré characters in other texts, as figures for the differences inhabiting all identities (subjective, cultural, national, etc.). I am trying to indicate, on the other hand, the sexual-political consequences of such a move, namely, the designation of men alone as subjects and beneficiaries of liberatory symbolic practices.

34. At the International Writers' Meeting in Montreal, Oct. 15, 1976, Boudjedra said he was very suspicious of the trend to valorize orality, which is "tied to a return to the countryside and to the view of the *noble savage*. It's very dangerous. It comes in part from Western ethnology and sociology which try to apply their schemata to Algeria. . . . In Algeria, the question of orality is closely linked to a backward-looking ideology (*passéisme*)," which Boudjedra wants to distinguish from nostalgia for the stories and storytelling that are dying with the storytellers of his grandmother's generation. "*Passéisme* is a reactionary political ideology. In my country, the people who espouse *passéisme* are religious fundamentalists who want people to live today as they did in ninth-century Islam" (quoted by Jean Royer in *Ecrivains contemporains: Entretiens I: 1976-1979* [Montreal: L'Hexagone, 1982], pp. 89-90). In *L'Insolation*, the figure of *la femme sauvage* is linked to a colonialist notion of the noble savage and to *passéisme*, whereas Djoha embodies those aspects of orality that disrupt oppressive social relations and can be turned to progressive purposes. An analogous figure is Tahar Ben Jelloun's Moha in *Moha le fou, Moha le sage* (Paris: Seuil, 1978).

35. In "Le Jeu sur l'intertextualité dans *L'Insolation* de Rachid Boudjedra," *Itinéraires et Contacts de cultures* 4-5 (1984): 235-46, Charles Bonn details the reinscription

of writings by Kateb in Boudjedra's novel, claiming, for instance, that Nadia is an "ogress" like Nedjma and like Moutt of *Le Polygone étoilé* (Paris: Seuil, 1966). Because he is concerned to show that Boudjedra's affiliation with Kateb is literary rather than national, cultural, or political, Bonn leaves sexual politics aside, missing the fact that while Nadia has only destructive power (except insofar as she elicits the monologue of the male narrator, Rachid), the repellent Moutt forces others to "provide for her," to satisfy her hunger so that "a song of eternal youth" (73) may be brought to *her* lips—not just to the lips of male creators. Similarly, although Bonn rightly points out that Samia is in many ways a "double" of Nedjma insofar as she is loved by a character named Rachid, guarded by a black man associated with tribal traditions, and so on, he overlooks the fact that Samia entirely lacks her literary predecessor's potency as a maker of social meanings.

36. Hafid Gafaiti, "L'Affirmation de la parole féminine dans l'oeuvre de Rachid Boudjedra," *Itinéraires et Contacts de Cultures* 11 (1990): 49-54. Rachid Boudjedra, *La Pluie*, trans. Antoine Moussali (Paris: Denoël, 1987). This novel was originally published in Arabic.

37. Rachid Boudjedra, *Le Démantèlement* (Paris: Denoël, 1982).

38. In "Phantasmatic Identification and the Question of Sex," a lecture delivered at Cornell University on Nov. 6, 1991, Judith Butler elaborated a critique of this association in the work of Julia Kristeva, challenging Kristeva's reliance on Lacanian orthodoxy regarding the constitution of the symbolic and its supposedly necessary exclusion of homosexual desire. On Kristeva's reluctance to transform the symbolic, see Butler's "The Body Politics of Julia Kristeva," *Hypatia: A Journal of Feminist Philosophy* 3 (Winter 1989): 104-18.

39. Fettouma Touati, *Le Printemps désespéré* (Paris: L'Harmattan, 1984); in English, *Desperate Spring: Lives of Algerian Women*, trans. Ros Schwartz (London: Women's Press, 1987); Hafsa Zinaï-Koudil, *Le Pari perdu* (Algiers: Entreprise Nationale du Livre, 1986); Myriam Ben, *Sabrina, ils t'ont volé ta vie* (Paris: L'Harmattan, 1986). Future references to these texts will appear in parentheses. Myriam Ben's novel was published in the series "Ecritures arabes," which, according to its director Marc Gontard (whose blurb appears on the back cover of *Sabrina*), "is intent on discovering new novelistic or poetic writing, new modes of expression capable of unsettling the hackneyed forms of the dominant literary discourse." Ironically, in terms of its clichéd language and plot, *Sabrina* is really no different from Zinaï-Koudil's *Le Pari perdu*, which is published in Algiers. Ali Ghalem's 1982 film *Une Femme pour mon fils* (A wife for my son) is conceived in the same spirit as the novels under discussion here.

40. I am thinking especially of the many reviews, annotated bibliographical entries, and essays of Jean Déjeux on this subject, notably his *Femmes d'Algérie: Légendes, traditions, histoire, littérature* (Paris: La Boîte à Documents, 1987), and of Charles Bonn's discussions of Assia Djebar and Yamina Mechakra in *Le Roman algérien*, pp. 79-111, 163-86.

41. Simone Rezzoug, "Ecritures féminines algériennes: Histoire et société," *Maghreb Review* 3-4 (1984): 86.

42. Yamina Mechakra, *La Grotte éclatée* (Algiers: Entreprise Nationale du Livre, 1986); originally published in Algiers by Société Nationale d'Edition et de Diffusion in 1979. A similar strategy is evident in the title story of Leila Abouzeid's *Year of the Elephant: A Moroccan Woman's Journey toward Independence*, trans. Barbara Parmenter (Austin, Tex.: Center for Middle Eastern Studies, 1989), where the protagonist Za-

hra is divorced and falls into destitution after carrying bombs in the struggle for independence. Like Mechakra, Abouzeid creates a protagonist of an earlier generation, both to take advantage of the symbolic value accorded women's role in the independence struggle and, as Rezzoug notes (88), to avoid charges of writing autobiographically, that is, writing merely to advance her personal interests. Abouzeid's collection of short stories was originally published in Arabic in the *Al Mithaq* newspaper in Rabat in 1983. It was subsequently published in Morocco in 1984 by Dar Al Maarif, then in Beirut by Dar Al Afaq Al Jadida in 1987.

43. Assia Djebar, *Les Enfants du nouveau monde* (Paris: Julliard, 1962).

44. Djebar discussed the film after a screening at the conference "Femmes, Ecritures, Sociétés" at Queen's University, Kingston, Ontario, Oct. 1991. Because the film was to have been shown on television, only little girls and older women appeared on camera because young women did not want to dishonor their families or ruin their chances of getting a husband by having their images broadcast on the national airwaves.

45. Assia Djebar, *Fantasia, an Algerian Cavalcade*, trans. Dorothy S. Blair (London: Quartet, 1985), originally, *L'Amour, la fantasia* (Paris: Lattès, 1985); and *A Sister to Sheherazade*, trans. Dorothy S. Blair (London: Quartet, 1987), originally *Ombre sultane* (Paris: Lattès, 1987). Future references will appear in parentheses in the text.

46. I am indebted to Anne Donadey Roch's "Writing the Trace: Assia Djebar's *L'Amour, la fantasia* as a Bilingual Palimpsest," delivered at the meeting of the Modern Language Association, Dec. 1990.

47. In Djebar's text, "tant d'anonymes ensevelies" (88).

48. Rabia Abdelkrim-Chikh, "Les Enjeux politiques et symboliques de la lutte des femmes pour l'égalité entre les sexes en Algérie," *Peuples Méditerranéens* 48-49 (July-Dec. 1988): 276.

49. Julia Kristeva, "Un nouveau type d'intellectuel: Le dissident," *Tel Quel* 74 (Winter 1977): 71.

Chapter 3. Exile

1. Edward Said, "The Mind of Winter: Reflections on Life in Exile," *Harper's* 161 (Sept. 1984): 50.

2. Paul Smith, *Discerning the Subject* (Minneapolis: University of Minnesota Press, 1988), pp. 126-27. On the subject of intellectuals and political dissidence in Eastern Europe, the Soviet Union, and Italy (regarding Pasolini's assassination in 1974), see, for example, *Tel Quel* 76 (Summer 1978), most of which is devoted to this topic; see also the interview with Bernard Henri-Lévy, "La Preuve du pudding," *Tel Quel* 77 (Fall 1978): 25-35, on the *nouveaux philosophes*, the New Right, and dissidents' criticism of various forms of oppression on the left.

3. Smith, *Discerning the Subject*, p. 170 n. 6. The Kristeva citation is from "Mémoire," *L'Infini* 1 (1983): 39-54.

4. Tahar Ben Jelloun, *Les Amandiers sont morts de leurs blessures* (Paris: Maspero, 1976), pp. 14-15; my translation.

5. Julia Kristeva, *Strangers to Ourselves*, trans. Léon Roudiez (New York: Columbia University Press, 1991), pp. 1-2; originally *Etrangers à nous-mêmes* (Paris: Fayard, 1988). Future references appear in parentheses in the text.

6. Julia Kristeva, *Lettre ouverte à Harlem Désir* (Paris: Editions Rivages, 1990).

7. Smith, *Discerning the Subject*, p. 129. Smith is discussing *Pouvoirs de l'horreur* (Paris: Seuil, 1980).

8. Jean Baudrillard, *Simulacres et simulation* (Paris: Galilée, 1981), p. 102. All translations of Baudrillard are mine.

9. Ibid., pp. 16, 34.

10. On the dissolution of the referent and its political implications, especially in Derrida and Barthes, see Smith, *Discerning the Subject*, pp. 41-55, 100-16. For a more general discussion, see Terry Eagleton, "Aesthetics and Politics," *New Left Review* 107 (Jan.-Feb. 1978): 21-34, and Janet Wolff, *The Social Production of Art* (New York: St. Martin's Press, 1981), p. 65.

11. Baudrillard, *Amérique* (Paris: Grasset, 1986), pp. 35-36.

12. Ibid., pp. 70-72, 106-7.

13. Baudrillard, *Simulation*, pp. 104-10.

14. Michel Foucault, "Two Lectures," in *Power/Knowledge: Selected Interviews and Other Writings, 1972-77*, ed. Colin Gordon, trans. Colin Gordon, Leo Marshall, John Mepham, and Kate Soper (New York: Pantheon, 1980), p. 83.

15. Foucault, "Intellectuals and Power," in *Language, Counter-Memory, Practice*, ed. Donald Bouchard, trans. Donald Bouchard and Sherry Simon (Ithaca, N.Y.: Cornell University Press), p. 206.

16. Rhada Rhadakrishnan, "Toward an Effective Intellectual: Foucault or Gramsci?" in *Intellectuals: Aesthetics, Politics, Academics*, ed. Bruce Robbins (Minneapolis: University of Minnesota Press, 1990), p. 68. In this section I am presenting a much abbreviated version of Rhadakrishnan's analysis and helpful extension of leftist critiques of Foucault's work in order to indicate their relevance to my discussion of exile. Future references to this essay will appear in parentheses in the text.

17. Edward Said, "Foucault and the Imagination of Power," in *Foucault: A Critical Reader*, ed. David Couzens Hoy (Oxford and New York: Basil Blackwell, 1986), p. 153.

18. Gayatri Chakravorty Spivak, "Can the Subaltern Speak?" in *Marxism and the Interpretation of Culture*, ed. Cary Nelson and Lawrence Grossberg (Urbana and Chicago: University of Illinois Press, 1988), p. 275.

19. Foucault, "Theatrum Philosophicum," in *Language, Counter-Memory, Practice*, ed. Bouchard, p. 185.

20. Gilles Deleuze and Félix Guattari, *Kafka: Pour une littérature mineure* (Paris: Editions de Minuit, 1975), pp. 37, 41. The translations of all passages quoted from this book are mine. Future references will appear in parentheses in the text. For a critique of Deleuze and Guattari in terms of a "cosmopolitanism" that acknowledges its reliance on the symbolic rather than relying on the fantasy of a "world" or a "nature" that precedes the symbolic ("nomadization without identity, deterritorialization without unity"), see Guy Scarpetta, "Déracinements," *Tel Quel* 89 (1981): 74-91, especially p. 76.

21. Homi Bhabha, "DissemiNation: Time, Narrative, and the Margins of the Modern Nation," in *Nation and Narration*, ed. Homi Bhabha (New York: Routledge, 1989), p. 291. Although Bhabha's style is disconcerting, this essay is interesting for its attempt to affirm the critiques of community generated in France in the early 1980s—critiques that rely on dispersion of identities as the means to resist totalizing and, ultimately, totalitarian forces that bind communities—while at the same time legitimating "gathering" as a productive political force for peoples whose scattering has precluded effective political action. I think Bhabha's essay implicitly takes issue

with the advocates of dispersion by suggesting that the gathering of peoples and identities is in no way reducible to a repressive representation, much less a fascistic fixation. Bhabha refers explicitly to the work of Jacques Derrida, especially *Dissemination*, trans. Barbara Johnson (Chicago: University of Chicago Press, 1981), and of Claude Lefort; see, for example, Lefort's *Essais sur le politique* (Paris: Seuil, 1982). Indirectly (through his references to the notion of finitude, for instance), Bhabha also refers to Jean-Luc Nancy's *The Inoperative Community*, ed. Peter Conner, trans. Peter Conner, Lisa Garbus, Michael Holland, and Simona Sawhney (Minneapolis: University of Minnesota Press, 1991); originally "La Communauté désoeuvrée," *Aléa* 4 (1983): 11-50. Along these same lines, see *Le Retrait du politique*, ed. Philippe Lacoue-Labarthe and Jean-Luc Nancy (Paris: Galilée, 1983). Bhabha's notion of gathering resonates with the reflection on deconstructive political theories and socialist activism in Ernesto Laclau and Chantal Mouffe, *Hegemony and Socialist Strategy: Towards a Radical Democratic Politics* (London: Verso, 1985). See also "Location, Intervention, Incommensurability: A Conversation with Homi Bhabha," *Emergences* 1 (Fall 1989): 63-88.

22. Alain Boureau, "Le Discours critique sur la littérature maghrébine d'expression française," *Oeuvres et Critiques* 2 (Winter 1979): 118, 122.

23. Michel de Certeau, "Idéologie et diversité culturelle," in *Diversité culturelle, société industrielle, état national* (Paris: L'Harmattan, 1984), pp. 231-32; my translation.

24. Michel de Certeau and Luce Giard, *L'Ordinaire de la communication* (Paris: Dalloz, 1983), p. 134; my translation. For an interesting analysis of one such "system of translation," see Azouz Begag, *L'Immigré et sa ville* (Lyon: Presses Universitaires de Lyon, 1984), on the way Maghrebian immigrants of the older generation use the public transportation system. Begag shows that for many Maghrebians, integration into the community means, ideally, acquiring and preserving a certain anonymity both in their housing complexes and in their commute to work. The car is favored over the bus or metro partly for this reason; adults neither stand out as "others" in the crowd nor find themselves compromised by the rowdy behavior of Maghrebian youths, which, in the opinion of some adults, explains and partially justifies French racism. Because of their situation in Lyon, the immigrants Begag studies don't resemble the social scientist's ideal *homo economicus* in their use of public transportation. Rather than determining their means of transportation and their route based on minimal expenditures of time and money, immigrants often take the bus, for instance, rather than the metro (which is usually cheaper and faster) because for illiterates in particular the underground network is confusing. Use of public transportation varies, too, in terms of gender; for example, women's use of public transportation is shaped both by the husband's prohibitions against certain types of circulation and by the women's sense of their Arab-Islamic identity. Immigrants also use taxis in ways that disconcert taxi drivers and the "general population," for example, when moving from one residence to another. Begag incorporates systems of translation such as these into his autobiographical novel *Le Gone du Chaâba* (Paris: Seuil, 1986), as does Farida Belghoul in *Georgette!* (Paris: Bernard Barrault, 1986).

25. Nancy Huston and Leïla Sebbar, *Lettres Parisiennes: Autopsie de l'exil* (Paris: Bernard Barrault, 1986), pp. 125-26. Translations are mine. Future references will appear in parentheses in the text.

26. Alice A. Jardine and Anne M. Menke, "Exploding the Issue: 'French' 'Women' 'Writers' and 'The Canon'?" *Yale French Studies* 75 (1988): 229-58.

27. François Furet, *La République du Centre: La Fin de l'exception française* (Paris: Calmann-Lévy, 1989), p. 55; my translation. Future references appear in the text.

28. For a discussion of the New Right's repressive use of liberal discourse in France and elsewhere, see Laclau and Mouffe, *Hegemony and Socialist Strategy,* pp. 171-75.

29. Jacques Donzelot, *L'Invention du Social: Essai sur le déclin des passions politiques* (Paris: Fayard, 1984), p. 237; my translation.

30. Tahar Ben Jelloun, *Hospitalité française: Racisme et immigration maghrébine* (Paris: Seuil, 1984), p. 87; my translation.

31. Adil Jazouli, "Intégration et assimilation," *Hommes et Migrations* 1114 (July-Sept. 1988): 107-8; my translation. Among other things, Jazouli is referring to the massive protests organized in December 1986 when an Algerian student, Malek Oussekine, was murdered by armed policemen.

32. *Le Nouvel Observateur,* Feb. 22-28, 1990, p. 23.

33. For a highly nuanced reading of orientalism's complex and contradictory manifestations in connection with emerging European nationalisms, gender, and class struggle, see Lisa Lowe, "Nationalism and Exoticism: Nineteenth-Century Others in Flaubert's *Salammbô* and *L'Education sentimentale,"* in *Macropolitics of Nineteenth-Century Literature: Nationalism, Exoticism, Imperialism,* ed. Harriet Ritvo and Jonathan Arac (Philadelphia: University of Pennsylvania Press, 1991), pp. 213-42. Edward Said's groundbreaking *Orientalism* (New York: Pantheon, 1978) must be mentioned here as well.

34. Leïla Sebbar, *Shérazade, brune, frisée, les yeux verts* (Paris: Stock, 1982), p. 98. Translations are mine. Future references appear in the text. Since I wrote this chapter, the novel has been translated: *Sherazade: Aged 17, Dark Curly Hair, Green Eyes, Missing,* trans. Dorothy Blair (London: Quartet, 1991).

35. In *The Colonial Harem,* trans. Myrna Godzich and Wlad Godzich (Minneapolis: University of Minnesota Press, 1986, pp. 130-31 n. 24), Malek Alloula points out that the Turkish term *odalisque,* as it is used by orientalists, is a misnomer since it designates not the indolent wife but the woman who serves her.

36. For an illuminating discussion of this dynamic in the cultural politics of *métissage,* see the introduction to Françoise Lionnet's *Autobiographical Voices: Race, Gender, Self-Portraiture* (Ithaca, N.Y.: Cornell University Press, 1989), especially pp. 11-12.

37. Assia Djebar, *Femmes d'Alger dans leur appartement* (Paris: des femmes, 1980), p. 189; in English, "Forbidden Sight, Interrupted Sound," trans. Lee Hildreth, *Discourse* 8 (Fall/Winter 1986-87): 54-55.

38. For a feminist critique of the uses of the primitive in anthropology, see Marianna Torgovnick, *Gone Primitive: Savage Intellects, Modern Lives* (Chicago: University of Chicago Press, 1989).

39. The book referred to is former army photographer Marc Garanger's *Femmes algériennes 1960* (Paris: Contrejour, 1982), which I discussed in chapter 1.

40. In a review of Sebbar's first novel, which I discuss in the next section of this essay, Jacqueline Arnaud writes, "Leïla Sebbar has given us an original work that, by virtue of its look at the immigrant milieu from the inside, as it were, perhaps prefigures a literature no longer about immigration but of immigration. It won't be long before the 'second generation' of immigrants has its writers" (*Annuaire de l'Afrique du Nord* [1981]: 1221-22). Begag's *Le Gone du Chaâba,* Belghoul's *Georgette!,* and Mehdi Charef's *Le Thé au harem d'Archi Ahmed* (Paris: Mercure de France, 1983) are

perhaps the best-known examples of this writing of the "second generation." All three writers deal with issues similar to those I have discussed here, although for them (Begag and Belghoul especially), painful cultural conflicts and the means of negotiating them are treated mainly in terms of their schooling. Like Sebbar, Belghoul focuses on girls' and women's experiences and goes further than either Begag or Charef in working into the language of her text the conflicting and ambiguous processes of acculturation to which immigrant children are subject. In school, Belghoul's seven-year-old protagonist is confronted with a teacher who requires her to write her assignments as if her semiliterate father had not had a hand in marking the pages of her notebook, and as if his voice—his references to the Koran, his violent outbursts denouncing the French—should not be heard. The title of the novel designates the social position arbitrarily assigned the unnamed female protagonist by an eccentric elderly Frenchwoman who wants her to stand in for the sons that have deserted her; once she learns how to write, the little girl is to write the woman letters as if she were her son. The name Georgette also designates the horror of the girl's father, were he to discover that she had assumed a position defined by and for the French. If I have devoted my analysis to Sebbar, who is not herself a Beur, it is because I think her texts offer the most interesting and complex articulations of the "second generation's" situation. Moreover, Sebbar—a French writer in exile from Algeria, the daughter of an Algerian father and a French mother—occupies a hinge position between French natives, expatriates, and immigrants, and uses this position to rethink Frenchness in productive ways.

41. Leïla Sebbar, *Fatima ou les Algériennes au square* (Paris: Stock, 1981), p. 9; my translations. Future references will appear in parentheses in the text.

42. Daniel Sibony, *Ecrits sur le racisme* (Paris: Bourgois, 1988), p. 8; my translation. Future references will appear in parentheses in the text.

43. Laclau and Mouffe, *Hegemony and Socialist Strategy*, pp. 162-63. In Algiers no less than in Paris women's subjection to oppressive conditions, imposed by the intersection between archaic cultural traditions and global patterns of dependency, is inextricably tied to the housing crisis. See "Que veulent les Algériennes?" *Afrique Magazine* 66 (Jan. 1990): 22-29.

44. I am indebted here to Nancy K. Miller's critique of Barthes and textuality in terms of the politics of male weaving. See her "Arachnologies: The Woman, the Text, and the Critic," in *The Poetics of Gender*, ed. Carolyn G. Heilbrun and Nancy K. Miller (New York: Columbia University Press, 1986); reprinted in Miller's *Subject to Change: Reading Feminist Writing* (New York: Columbia University Press, 1988), pp. 77-101.

Chapter 4. Out of France

1. Roland Barthes, *A Lover's Discourse: Fragments*, trans. Richard Howard (New York: Hill and Wang, 1978), p. 188; originally *Fragments d'un discours amoureux* (Paris: Seuil, 1977), p. 223. Barthes is quoting Tahar Labib Djedidi's *La Poésie amoureuse des Arabes: Le Cas des Urdites. Contribution à une sociologie de la littérature arabe* (Algiers: Société Nationale d'Edition et de Diffusion, [1974?]).

2. Evelyne Sullerot, *L'Aman* (Paris: Fayard, 1981); Marie Cardinal, *Au pays de mes racines* (Paris: Grasset, 1980); J. M. G. Le Clézio, *Désert* (Paris: Gallimard, 1980); Michel Tournier, *La Goutte d'or* (Paris: Gallimard, 1986); Guy Hocquenghem, *L'Amour en relief* (Paris: Albin Michel, 1982). Only the latter two novels appear in trans-

lation: Tournier, *The Golden Droplet,* trans. Barbara Wright (New York: Doubleday, 1987); and Hocquenghem, *Love in Relief,* trans. Michael Whisler (New York: Seahorse Press, 1986). All references are to these editions and appear in parentheses in the text. All translations of the Sullerot, Cardinal, and Le Clézio novels are mine.

3. In *Autobiographical Voices: Race, Gender, Self-Portraiture* (Ithaca, N.Y.: Cornell University Press, 1989), Françoise Lionnet treats Marie Cardinal as a Francophone writer in her reading of *Les Mots pour le dire* (Paris: Grasset, 1975); in English, *The Words to Say It,* trans. Pat Goodheart (Cambridge, Mass.: Van Vactor and Goodheart, 1983). While I agree with her that *Les Mots pour le dire* opens a space between French and French-Algerian identity, showing how the interaction of patriarchy and colonialism produces the female protagonist's madness and bodily suffering, I am nonetheless reluctant to identify Cardinal as a Francophone, rather than a French, writer. Granted, as Cardinal's novel suggests, both the French-Algerian narrator and Algerians as a national group are subject to domination by the interrelated systems of patriarchy and colonialism: the "blood of civil war which ran into the gutters and overflowed onto the sidewalks, following the geometric patterns in the cement of civilization" (88) is associated with the menstrual "blood" (4) that flows incessantly in the narrator when she succumbs to madness as a result of her mother's "villainy" (105), just as the "torture" of Algerians by the French (88) recalls "the words [my mother] was about to inflict on me like so many mutilating swords" (135). Still, it seems to me that the minority positions Cardinal presents (feminist, anticolonial, Pied-Noir) are *French* minority positions that differ significantly from those of the Algerian people. They differ, too, from the minority positions presented, for instance, in Sebbar's portrayal of Maghrebian immigrants whose histories are deeply embedded in French society and culture. Cardinal's insistence on her Algerian identity, while critical of hegemonic notions of Frenchness, clearly indicates the need to mark a difference that might otherwise pass unnoticed. Sebbar's situation as the daughter of a French woman and an Algerian man is just the reverse: as I showed in the last chapter, the "marked" feature of her Algerianness blinds the French public to what for them is the "unmarked," French aspect of her identity. For me, the point here is not that the Algerian people are more Algerian than Cardinal, or that Sebbar (who identifies herself as French) is more Algerian than Cardinal, or that the minority positions Sebbar traces are more authentic than Cardinal's in relation to hegemonic French culture, for these judgments rely on the very notion of ethnic or national "purity" that Lionnet criticizes so effectively. Rather, in keeping with Lionnet's advocacy of *métissage* as a reading strategy that attends to "our heterogeneous and heteronomous identities as postcolonial subjects" (8), I want to take account of differences between minority positions (not just between minority and hegemonic positions) as sites of *conflict* as well as solidarity. In the texts to be analyzed here, the interaction of these differences reinforces existing inequalities or introduces new ones as often as it fosters what Lionnet calls "the free play of meaning" (198).

4. Lionnet, *Autobiographical Voices,* p. 5.

5. See Fredric Jameson, "Postmodernism, or The Cultural Logic of Late Capitalism," *New Left Review* 146 (July-Aug. 1984): 53-92.

6. *Le Maghreb dans l'imaginaire français: La Colonie, le désert, l'exil,* ed. Jean-Robert Henry (Aix-en-Provence: Edisud, 1985), p. 8. Here I am summarizing Henry's very helpful and thorough presentation of this literature.

7. "The New French Culture: An Interview with Guy Hocquenghem" by Douglas Crimp, *October* 19 (Winter 1981): 111.

8. Guy Hocquenghem, "Interview," p. 106, and Hocquenghem, *Lettre ouverte à ceux qui sont passés du col Mao au Rotary* (Paris: Albin Michel, 1986), pp. 136-38.

9. Guy Hocquenghem, *La Beauté du métis: Réflexions d'un francophobe* (Paris: Editions Ramsay, 1979), p. 20. Here Hocquenghem is responding to an ideal of Giscard's: "Je veux rendre chaque Français propriétaire de la France" ("I want to make each Frenchman France's owner").

10. Armand Mattelart, Xavier Delcourt, and Michèle Mattelart, *International Image Markets: In Search of an Alternative Perspective*, trans. David Buxton (London: Comedia Publishing Group, 1984), p. 9; originally *La Culture contre la démocratie? L'Audiovisuel à l'heure transnationale* (Paris: La Découverte, 1984), p. 18.

11. Mattelart, Delcourt, and Mattelart, *La Culture contre la démocratie*, pp. 19-25; *International Image markets*, pp. 9-12.

12. Hocquenghem, *Lettre ouverte*, pp. 133-34.

13. Ibid., p. 162. To illustrate the new consensus among artists, intellectuals, and politicians of the left and right, Hocquenghem points out that Mitterrand's friend and supporter Marguerite Duras ("that old destroyer") publicly defends the Socialist government's sinking of the Greenpeace ship monitoring French testing of nuclear weapons in 1984. For a different view of the collapse of oppositional politics in France, see Jean Baudrillard's sly but basically affirmative account, *La Gauche divine: Chronique des années 1977-1984* (Paris: Grasset, 1985).

14. Quoted in Hocquenghem, *Lettre ouverte*, pp. 172-73.

15. See Régis Debray, "Il faut des esclaves aux hommes libres," in *Le Tiers Monde et la gauche*, ed. Jean Daniel and André Burguière (Paris: Seuil, 1979), pp. 89-96. This article was first published in *Le Monde Diplomatique*, Oct. 1978. Criticizing French intellectuals who contemptuously dismiss the usefulness of human rights discourses, Debray writes: "To isolate the 'Europe of Freedoms' dear to CIEL (the Committee of Intellectuals for the Europe of Freedoms) from the third world, whose permanent exploitation ensures the maintenance of these very freedoms, is to kill two birds with one stone: Europe is cut off from its bloody historical formation, so that the shadow cast by the crimes of yesterday and today are effaced from the present; and politics is freed from the obscure substructures of the economy, just as the metaphysical purity of principles is freed from the sordid details of administration. 'The rights of man,' said a recent guest at the Elysée Palace, without the slightest trace of irony, 'is the return of transcendence to politics' " (90; my translation). See also Debray, *Les Empires contre l'Europe* (Paris: Gallimard, 1985).

16. Hocquenghem, "Interview," p. 115, and *Lettre ouverte*, pp. 67-72.

17. Hocquenghem, "Interview," p. 113.

18. A third axiom at work in the novel holds that organized feminist movements are oppressive phallic institutions that are, in any case, historically obsolete since the battle for women's equality has supposedly been won in the West. Since I cannot analyze this here, I will simply point out that Edith's interpretations of events are used to discredit 1950s feminism, whose supposed elitism excludes true women like Edith, as is clear from the protagonist's relation to her condescending activist friend, Brigitte. Similarly, 1980s feminism is dismissed as a necessarily imperialist phenomenon, evidenced in the plans of Edith's daughter, Nadine, to go to Algeria to enlighten Algerian women on the matter of their oppression. Significantly, it is not just feminist movements that are discredited, but nearly all females; for exam-

ple, the wife of Edith's nephew, who is said to be cold and ungiving, and Edith's au pair girl from Germany, Brunehilde, a burlesque figure who, like Edith, is seduced and abandoned, but unlike her, never makes good despite her good-heartedness. The effect of discrediting various feminisms and individual women is to allow Edith (clearly a stand-in for Sullerot herself) to shine as the star of true womanhood under Giscard: she is the female embodiment of the neoliberal values being celebrated in France in the late 1970s, particularly individualism. Other than Edith, the only "good" women are Edith's and Sedik's mothers, idealized characters who function to advance Sullerot's sentimental view of maternity as the basis for equitable social relations.

19. Tony Hodges, *Western Sahara: The Roots of a Desert War* (Westport, Conn.: Lawrence Hill, 1983). Leo Kamil, *Fueling the Fire: U.S. Policy and the Western Sahara Conflict* (Trenton, N.J.: Red Sea Press, 1987). "The Superpowers and the Western Sahara: A North South Conflict," *Activist Review* (Cambridge, Mass.) 9-10 (Sept.-Oct. 1987): 1-4. I thank Kathryn Milun for discussing the concept of *terra nullius* and the Western Sahara conflict with me.

20. See Kamil, *Fueling the Fire*, pp. 26-27, 50-62.

21. Marguerite Duras, *Green Eyes*, trans. Carol Barko (New York: Columbia University Press, 1990), pp. 131, 140; originally *Les Yeux verts* (Paris: Cahiers du Cinéma, 1987), pp. 170, 182. Marlowe Miller's dissertation, "Family, War, and Writing: H.D., Virginia Woolf, and Marguerite Duras" (University of California, San Diego, 1991), alerted me to these passages on power and sorrow, which originally appeared in *Cahiers du Cinéma*, June 1980.

22. Kamil, *Fueling the Fire*, p. 73.

23. See especially Julia Kristeva, *Révolution du langage poétique* (Paris: Seuil, 1974), in which she argues that the political limitation of the semiotic in Mallarmé and Lautréamont is that it remains within the aesthetic realm, that is, it celebrates the expression of heterogeneity without reengaging the thetic instance.

24. For discussions of shifts in the semiotic/symbolic relation in Kristeva's work, see Paul Smith, *Discerning the Subject* (Minneapolis: University of Minnesota Press, 1988), which I discuss in chapter 3; and Jacqueline Rose, *Sexuality in the Field of Vision* (New York: Verso, 1986), pp. 141-64. Of course, with the publication of *Etrangers à nous-mêmes* (Paris: Fayard, 1988), her novel on intellectuals and popular passions, *Les Samouraïs* (Paris: Fayard, 1990), and especially her *Lettre ouverte à Harlem Désir* (Paris: Editions Rivages, 1990), Kristeva reengages with current political problems.

25. Kathleen Woodward, "The Look and the Gaze: Narcissism, Aggression, and Aging," *SubStance* 58 (1989): 80.

26. Sigmund Freud, "On Narcissism: An Introduction" (1914), in *The Standard Edition of the Complete Psychological Works of Sigmund Freud*, ed. James Strachey (London: Hogarth, 1964-74), vol. 14, p. 89.

27. J.-B. Pontalis, "Dream as Object," trans. Carol Martin-Sperry and Masud Khan, *International Review of Psycho-Analysis* 1 (1974): 128. The passages I have cited from Freud and Pontalis are taken from Woodward's illuminating discussion of narcissism in their work and in that of Heinz Kohut.

28. It is unfortunate that in U.S. cultural studies, feminist writing and political action are increasingly seen as divided, in Angela Gilliam's words, between "those who believe that the major struggle for women is increasing their access to, and control over, the world's resources and those who believe the main issue is access

to, and control over, orgasms" ("Women's Equality and National Liberation," in *Third World Women and the Politics of Feminism*, ed. Chandra Talpade Mohanty, Ann Russo, and Lourdes Torres [Bloomington and Indianapolis: Indiana University Press, 1991], p. 217). Apart from the obvious fact that feminist work on sexuality, pleasure, and language over the last twenty years can hardly be reduced to concern with orgasms, Gilliam's formulation of the problem is unhelpful since it merely asserts the need to tie sexuality to the economic and the political rather than indicating how the connections are to be made in a particular cultural-political situation. As I have been trying to show, the writing of women like Cardinal suggests multiple and contradictory ways of making these connections, which themselves should be the object of feminist critique.

29. Jacques Lacan, "Le Stade du miroir comme formateur de la fonction du Je" (1936), in *Ecrits* (Paris: Seuil, 1966).

30. Jacques Lacan, "Remarque sur le rapport de Daniel Lagache: 'Psychanalyse et structure de la personnalité,' " in *Ecrits;* cited by Rose, *Sexuality in the Field of Vision,* p. 186.

31. There is a striking contrast between this narrator's claim to have opposed colonialism even as a young adult and the one made by the narrator of the earlier novel, *The Words to Say It.* Toward the end of her psychoanalysis, the latter says:

> C'est maintenant seulement que je me rendais compte que je n'avais jamais vraiment lu un journal, jamais vraiment écouté les nouvelles, que j'avais pris la guerre d'Algérie pour une affaire sentimentale, une triste histoire de famille digne des Atrides. Et pourquoi cela? Parce que je n'avais aucun rôle à jouer dans cette société où j'étais née et où j'étais devenue folle. Aucun rôle sinon donner des garçons pour faire marcher les guerres et les gouvernements et des filles pour faire, à leur tour, des garçons aux garçons. Trente-sept ans de soumission absolue. Trente-sept ans à accepter l'inégalité et l'injustice sans broncher, sans même les voir! (285)

> It is only now that I understand that I had never really read a newspaper or listened to the news. I'd looked upon the Algerian war as a sentimental matter, a sad story worthy of the Greeks. And why was that? Because I had no role to play in the society where I was born and had gone crazy. No role, that is, other than to produce sons to carry on wars and found governments, and daughters who, in their turn, would produce sons. Thirty-seven years of absolute submission. Thirty-seven years of accepting the inequality and the injustice, without flinching, without even being aware of it! (264)

As Françoise Lionnet shows in *Autobiographical Voices,* the narrator of *The Words to Say It* analyzes her blindness to both colonial and sexual domination in terms of relations between the two forms of oppression. What interests me about the difference between this narrator's presentation of her personal history and that of the narrator in *Au pays de mes racines* is that it marks a shift in French politics: self-criticism and work for change in the social world have been replaced by a certain complacency. The inconsistency in Cardinal's autobiographical self-presentation may well indicate a shift in the writer's politics as well. However, it would be a mistake to view the inconsistency simply as a flaw in Cardinal's writing. I agree with Cardinal that critics who regard her essentially as a writer of testimonials—critics who might point to such an inconsistency as a flaw—at once trivialize testimonial writing as an exercise in passive transcription of "real" individual experience and, in the same gesture, seek to deny Cardinal's status as a writer. For Cardinal's own view of her project as a writer, see her interview with Jean Royer, "Marie Cardinal," in *Ecrivains contemporains* (Montreal: L'Hexagone, 1982), pp. 58-63. On women's testimonial writing as self-construction, expression of collective identity, and political critique in Latin America, see Doris Sommer, " 'Not Just a Personal Story': Women's *Testimonios* and the Plural Self," in *Life/Lines,* ed. Bella Brodzki and Celeste Schenck (Ithaca, N.Y.: Cornell University Press, 1988), pp. 107-30.

32. Royer, "Marie Cardinal," pp. 62-63.

33. Ibid., p. 60.

34. Albert Camus, "The Adulterous Woman," in *Exile and the Kingdom,* trans. Justin O'Brien (New York: Knopf, 1958), pp. 3-33; originally "La Femme adultère," in *L'Exil et le royaume* (Paris: Gallimard, 1957), pp. 11-41. Further references will appear in parentheses in the text.

35. Albert Memmi, *Le Désert* (Paris: Gallimard, 1977); Driss Chraïbi, *Naissance à l'aube* (Paris: Seuil, 1986).

36. For an analysis of Le Clézio's treatment of the history of Saharawi resistance, see Kathleen White Smith, "Forgetting to Remember: *Anamnesis* and History in J. M. G. Le Clézio's *Désert," Studies in Twentieth Century Literature* 1 (Fall 1985): 99-114.

37. In *La Prière de l'absent* (Paris: Seuil, 1981), Tahar Ben Jelloun's narrator notes with irony that the ancestors who made of Ma al-'Aynayn "a myth, a saint, an image" concealed "the feudal, authoritarian, and even proslavery character of this tribal chief who dreamed of being the chief of an entire state" (224). Critical of nostalgia for the lost origin and idealization of the ancestral past, Ben Jelloun shows in his narrative that the three pilgrims en route to the tomb of Ma al-'Aynayn necessarily fail to recover their past as a means to salvation, for "an invisible wall of glass stood between them and the South" (219). For an analysis of the parallels and divergences between *Désert* and *La Prière de l'absent,* see Pierrette Renard, "Traversée du désert et quête initiatique," *Recherches et Travaux* 35 (University of Grenoble, 1988): 100-109.

38. For example, Marianne Alphant speaks of the "perverse reversal of colonialist ideology" in her review "La Chanson du gâs qu'a mal Tournier," *Libération,* Jan. 10, 1986, p. 31.

39. See my "Fascist Bonding and Euphoria in Michel Tournier's *The Ogre," New German Critique* 42 (Fall 1987): 79-112, and Alice A. Jardine's comments on *Vendredi ou les limbes du Pacifique* (Paris: Gallimard, 1967) in *Gynesis: Configurations of Woman and Modernity* (Ithaca, N.Y.: Cornell University Press, 1985), especially pp. 217-23.

40. See, for example, Jean Montalbetti, "Le Piège de l'image," *Magazine Littéraire* 226 (Jan. 1986): 18-19, and, in the same issue, Arlette Bouloumié, "Mythologies," pp. 26-29. The problem with these readings is not that they focus on myth, but that they use myth to dehistoricize both Tournier's work and the readings themselves.

41. This charge is leveled, for instance, by Marianne Alphant, "La Chanson du gâs," and by Angelo Rinaldi in his review of *The Golden Droplet,* "Connaissez-vous Pompignan?" *L'Express,* Jan. 10, 1986, p. 56. Of course Tournier has many admirers, as well. See Serge Koster, *Michel Tournier* (Paris: Editions Henry Veyrier, 1986); Salim Jay, *Michel Tournier, Idriss, et les autres* (Paris: Editions de la Différence, 1986); and Françoise Merllié, *Michel Tournier* (Paris: Belfond, 1988).

42. Rinaldi, "Pompignan," p. 56.

43. This impulse is evident in the Alphant and Rinaldi reviews cited above. But it also informs Alain Buisine's reading, which bemoans the vampiristic effect of Arthur Tress's photography on Tournier's writing in *The Golden Droplet:* "Arthur Tress [an American] would steal his writing from him simply by conferring on him a certain figural incarnation; he would withdraw from his texts a part of what had made them so magnificently *substantial.* . . . [Imaginative power] must remain virtual in relationship to the text, which would be literally bled white by its becoming representational—a hemorrhage of the imaginary would flow (no doubt irreversibly) from the storyteller's art to the cliché/photographic plate." This statement appears in "A Dispossessed Text: The Writings and Photography of Michel Tournier," trans. Roxanne Lapidus, *SubStance* 58 (1989): 28, 31; my emphasis.

44. Michel Tournier, "Ecrire à l'âge nucléaire," *Sud* 61 (1986): 171.

45. Michel Tournier, "Egypte: Du Rêve à Mokhatam," *Sud* 61 (1986): 194. See also "Extraits: 'Pages extimes,' " *Le Monde des Livres,* Aug. 6, 1982, p. 11, where Tournier enjoins his countrymen to adopt a New Year's resolution to increase their wealth: "[Wealth] makes people not only generous and disinterested but intelligent and good. Yes, one must dare to say it: poverty is the mother of all vices. . . . Look how our parents lived: the terrible harshness of that society; the pitiless exploitation of workers, women, and children; the colonial wars and wars of revenge; social barriers. And if all of that has improved somewhat, is it because we have become more virtuous? No, it's that we have become less poor."

46. Hocquenghem, *La Beauté du métis,* pp. 20, 137. The only point at which Amar's Tunisian/third-world identity becomes politically defensible in *Love in Relief* is when Larry, acting in collusion with the U.S. government, is about to destroy him by forcing him to choose between life imprisonment for drug trafficking and participation in his experiments. In a letter addressed but never sent to the jurors who will judge him, Amar says, "Your moral rules are as arbitrary to me as your perceptual world: I who come not only from Arabia, but from a continent that is invisible" (196).

Index

Compiled by Hassan Melehy

229

Winifred Woodhull is assistant professor of literature at the University of California in San Diego. She has published numerous articles on twentieth-century literature, critical theory, and cultural studies.